Her Lost Year

Her lost year

A Story of Hope and a Vision for Optimizing Children's Mental Health

Tabita Green
with Rebecka Green

simply enough press

This book is not intended to replace the advice of a trained health professional. If you know or suspect that you have a health problem, you should contact a health professional. The author specifically disclaims any liability, loss, or risk, personal or otherwise, that is incurred as a consequence, directly or indirectly, of the use and application of any of the contents of this book.

Readers should be aware that Internet websites offered as citations and/or sources for further information may have changed or disappeared between the time this was written and when it is read.

Published in the United States by Simply Enough Press, Decorah, Iowa.
SimplyEnoughPress.com

First Paperback Edition: July 2015

Library of Congress Control Number: 2015903065

ISBN 978-0-692-39349-9
eISBN 978-0-692-39350-5

Book design by Terry Rydberg and Erik Berg
Cover design by Samuel Sander
Cover art by Priscilla Åhlén Sundqvist

Printed in the United States of America

10 9 8 7 6 5 4 3 2 1

To Todd, for your love and support—and for giving Sophie a voice.

Contents

Part 5: Optimizing Children's Mental Health

Introduction

Sometimes an event takes place that changes the course of your life—and alters your view of the world—forever.

For me, this was a prescription for the antidepressant Zoloft handed to my then thirteen-year-old daughter by a smart, caring general practitioner in the late spring of 2010.

Prior to that fateful spring, my knowledge of mental health and psychiatry was limited to what I had learned from a psychology survey course in college, pop culture, and pharmaceutical ads. I had heard of Prozac (who hasn't?) and understood that it was a miracle drug that helped depressed people feel better. I had basic knowledge of schizoaffective disorder and remembered a couple of anorexia cases from my high school days. I had derived from movies such as *As Good As It Gets* that mental illness was a life sentence (unless deemed "situational"), but that it could be managed with medication. And frankly, that was all I wanted to know. Mental illness was something foreign and uncomfortable, not something I wanted to spend a lot of time thinking about.

Until our harrowing experience with the mental health system, I also trusted people in authority and professionals—to a fault. Growing up, I didn't question the rules and behavior management strategies at the private San Francisco school I attended as a young child. I never questioned the fact that girls had to wear skirts and dresses, while boys were allowed to wear pants. I also didn't question the punitive tally system, which kept us students under control and following the rules. Even as an adult, I continued blindly to trust experts and professionals, assuming they had my best interest in mind, such as the financial planner who highly recommended we invest in an expensive life insurance plan. Only much later did my husband, Todd, and I realize he had pocketed large portions of our early investments as commissions.

So it's no surprise that when several healthcare practitioners encouraged us to medicate our daughter, Rebecka, for feelings of depression and anxiety, emotions that most certainly stemmed from environmental factors, we trusted it was the right thing to do. Even when the outcomes were catastrophic, we continued to trust the professionals, despite our intuition telling us otherwise. And, being professionals ourselves, we wanted to respect the mental health experts and adhere to their treatment plans, because we'd have wanted others to trust us in our own areas of expertise.

However, after a year of following the advice of various physicians, and watching our only child's physical and mental health deteriorate at a break-neck pace, we decided enough was enough. Thus, while this is a story about trusting health professionals and pharmaceutical companies to the detriment of one child's physical and emotional health, more importantly, it is a story of two parents' inexhaustible determination to get their daughter back after a year of medications, hospitalizations, and extreme psychiatric symptoms. I'll also share what we learned along the way—about modern psychiatry, alternative treatment options, and strategies for optimizing mental health outcomes, some of which require social change.

Our experience during the lost year, the subsequent journey to break Rebecka free from modern psychiatric treatment, and the research for this book revealed that there is a lot we *don't* know about mental health. Nobody really knows what causes symptoms of mental illness, and some critics of psychiatry even question the practice of labeling people as mentally ill. Yet there is a widely held belief—perpetuated by the pharmaceutical industry—that mental illness stems from a chemical imbalance in the brain. Thus, many physicians prescribe medication in an attempt to restore this balance and treat the symptoms, while ignoring the real problems—unstable homes, ineffective parenting, physical and emotional abuse, poverty, lack of exercise, poor nutrition, low self-esteem, separation from nature, one-size-fits-all education, corporate money in politics, environmental toxins, stress, etc. They do this because there is a whole lot of money to be made for pharmaceutical companies, insurance companies, and psychiatry as long as we continue to trust the system—and it's what they've been taught to do. It also helps keep antiauthoritarian individuals—or kids who don't fit neatly into the box we call public school—under control.

Looking at mental illness through the lens of French philosopher Michel

Foucault's discourse analysis helped us make sense of our experience. According to Foucault, modern societies have a number of discourses, which shape who we are and what we hold to be true. Discourse reflects society's power relationships, for example economic and political power. At the risk of oversimplification, think of a discourse as a script. The script dictates our lines and our performance on a given topic or theme. We must abide by the script in order to be taken seriously by experts and even by society. The tricky part is that we are not conscious of the script, or at least not fully conscious. In the same way, a discourse is a "conversation" we participate in without being fully conscious of the rules we must follow to begin with. In the case of mental illness, the prevalent discourse says that mental distress is a biological, medical issue and that medical issues are best treated with medicine. This is what most of Rebecka's providers held to be true—with grave consequences.

It's important to note that overmedication is a side effect of a bigger, deeper problem: pathologizing the human experience. While medication caused a large part of Rebecka's most severe symptoms, the discourse that said that her thoughts and feelings and behaviors were not normal, but due to one or more diagnosable mental illnesses, certainly impeded her journey to emotional health, as she sought to uncover what was "wrong" with her. Nobody sat us down and said, "Looks like Rebecka is going through a rough patch. Let's take some time to figure out what's bothering her and see how we can make some changes in her environment to help her feel better." The reason nobody had this conversation with us is because the whole system is based on the medical model of mental illness. The complexity of our story reveals that the problem is bigger than "pills as a first resort," although this is a huge problem in itself.

While writing this book, I also learned that our experience with the mental health system is not a one-off. I have read a number of stories of people who started taking psychiatric medications in their teens and ended up either disabled or losing years or decades of their lives. And as soon as I started talking to people about this book, I realized that most everybody has a psychiatry story. Sometimes it's their personal story. Other times, it is the story of their child or a child of a friend or family member. Yet other times, it is stories of unnamed students, told by concerned teachers. While some stories end well (especially when medication is considered *one* component of an integrated treatment approach), others do not—or they don't until medication is removed from the mix. So while this book is anchored around our specific story, keep in mind that there are many other stories out there—similar, but always slightly different, because we are all unique individuals.

'Who This Book Is For

This book is for anybody who cares about the mental health and happiness of children, born and not yet born. It is a tale of caution and an invitation to discernment, but more importantly, a proclamation of hope and a vision for optimizing our children's mental health.

- **Parents and caregivers of children and teens who are suffering,** I want you to know that medication is not the only answer, and I want you to feel empowered—with the help of the information contained within these pages—to have constructive conversations with your child's doctor about the best treatment plan for your child. I hope you will study part 4 of this book closely, and consider some of the alternative treatment options available. If you decide—after reading this book, consulting with your child's doctor, and weighing the pros and cons of various approaches—that medication is required for your child's mental well being, I will not think less of you. You are the best judge of what's best for your child, because nobody knows her better than you do. And remember, you are not alone, though it can feel like it at times.

- **All other parents, caregivers, and parents-to-be,** I applaud you for considering the mental health of children important enough to pick up this book. You are a significant influence on the mental health of your child. Children take their cues from the adults in their lives and mirror those adults' behavior and moods. The good news is that children are born with a resilience that helps them overcome life's obstacles. It's our job to nurture this resilience and do our best to usher our children into adulthood equipped with skills to get them through life's inevitable downs.

- **Educators,** you spend a significant amount of time with our children. For that, I thank you. As schools become more focused on rigor, performance, and competition, your ability to provide a nurturing environment diminishes. I hope you will take to heart the message in this book that how we teach our children—and the skills we provide them—has a significant impact on their social and emotional well-being. I invite you to explore the ways in which education can be upgraded to support kids' mental health. While systems change is needed, it is also possible to start small in your own classroom.

- **Doctors, nurses, therapists, social workers, and all others who work in the mental health system,** I appreciate your willingness to devote your life to ease the suffering of others. While my family's experience with psychiatry was less than favorable, I also know that our practitioners did what they thought was best for Rebecka. This is why we must question the "truths" about the brain, mental illness, and medication that have been presented to us—often under the sponsorship of for-profit pharmaceutical companies. Please read this book with an open heart and mind and consider how mental health care could be done differently, by addressing the needs of children and families holistically. Be the change.

- **Concerned citizens, politicians, and business leaders,** we all play a role in determining whether our society is conducive to mental health or not. Right now, it is not. There are significant shifts that must happen in the way we engage politically, the way corporations operate, and the way we think about the planet's resources. I invite you to consider the suggestions I offer in this book for how we can create a society that is designed to optimize mental health. The future of our country and, indeed, our world depends on it.

As my friend Johanna Bergan once pointed out to me, *everyone* has mental health. We all have brains, and our brains can be exercised like any other muscle to function optimally in the bigger context of environmental and societal factors. The process of optimizing a child's mental health starts at conception, but it's never too late to start helping a child or a teen to nurture their innate resilience. We can all participate in creating a society where the mental health of all people is a top priority.

How This Book Is Organized

This book is divided into five parts. Leading up to part 1 is an introductory chapter, which briefly chronicles the first thirteen years or Rebecka's life. The point of this chapter is to demonstrate that on paper, Rebecka had a good childhood. Nobody would have guessed that by the time she reached adolescence, she would be suffering such mental distress. However, if you read carefully, you might find some clues that Rebecka was an anxious child and that some aspects of our home life didn't exactly set the stage for optimal mental health.

Part 1 describes in detail the events that led Rebecka into the vicious circle of mental illness. Without much warning, our family is torpedoed into a world of therapists, psychiatric medication, inconceivable side effects, more medication, self-harm, hospitalizations, psychiatrists, and stigma. While much of it doesn't "feel" right, we trust the professionals and follow their treatment plan, while Rebecka gets worse. My lofty plans to "rescue" Rebecka from her conglomeration of mental disorders fail miserably. We start to think she is lost to us forever.

In part 2, my husband and I finally start to educate ourselves on the matter, thanks to an empathetic colleague and friend, and realize that perhaps our gut instincts were right and the professionals were not. A number of interventions on our part, lots of hard work by Rebecka, support from a brilliant psychologist, and appropriate treatment allow Rebecka to break free from the shackles of mental distress—once and for all.

Part 3 summarizes what we learned about psychiatry and the mental health system, including how psychiatry evolved from being more focused on psychotherapy to primarily prescribing and managing medication; the close, seemingly unethical, ties between psychiatry, the pharmaceutical industry, and other industry organizations; and the reason why so many kids are diagnosed with mental disorders. This is not new news, but it is packaged in such a way that you don't need an MD or a PhD to engage the issues.

In part 4, I explore a number of alternatives to medication for treating mentally distressed kids and teens. I start by pointing out that some of the most effective "treatments" are simply doing what's natural—eating real food, moving our bodies, getting sufficient sleep, and being in nature. Beyond that, I delve into the mental-health benefits of mindfulness and also having a sense of belonging and purpose. In addition, I describe some of the most helpful mental health therapies for kids and teens, based on personal experience and extensive research.

In the final part, I start to wonder why so many kids are distressed in the first place and offer a vision for a society designed to optimize mental health. I then proceed to cover four key areas, which require significant changes and upgrades to move us in the direction of such a society. These areas are consumerism, government, parenting, and education. Along the way, I provide suggestions for how you, the reader, can take action for positive change. Part 5 ends with a call to action to join the movement to optimize our children's mental health. Everybody is needed and everybody can help.

The Book I Wish I'd Read

My intent with this book is not to shame parents and children who have succumbed to the pressures of modern psychiatry. Nor is it to blame well-intentioned physicians for doing what they know to ease the suffering of their young patients. Mental suffering is real and devastating, and while many children are being labeled as "mentally ill" when they shouldn't be, there are also many children who suffer in silence and do not receive appropriate treatment—a topic covered extensively in Judith Warner's *We've Got Issues*.

Rather, I want to present to you the book I wish somebody had handed me in the spring of 2010 (or, even better, in the summer of 1996, when the cells that became Rebecka started to divide), a book written with the parent and caregiver in mind. A book that urges the reader to be aware of our society's discourses on mental illness, to question psychiatric medication as a first-line treatment for kids, to trust gut instincts, to consider the full spectrum of treatment options, to simplify life, and to use parenting strategies proven to build resilience and prepare kids for life's inevitable ups and downs. A book filled with hope—and a call to action.

While it is troubling to realize we can't blindly trust the mental health authorities, it is ever so encouraging to know that improved mental health is available to all and within our reach. The event that led to my family's tumultuous encounter with the mental health system—and the process of writing this book—changed my life. It is my most fervent and humble wish that reading this book may be such an event for you.

A Few Style and Content Notes

- Tabita is the primary author of this book. Rebecka is a contributor to the first two parts. Thus, "I" refers to Tabita, and "we" refers to Tabita and Rebecka in the context of authorship.

- Rebecka's voice is heard throughout the first two parts in clearly marked passages. The words are hers, and they have been edited only for grammatical correctness.

- Aside from the Mayo Clinic, hospital names have been changed.

- Aside from Valentin Clinic and Mayo Clinic personnel, all therapists' and psychiatrists' names have been changed or abbreviated to protect their identities. In all other cases, I've noted when I've changed somebody's name.

- I refer to "disordered eating" and "eating disorder" somewhat inter- changeably. However, I most often use "disordered eating" to refer to the behavior and "eating disorder" to signify the diagnosis.

- Some of Rebecka's psychiatric experiences were quite graphic and highly disturbing. We have chosen not to include them in the book, because they're too painful to relive and too personal to share.

The First Thirteen Years

Pregnancy

"I'm pregnant," I said, and waved the home pregnancy test in front of my husband Todd's face. He sat down on the bed, in shock. This was not the plan. In fact, we were on the five-year plan, and we'd only been married a little over a year. Todd was in seminary in Atlanta. I worked at a boarding school close to Little Five Points, a district on the east side known for its alternative culture—and we lived at said school, working as house parents in exchange for free room and board.

Our "apartment" was a big room with a bathroom smack in the middle, creating a living space in the shape of a 'C.' One side of the bathroom was our bedroom/office; the other side was our living room. We had a small dorm-style refrigerator, a microwave, and a "pantry" (an office file folder box I had covered with sticky shelf paper to make it look more kitchenesque).

We ate most of our meals in the roach-infested kitchen downstairs with the dozen or so misfit teens that happened to be living on the second floor of the school at any given time. Our next-door neighbor, a sixteen-year old male, who we suspected might be abusing Alka-Seltzer Plus to get "high," played his stereo with the bass at max capacity, shaking our walls in the process.

Were we going to bring a baby home to this? If not, how were we going to be able to afford raising this child? Todd had one more year of seminary. I was making a meager $12,000 a year, which was fine with the free room and board deal, but wouldn't stretch far should we need to get a real apartment and start buying our own food.

I wasn't overly worried about it. I had emigrated to the United States just a year ago from Sweden, where the social welfare safety net takes care of you when you get into a pickle like this. Todd, on the other hand, was stressed-out. He knew how the US system worked, and in his head, he was already calculating the cost of college. He decided to call his dad. Talking to a parent can be quite comforting. Todd emerged from the phone call calm and confident and gave me a big hug. We were pregnant! Everything would be just fine.

The first two trimesters of the pregnancy were a breeze. Yes, I had a little morning sickness, but no vomiting nastiness like you see in the movies and hear friends talk about. I was eager to start "showing," because I felt self-conscious walking up and down the aisles of Babies "R" Us, pining for baby gear without a big, round belly. Finally, around month seven or so, people could see that I was pregnant. I continued working and directing the children's choir at our church with gusto.

In the third trimester, I started having early contractions. My midwife prescribed medicine to stop the contractions (to be taken every four hours) and bed rest. Not strict bed rest, but the kind where you get to sit on the couch all day and read the *Lord of the Rings* trilogy from beginning to end. Or read *What to Expect When You're Expecting* all the way to the last, scary chapters about everything that can go wrong. Aside from worrying about going into labor early, bed rest was awesome (for me, at least). Our church gave Todd a charity job as a part-time janitor, paying ten dollars per hour. This was our only income. We made it work.

I followed the rules, carried to term, and gave birth to a healthy, seven-pound, eleven-ounce baby girl close to midnight on Good Friday, March 28, 1997. We named her Rebecka Suzanne.

The Early Years

We brought Rebecka home to the boarding school studio apartment when she was two days old. She was instantly the center of attention among the students at the school, our friends at Columbia Theological Seminary, and at church. She was a real little charmer and brought smiles to people's faces.

The only trouble during infancy was some minor colic, which Todd learned to cure by dancing with Rebecka to ABBA's "Dancing Queen." I stayed home with her until the start of the following school year. Rebecka was five months old when she started going to a home daycare while I was at school. It was too early, in my opinion, but we had moved into seminary housing and sorely needed a source of income. I decided to be okay with it. She showed little separation anxiety, and we concluded that we had a very flexible and well-adjusted baby.

On Rebecka's first birthday, Todd had an interview with a church in Waco, Texas. Our whole family attended, and to this day we are convinced that Rebecka sealed the job. She charmed the entire search committee and had the senior pastor wrapped around her little finger. She looked like a cherub with her chubby cheeks and blonde curls. A few months later, we went with the church's youth group on a mission trip to New Mexico. During one of the feel-good bonding activities, somebody said "Twinkle, twinkle little star." Rebecka didn't miss a beat and filled in the rest with perfect pitch: "Howwa wowwa wowwa aahh."

However, it was not until she turned two that we started to pick up on the fact that Rebecka was a gifted child. At her second birthday party, she received an alphabet puzzle. She showed us how she could name all the letters, and not just in order. We could point to any letter, and she could immediately tell us the name. We were proud of our smart kid, but didn't think too much about it.

By the time she reached preschool, she was bilingual in English and Swedish and was also studying Spanish. Everything came easily for Rebecka. She wasn't an off-the-charts genius, but she was up there.

We enjoyed four wonderful years in Waco. Rebecka had surrogate grandparents who spoiled her and made her feel comfortable and special. We had a lot of friends in the congregation who showered us with generosity—including lots of hand-me-downs from a family with three daughters. We didn't have much, but we had enough. Rebecka had a good early childhood.

Elementary School

The year Rebecka turned five, we moved to Nashville so Todd could attend graduate school at Vanderbilt University to pursue a PhD in Religious Studies. I had just completed my BA in computer science at Baylor University and had managed to find an entry-level programming job at a software company.

We purchased a twelve hundred-square-foot townhouse close to one of the best elementary schools in Nashville, Granbery Elementary. In first grade, Rebecka was tested for the gifted program. The tests indicated extremely high verbal skills and slightly above average logical/spatial skills. The counselor explained to us that having a big gap between the different types of skills could be stressful because verbal-related skills would come so easily while other skills would require more work. "Nothing to worry about," she said, "but something to keep in mind."

Rebecka was accepted into the gifted program, Encore. She seemed somewhat ambivalent toward it and asked to quit once or twice, but overall, it was a good experience. Her first-grade assessment stated:

> Rebecka seems to enjoy the challenges of Encore. She is always ready to begin the day and eagerly participates in all activities. Rebecka is a good listener, asks meaningful questions and uses high level thinking to solve problems.

When Rebecka was in second grade, we noticed that she had started to develop some mild tics. She moved her head in repetitive motions, blinked a lot, and made some grunting noises. It wasn't extremely noticeable, but as parents, we definitely picked up on it. Being a worrier, I researched Tourette syndrome and contacted the school counselor to see if we should be concerned. The counselor indicated that it was probably stress. Indeed, the annual standardized testing was coming up and Rebecka was worried about it, although she never verbalized this to us. As soon as the tests were over, her symptoms abated. They returned the following year around the same time, and then vanished for good.

Rebecka had all sorts of extracurricular opportunities in a city like Nashville. She tried a variety of sports and types of dance. She was a member of the Nashville Children's Choir—landing a coveted spot in the Touring Choir in fifth grade, which included participating in a recorded Christmas at Belmont concert with American Idol finalist Melinda Doolittle. She also attended an amazing Sunday school program at a Presbyterian church.

And she had Sophie, our bichon frise, who had been Rebecka's Christmas present when she was eight. She loved that dog (still does!), took dog-training classes, and taught her all sorts of fun tricks, including "roll over," "sit," and "shake." Sophie was the sibling she never had, but without the fighting!

In lieu of brothers and sisters to play with, Rebecka often had friends over after school and for sleepovers and frequently went to visit her friends' homes. Several of her classmates lived in the neighborhood, and as she got older, she was allowed walk to their houses on her own. She loved the independence.

As I advanced in my career, we were able to buy a nice, large home with a recreation room covering our double garage. This was Rebecka's domain.

She spent countless hours with her friends playing Dance Dance Revolution, watching movies, and eating lots of popcorn. This was also where we celebrated Stuffed Animal Church when we weren't in the mood to attend our regular church. Rebecka adored her stuffed animals, and Todd made them come alive by giving them different voices.

Rebecka *loved* living in Nashville.

However, we knew that Nashville was not a permanent home for our family. As Todd's PhD work drew to a close, he started looking for teaching positions. College teaching jobs are not easy to come by—and the chances of one opening up in Nashville were slim to none. We were able to buy a sixth year in Nashville when Todd got a temporary position at the Vanderbilt Divinity School, replacing a professor on sabbatical. However, the search for a more permanent position continued.

One spring day in 2008, Todd received an invitation to teach at Luther College in Decorah, Iowa. Unfortunately, it was not a tenure-track (permanent) position, but rather a visiting professorship, renewable for up to three years. However, it was the best option out there, so we started brainstorming how to make it work. Over the years, I had worked my way up the corporate ladder and was now a vice president at the same company I had started with six years prior. It was a nice job—despite frequent travel to our Wisconsin office—and I was hesitant to give it up. Yet the thought of staying in Nashville and having Todd be so far away was not appealing. Plus, I couldn't continue traveling at the same rate if I was operating as a single parent. Quitting my job and moving to Decorah seemed risky, because we had our house in Nashville and with the recession, we had no idea how long it would take to sell.

We looked at the map and realized that Decorah was only a four-hour drive from the Wisconsin office. One option would be for me, Rebecka, and Sophie to move to Wisconsin and for Todd to move to Decorah. We could spend the weekends and summers together. Anyway, it might only be for a year, because Todd would continue his search for a permanent position.

During this whole process, we contemplated the impact the different options might have on Rebecka. However, considering how flexible and social she seemed to be, we didn't think she would have trouble adjusting to any of these situations. In the end, she and I both voted for the option to move to Wisconsin, and so it was decided.

❧

Middle School

In July of 2008, Todd and I said goodbye to Nashville and drove the 570 miles up to Brookfield, a suburb west of Milwaukee. We had carefully handpicked Brookfield due to its proximity to my office and, more importantly, the great reputation of the schools there. Rebecka was excited about all the opportunities available at the school through clubs and other organizations. She arrived in Wisconsin a couple of weeks later by plane. She had wanted to spend some extra time with her friends before moving north.

We worried that Rebecka would miss the big house in Nashville and be upset that she would have to live in an apartment, but she took it in stride. "I think I'll actually like living here," she said after the initial tour. I appreciated the smaller space in terms of ease of cleaning. Rebecka liked the fact that you could get anywhere in the apartment in less than ten steps. (She wasn't really into physical exercise.)

We settled into our routine. I got up at 4:45 a.m. every morning to get my workout in before it was time for Rebecka to board the bus at 6:40 a.m. She came home after school and completed her homework and took Sophie for a walk. I tried to come home no later than 5:30 p.m. to prepare dinner and do other mom things. This arrangement forced me to cut down on my work hours, which was a good change.

Todd made the trek from Iowa to Wisconsin most weekends, but once a month, Rebecka and I drove with Sophie to visit him in Decorah. He was renting a house there, and we joked about going to our vacation home. In fact, those weekends were some of the most relaxing of my life. Decorah is the cutest little town, surrounded by bluffs and cornfields, with air so fresh you can taste it. In the mornings, I'd step outside and take deep breaths to fill my lungs with the freshness.

As the fall semester of sixth grade went along, I noticed that Rebecka wasn't spending much time with friends. She rarely brought friends to the apartment, and she didn't go to other people's houses very often. It wasn't like her not to make friends, but I had trouble figuring out what was going on. We visited the only Presbyterian church in the area, but there were hardly any children there. In fact, there weren't a whole lot of people under seventy! So there weren't a lot of friend opportunities there. The semester ended without any close friendships having been formed.

At the same time, Rebecka's generally cheerful disposition changed dramatically. She was moody and at times not very pleasant to be around. I thought maybe this was just related to puberty; she was eleven going on twelve, after all. But something didn't feel right.

During a Christmas visit to Sweden, normally a fun event, Rebecka continued to be quite moody and unpleasant. I wanted to figure out why Rebecka was feeling bad and acting the way she was. Then it dawned on me. She had been living virtually in Nashville for the past six months. With modern technology it was much easier to stay connected using texting and online chat. She had also been spending more time than she should watching TV, likely contributing to her moodiness.

Of course, Todd and I wanted her to stay connected to her old friends, but not to the detriment of her ability to make some new connections in Wisconsin. We devised a plan. The evening we got back to our little apartment in Brookfield, we broke the news to Rebecka: no more TV and computer for a while. Cold turkey. She still had her cell phone, but it would be restricted. She cried and cried, but we stood our ground. That was a Sunday.

Two days later, Rebecka and I were having our weekly dinner at Noodles & Company. We were chatting pleasantly and Rebecka remarked: "You know, I feel like my mood is much better from not watching TV." I agreed. It was nice to have our pleasant daughter back. She thrived in school and received a straight-A report card at the end of the spring semester. She also made some friends.

Things seemed to be going well. Rebecka decided to sign up for confirmation at a Lutheran church during her seventh grade, since several of her friends were doing the same. She also participated in a theater class. Maybe middle school wouldn't be so bad after all...

Part 1

❦

A Vicious Circle

Pills as a First Resort

(January 1–August 2, 2010)

Mental health medications do not cure mental illness.
However, they can often significantly improve symptoms
and help promote recovery and are recognized as
first-line treatment for most individuals.

—National Alliance on Mental Illness (NAMI) website

During our time in Brookfield, I became increasingly unhappy with my job. Not because the job changed, but because I changed. I became acutely aware of the environmental problems we face and the importance of moving beyond consumerism for a sustainable future.

The business I worked for created software for the retail industry. The goal of our software was to help manufacturers and retailers sell more. This business goal directly contradicted my newly developed values of sustainability and anti-consumerism. For the first time in my life, I understood the importance of doing work that aligns with your values.

The problem was, I was stuck. At the time, Todd had a year and a half left on his visiting professor contract, and we didn't know what would happen after that. It didn't seem fair to move Rebecka for what could potentially be just one year so that we could all live together and I could quit my job. When we decided in early 2010 that Rebecka and I would stay in Wisconsin, I mourned the situation. I cried a lot, and even though I tried to hide it from Rebecka, she knew. She felt guilty that I was sad because of a decision we had made to protect her happiness.

Rebecka was sick a lot that winter. According to her school records, she missed fifteen days of school in the first three months of the year. At one point, when she complained of a severe headache and lightheadedness, we ended up at the urgent care clinic. The doctor on call ordered rest in a dark room, thinking that it might be a migraine. Her primary doctor wasn't able to pinpoint what was wrong either, but prescribed several rounds of antibiotics. It was strange, because for most of her life, Rebecka had been a very healthy kid. She would get sick once a year—at most.

In addition to frequent illnesses, Rebecka's eating patterns changed that spring of seventh grade. Since the time Rebecka was in kindergarten, I had packed a lunch for her every morning. Not because I didn't want her to eat the school food, but because *she* didn't want to eat it. It was "nasty," she said. Then one day, she came home from school and announced that she wanted to start eating school food. "Nobody brings food from home," she explained. I was relieved. This would save me time every morning, and I was always looking for ways to save time. I didn't even look at the school lunch menu to see what they were serving. Having been born and (mostly) raised in Sweden, where school food is quite wholesome, I assumed that if they served it at school, it was healthy and safe.

At the same time, Rebecka was increasingly starting to refuse breakfast, or eat a very small breakfast. She said it made her stomach hurt. Knowing how important breakfast is for general health and learning, I tried to coax as much food as I could into her without making it a daily battle. She ate well at dinner, so I didn't worry too much about it.

Rebecka continued to be sick a day here and a day there, usually with a low-grade fever and no other symptoms. I was at a loss as to what to do, but allowed her to stay home from school the days she didn't feel well. Honestly, it was a nice excuse for me to work from home, away from all the pressure and conflicted feelings associated with my office.

One weekend in the middle of April, Rebecka and I visited Todd in Decorah. The weather was just starting to warm up after a long winter, and I was thoroughly enjoying our mini-vacation. I visited the local food co-op for lunch, while Todd and Rebecka went to get pizza. After lunch, Rebecka and I had a pedicure appointment, so Todd dropped her off outside the spa and told me, quite seriously, that Rebecka had something to tell me.

Once we were situated in our pedicure chairs, Rebecka didn't beat around the bush.

"I've been feeling really depressed lately."

I looked quizzically at the slim, strawberry-blonde girl sitting in the chair beside me. I was confused. She didn't seem depressed. She didn't sit in her room for hours on end, refusing to socialize. Rather, she had become quite the social butterfly—a big change from sixth grade, when she'd been the new, awkward girl, missing her Nashville friends terribly, and keeping in touch with them via Internet and cell phone at the expense of making friends at her new school.

"I cry in the bathroom sometimes," she said. "You know when I'm in there for a long time in the evenings?"

She *had* been spending considerable time in the bathroom, but I assumed this had to do with her new love of makeup and obsession with looking her absolute best at all times (which seemed developmentally appropriate—at least in our culture).

I said I was sorry she was sad. But I couldn't wrap my head around it. When I was thirteen years old, I wouldn't have had the vocabulary to express sad emotions in terms of "depression." Could this simply be puberty hormones at work? I mean, everybody feels down from time to time, right?

She insisted she didn't know why she was sad. She would just start crying.

"Next time it happens, let me know," I said. "We'll work through it together." Secretly, I hoped it would just go away.

Around the same time, Rebecka also confided in me that a couple of her good friends had been diagnosed with anorexia. We talked about how sad that was and how Rebecka might be a supportive friend as they worked through it. Rebecka told stories of trying to convince her anorexic friends to drink milk-shakes and other junk food to put the pounds back on. I was glad to hear that she was trying to be a good friend and help in her own way.

Rebecka was slimming down a bit herself, but I didn't think much of it, because she was simply starting to look more like the rest of the girls her age: growing lengthwise, rather than getting wider. However, one day in the beginning of May, it struck me that she had slimmed down considerably. As we were sitting together in our small living room, I said, "It looks like you have lost a lot of weight." She looked surprised. She said she hadn't been trying to lose weight, but got up and walked into the master bathroom to step on the scale.

She came out looking even more astonished. "I think I've lost twenty pounds," she said. Her weight was hovering around a hundred pounds. And she was almost as tall as I was, or around five feet five.

After all the talk about her anorexic friends, the next question just slid out of my mouth. "Do you think you may be anorexic?" I asked.

"Of course not," she responded. Wasn't she the one who was always trying to get her friends to eat more? I decided to believe her.

rebecka: on losing initial weight

Of all the events that took place in the years of my early adolescent life, I remember the matters relating to my eating and weight much better than anything else. In the middle of my seventh-grade year, I had finally started to make friends. For a year and a half I was the weird, lonely new girl from Tennessee with frizzy hair and thick braces. My rise to popularity seemed to be directly correlated with my discovery of makeup, layered hair, and the removal of my braces. In short, I was getting past my awkward phase and turning into something much more beautiful. Acknowledging that I sound full of myself, I was a fairly good-looking thirteen-year-old. In fact, to this day I know I received more compliments on my looks at the age of thirteen than any other age. I was also surrounded by other good-looking thirteen-year-olds. People knew who I was now; they knew I was someone to pay attention to. During this time, my best friend was struggling with a cruel eating disorder. Despite typical eating-disorder cattiness, I knew she always had it worse than I did. The fact that I knew she was sick made me sad, and I quite possibly absorbed her behaviors and made them my own. Still, I place no blame on her. She let her sickness rule her, and I let her sickness rule me.

When I went through my first bout of womanly puberty, I reached a healthy 120 pounds. This was a normal weight for my age and height, and I thought nothing of it. However, as time passed, my chronic stomachaches took over, and the desire to look good in public outweighed my need to eat at lunch. I was unconsciously performing the very acts that would take over my life in the near future. It only took five weeks for me to drop from that healthy weight of 120 to a slim one hundred pounds. The pounds slipped through my fingers like grains of sand, and I was powerless to stop it. I didn't notice the difference until there were no grains of sand left, and all I had was a ghastly thin physique and a worried mother.

When my mother brought up my thinning appearance, I thought nothing of it. Sure, the proof was in the scale that revealed the number neither of us saw coming, but in my mind I was healthy and eating much like any other teenager. Perhaps it was my denial that set the eating disorder off in full swing. Or maybe it was the fact that I had officially reached the standard of American beauty with my new body. I don't think there was one definite cause as to why the disorder took my life into a dark, empty hole filled with ghosts encouraging restricting and purging. I do know, however, that that initial weight loss made something in my brain click, and that click would become a burden on my family and me for several years to come.

The very next day, on our fifteenth wedding anniversary, I got a call from the mother of one of Rebecka's friends. I had gone for a hike during my lunch break and was heading back to my car when the phone rang. I didn't recognize the number, but it was local, so I thought I'd better answer. The mom introduced herself (I'll call her Beth), and I quickly made the connection that this was the mom of one of Rebecka's anorexic friends (I'll call her Ashley).

"I wouldn't intrude in this way if I didn't think Rebecka might be in danger," she started. (Knot in stomach.) "Ashley told me last night that Rebecka came to her and said that you were worried that she has an eating disorder."

I tried to shrug it off. "Yes," I said, "she *has* lost a lot of weight, but she says it was unintentional."

Beth then proceeded to tell me about taking Ashley in to see the doctor due to significant weight loss and discovering that Ashley's heart rate was dangerously low. Ashley had been hospitalized for several days while the hospital staff worked on stabilizing her condition.

I was in shock. I hadn't realized that Ashley's condition was so severe. I also learned that Ashley was now in an outpatient day program designed to help teens with eating disorders. I felt myself being hurled into a world that I didn't want to know anything about. And I certainly didn't want to have to know the best place to take a child with an eating disorder, or the various treatment options.

I expressed my deepest sympathy to Beth and managed to stay calm and collected as we ended the call. But my heart was racing, the adrenalin was flowing, and all I knew was that I had to get Rebecka to the doctor. Today.

I called the doctor's office as soon as I got off the phone with Beth, and relayed our story for the first of countless times. I explained that Rebecka had been feeling depressed, and that I had just noticed that she had lost twenty pounds. I mentioned that she wasn't eating breakfast and had friends who struggled with anorexia. And that one friend's mom had just scared me half to death. "Can we come in today?" I concluded.

Rebecka's regular doctor was not available, but we could see a Dr. O.

"Okay," I said, imagining my child's heart rate at less than fifty beats per minute and every beat potentially being the last.

We arrived at the doctor's office later that afternoon and went through the standard procedure of checking the pulse lying down, then standing up. Everything was fine. In fact, Dr. O homed in more on the feelings of depression than the potential eating disorder. He gave us two options:

1. Find a therapist for Rebecka and consider family therapy as well.
2. Find a psychiatrist. ("But you probably don't like that option," he said. No, I did not.)

Thus began the hunt for the perfect therapist. I wasn't happy about the thought of Rebecka's needing to see a therapist. (What parent wants to admit that their child has problems?) But it was much more appealing than the psychiatrist option, because, in my mind, seeing a psychiatrist indicated a need for psychopharmaceuticals—and Rebecka's situation did not seem severe enough to warrant medication. Our hope was that she could work through her struggles with the support of a good therapist.

So how does one go about finding a therapist? Let alone a therapist that clicks with your young, intelligent, and very particular teenage daughter?

Dr. O had given me a card listing his partners in the mental health world. I made sure the practitioners were covered by our health insurance and called to set up the appointment.

We got a time with a psychotherapist by the name of Pam Davis.

As we sat in the waiting room before our first appointment, I surveyed the room. Nobody looked happy. *What kind of problems do these other people have?* I wondered. I felt self-conscious being there, and the stigma surrounding mental illness enveloped me.

When we were finally called for the intake appointment, the therapist led us to a typical counseling room with a couch and, in this case, a bunch of toys and other props. She was clearly used to working with children. But was she used to working with teens? I could see how you might need a different personality (and different props) to work with teenagers versus children.

Ms. Davis started off by explaining matter-of-factly that anything Rebecka said was confidential. If Mom or Dad called asking questions, she would let Rebecka know. I understood she was trying to build trust with Rebecka, but it felt like a slap in the face. Were we not to be involved in this process? This was our child, after all, and Todd and I knew her better than anybody else.

Rebecka liked this aspect of therapy, but unfortunately, Ms. Davis was not a very warm person. In fact, she felt almost abrasive. But I decided to trust the professional. She must know what works, I reasoned. She had a job, after all.

Rebecka visited Ms. Davis two more times that May before deciding it wasn't working. They hadn't warmed to each other, and Rebecka didn't feel like any progress was being made. Of course, these things take time, but all the same, if Rebecka had made up her mind that it wouldn't work, it probably wouldn't.

In the middle of May, Rebecka got sick again, and on May 20, she collapsed at school. I had been out of town for work and drove straight from the airport to our apartment to find Rebecka writhing in severe abdominal pain. Since I had no way to discern whether this was benign or dangerous pain, I took her to the ER.

It was a nice suburban urgent care-type ER, so we didn't have to wait long to see a nurse. We told her the story of depression, weight loss, and collapsing at school. She asked the mandatory questions about suicidal thoughts and sexual activity. No and no, was the answer.

The ER doctor decided to do a computed tomography (CT) scan to make sure Rebecka didn't have appendicitis. I had a vague notion that CT scans are not good for you, but went along with it. Thankfully, there was nothing wrong with her appendix. Rather, she was very constipated—which we later learned can be a symptom of eating disorders and stress. We were sent home with instructions to buy magnesium citrate to relieve the constipation.

During this time, I was trying to find a new therapist for Rebecka. I can't remember how we found Patti Pitt, but she became therapist number two. By this time, Todd was home for the summer, so he took Rebecka to the first session. Similar to my experience with therapist number one, he was given no opportunity to speak alone with Ms. Pitt to give his two cents about what was going on. And at the end of one sixty-minute session, Ms. Pitt proclaimed she would like to "kick-start" the process with medication.

We were astonished. Really? Medication after one visit? The reason we were seeing a therapist was to avoid medication!

A Note on My General Philosophy on Medication

I have mixed feelings about medication—especially medication that masks symptoms that are caused by an underlying issue that should be addressed.

For example, I'm hesitant to take headache medicine, because the headache is a sign that I'm either not sleeping enough, not drinking enough water, not eating enough (rarely the case), or that I worked out too hard. Of course, in the last scenario, the damage is already done and it might make sense to pop a pill and just remember that doing intense running intervals after weeks of not doing any is not such a good idea.

On the other hand, I have nothing against taking medicine for menstrual cramps or curing strep throat with a dose of amoxicillin.

Prior to 2010, I had very little experience with psychiatric medications. In fact, all I knew was that they kept my brother-in-law from being much worse, and that my youngest brother should probably be taking them. I had even indicated as much to my mom. Like most people caught up in the prevalent discourses on mental illness, I thought these medications were miracle pills that helped people with brain disorders function better.

However, I did have reservations about giving these types of medications to children, but I cannot tell you why. It was a gut feeling.

So although I am more conservative than some when it comes to medication, I didn't have strong feelings against psychiatric medications—at least to treat mentally ill adults—prior to 2010, when we were faced with the prospect of having to administer this type of medication to our thirteen-year-old daughter.

At the end of May, Todd took Rebecka to see her pediatrician as a follow-up to the ER visit. They emerged with a prescription for Zoloft of twenty-five milligrams a day—half of the recommended initial adult dosage. The doctor's reasoning: perhaps anxiety is causing the stomach pain. Combined with the suggestion by Patti Pitt, it was enough to get us to comply. The doctor did indicate that there had been cases of suicidal behavior reported with the use of Zoloft, but that it wasn't anything to worry about.

I remember receiving the news and feeling my heart sink. A good friend from work was outraged. "She doesn't need medication," he fumed. "She's thirteen and going through puberty. Of course she's going to feel depressed. And the fact that she's not eating properly is probably causing the stomach pain!"

Medication Facts: Sertraline (Zoloft)

» Sertraline is an antidepressant in the SSRI (selective serotonin reuptake inhibitor) class.

» Pfizer brought Zoloft (trade name) to market in 1991.

» The Zoloft label indicates that it may be used to treat major depressive disorder in adults, obsessive-compulsive disorder (OCD) in children, teens, and adults, panic disorder in adults, posttraumatic stress disorder (PTSD) in adults, premenstrual dysphoric disorder (PMDD) in adults, and social anxiety disorder in adults.

» Warnings include clinical worsening, suicide risk, serotonin syndrome, and the possibility that some patients will develop bipolar disorder.

» There is a long list of "adverse events," including hallucinations and suicidal ideations. Please see FDA label for full list.

» Regarding pediatric use, the label states: "Safety and effectiveness in the pediatric population other than pediatric patients with OCD have not been established. . . . Anyone considering the use of ZOLOFT in a child or adolescent must balance the potential risks with the clinical need."

» Zoloft was the third-most-prescribed psychiatric drug in 2011, with about 37 million prescriptions (up 8 percent since 2009).

Sources: Drugwatch.com, US Food and Drug Administration (FDA), PsychCentral

I agreed, but at the same time, we wanted to trust the professionals. (This became a recurring and detrimental theme over the next twelve months.) So we continued with the medication. Maybe it would help.

rebecka: on starting medication

*I was very indifferent. If there was a magic pill that could
make me feel happy again, I was willing to try it.*

At a follow-up visit a few weeks later, Rebecka reported no improvement in her mood or in her stomach. But the medication continued. "Give it some time. It can take several weeks to experience relief," the doctor said. There was no discussion about diet, exercise, stress management, meditation, acupuncture, or other natural approaches to help our daughter cope with her distress and feel better.

We continued to trudge through June, visiting Patti Pitt and administering Zoloft. Rebecka acted pretty normal for the most part. She wasn't sitting in her room and staring at the wall or anything. Rather, she continued to be quite social. But she admitted to engaging in self-harm, primarily using sharp objects (shampoo bottle tops, paperclips, hairclips) to scratch her skin, a behavior that had been going on since the spring, before Rebecka started taking Zoloft. I'd never even heard of such a thing before (why would you willingly hurt yourself?), and it scared me. Todd and I started to wonder in earnest what had gone wrong.

Rebecka had always been the perfect child. In fact, we often joked that the reason we only had one child was because we could never have a more perfect second child. She slept through the night at two months and hit all the developmental milestones in a timely manner, charming everybody around her along the way. She was fun-loving, intelligent, musical, friendly, and well behaved.

In my mind, Rebecka the perfect child and Rebecka the self-harming teen did not go together. The easiest explanation we could think of—based on what we knew about mental illness, which wasn't much—was that Rebecka must have had an underlying mental illness gene that was now starting to rear its ugly head. Perhaps this was her destiny.

In early July, we went to Sweden for our annual visit. During this trip, Rebecka's fear of eating became much more apparent. She requested very small portions of food, ate junk food in place of real food, and made every meal a less-than-pleasant experience. She kept track of her food intake in a little notebook, making sure not to eat more than a thousand calories per day.

I tried to explain that the body's metabolism slows down when calorie intake is dangerously low, but this information went in one ear and out the other. Of course, we learned later that there is no way to reason with a person with an eating disorder. However, despite the significant weight loss and clearly disturbed eating patterns, neither her doctor nor her therapists had suggested we seek help specifically for her disordered eating. Perhaps the thought was that Zoloft would magically cure it.

One specific event that sticks out in my mind from that trip occurred during a picnic we were having on July 4 to celebrate my sister's birthday. I mentioned something about moving from Brookfield and my excitement about it. I was so ready to get settled somewhere, build deep relationships, and get involved in the community. Rebecka, on the other hand, started crying. I knew this topic was sensitive, but I didn't realize just how much Rebecka dreaded our inevitable move. She finally had friends, and a boyfriend, and she enjoyed her Brookfield life. And soon it would all be taken away. After consolation from a couple of different people, she eventually composed herself. But Todd and I knew this was not a normal reaction. The topic became taboo until further notice.

Toward the end of our trip, while sitting next to me in the car outside the house we were borrowing, Rebecka admitted to continued cutting. Her confession made me feel like the ground was crumbling below my feet. I wanted somebody to throw me a buoy and pull us all to safety.

But there was no buoy. Just Zoloft and a therapist named Patti Pitt.

I pleaded with Rebecka to tell me next time she felt like cutting. We could work through it together. She promised—mostly for my sake.

The next day, we told Rebecka that we would have to cancel an upcoming trip to Nashville to see her old friends if she wouldn't eat properly. Nobody had told us that setting consequences would work for eating disorders, but intuitively, it felt like the logical thing to do. Like magic, she started eating normally again. This trip clearly meant a lot to her.

When we returned to Wisconsin, Rebecka attended summer camp at the Milwaukee Art Museum. She had no trouble making friends and seemed to enjoy the experience. We definitely didn't sense any anxiety. Maybe the medicine was helping after all!

The following week, Rebecka went back to the pediatrician for a medication follow-up. Rebecka said the Zoloft was not helping her mood and complained that she had been experiencing obsessive-compulsive thoughts, especially related to cutting. She also confessed that she had been having suicidal thoughts.

The doctor decided to switch her to Prozac, which is supposed to be better for obsessive-compulsive thoughts. In hindsight, I thought this was quite ironic, considering that the *only* disorder Zoloft is approved to treat in children is OCD. Again, there was no discussion regarding other methods of treating the feelings of depression and undiagnosed eating disorder. We left the doctor's office with a prescription for twenty milligrams a day.

Medication Facts: Fluoxetine (Prozac)

» Fluoxetine is an antidepressant in the SSRI (selective serotonin reuptake inhibitor) class.

» Eli Lilly brought Prozac (trade name) to the US market in 1988.

» The Prozac label indicates that it may be used to treat major depressive disorder in adults and pediatric patients ages eight to eighteen, obsessive-compulsive disorder (OCD) in adults and pediatric patients ages seven to seventeen, bulimia nervosa in adults, panic disorder in adults, bipolar I disorder in adults (in combination with Zyprexa), and treatment-resistant depression in adults (in combination with Zyprexa).

» There is a long list of "warnings and precautions" that include clinical worsening and suicide risk. Please see FDA label for full list.

» There is also a long list of "adverse reactions," including anorexia, insomnia, and anxiety.

» Regarding pediatric use, the label states: "The safety and effectiveness in pediatric patients <8 years of age in major depressive disorder and <7 years of age in OCD have not been established. . . . Anyone considering the use of PROZAC in a child or adolescent must balance the potential risks with the clinical need."

» Prozac was the fifth-most-prescribed psychiatric drug in 2011, with about 24.5 prescriptions (up 6% since 2009).

Sources: Drugwatch.com, US Food and Drug Administration, PsychCentral

Side Effects from Hell

(August 3, 2010–September 7, 2010)

As [Eli Lilly] well knew, Prozac and other SSRIs could trigger
manic episodes, and so it instructed its sales representatives to tell
psychiatrists that Zyprexa 'is a great mood stabilizer, especially
for patients whose symptoms were aggravated by an SSRI.'
In essence, Eli Lilly was telling doctors to prescribe its second
drug to fix the psychiatric problems caused by the first one.

—Robert Whitaker, *Anatomy of an Epidemic*

Since Rebecka's eating habits had improved, we let her go to Nashville to see her friends. I was also going there for business, so at least I wouldn't be far away if she got sick again. We really wanted to encourage her good eating and reward her with this trip. Rebecka and I arrived in Nashville on August 3, 2010, and I dropped her off at the home of one of her friends, whom she hadn't seen for months. It was a joyful and sweet reunion. I decided not to worry, and went about my business for the next several days.

A few days later, toward the end of our trip, I met up with a good friend and mentor at the iconic Nashville eatery Tin Angel. We settled down in the cozy atmosphere, sipped our wine, and chatted about life and work while we waited for our dinner to arrive. Suddenly, my phone rang. It was Rebecka.

"Hi, Mom." She sounded good—almost excited. *Phew.* "So the last few days

I've been hearing voices."

Wait! What? "Okay…? What are they saying?"

"Oh, just different things. And I'm also seeing a little girl."

"Um. Are you worried?" *I'm freaking out.*

"No, not really. Actually, it's kind of interesting."

I relaxed a bit. "Do you want me to come pick you up? You can come spend the night with me at my hotel if you want."

"No, I'm fine. I'll see you tomorrow."

"Okay. I love you."

"Love you too."

Considering that my friend had just heard half of the conversation, I told her what was up. She offered to call off the dinner if I needed to go pick up Rebecka. However, I wanted to respect Rebecka's decision to stay with her friend one last night. Somehow, I managed to eat my dinner and get through the rest of the evening. Life was bordering on the bizarre.

The following day, I treated Rebecka to one of my favorite Nashville restaurants, Tayst. Rebecka spent almost the entire meal telling me where Alice—her name for the little-girl hallucination—was standing, and what she was doing. I tried to comprehend what was happening. I asked questions. I really had no idea what to think about it all. It was scary and amusing at the same time.

Rebecka was clearly fascinated by the experience. The fact that she wasn't worried about it had a calming effect on me as well.

The next day, when we were back in Brookfield, Rebecka had another follow-up appointment with her pediatrician. Todd accompanied her and listened quietly while Rebecka described the hallucinations to her doctor, who said that this case was now beyond her area of expertise and referred Rebecka to a psychiatrist.

Todd was stunned. Frustrated thoughts spun through his mind: Wait! You are responsible for starting her on a medication that led to this problem, and now you are basically abandoning us? Why did you prescribe antidepressants to her to begin with if you didn't feel qualified to handle the 'complications' that might arise? But he didn't say anything. He wanted to trust the system—trust the professionals.

I remember getting a call from Todd and feeling the sense of losing control growing exponentially. In my mind, a referral to a psychiatrist meant something was really wrong.

That same day, Todd took Rebecka to a bookstore where she purchased a psychology book, *The Complete Idiot's Guide to Psychology*. We were impressed that she wanted to learn more about psychology. In reality, she was probably freaking out and wanted to know what the hell was happening to her.

The following day, Rebecka hung out with two of her friends in the afternoon. They seemed to have a blast and took lots of pictures doing everything from riding around in a grocery store cart to having light-saber fights in the hallway of our apartment building. Looking back at pictures from this day, I see that Rebecka looks sort of happy, but tired and awfully thin. Like one of those sad celebrity pictures in magazines with headings such as "Angelina at the Academy Awards: Too Thin or Fashion Win?" and "Mary-Kate's Private Battle."

Hospitalization #1

Later that night, when we were already in bed, Rebecka came into our bedroom. She was shaking and clearly upset, but not crying. She told us rather matter-of-factly that she had been sitting in the living room, reading a book, when Alice had walked over to her and grabbed her hand (this was the first tactile hallucination) and led her to the kitchen, encouraging her to hurt herself. Rebecka was understandably jarred by this experience and indicated that she didn't feel safe.

I was terrified. So was Todd.

Beth, whose phone call had sent us to the doctor in the first place, had given us a card for Sanders Psychiatric Hospital. It was the only psychiatric hospital we knew about, so we gave them a call. I explained the situation, and the kind voice on the other end encouraged us to bring Rebecka in to be admitted. We packed a bag—the first of many—and headed out.

Sanders Psychiatric Hospital sits on a gorgeous property with lots of grass, flowers, and trees. We couldn't see much of this as we arrived, but it truly had the feel of the old-fashioned mental hospitals you see in movies. Once inside, we provided insurance information, hoping everything would be covered. (They would let us know in the morning, they said.) Then we made our way to the child and adolescent unit. A nurse inspected Rebecka from head to toe, noting any existing marks or injuries. A staff person checked her belongings for sharp objects and strings. And we answered a lot of questions.

The whole experience was surreal. We were admitting our child to a psychiatric institution—our only child, who earlier that day had seemed completely "normal" while hanging out with her friends. It was confusing, to say the least.

Rebecka got her own room, which was void of anything that could be used for self-harm, and which locked from the outside. She had a bathroom, but was not allowed to keep most of her toiletries with her—and no makeup. Electronic gadgets were also disallowed. I was happy about this.

We returned home in the early hours of August 13 and attempted to sleep. The apartment felt empty without Rebecka. And somehow, I knew our lives would never be the same. We had entered the mental "health" system, where pills are a first resort, new symptoms are treated with more pills, and Rebecka's condition yesterday, a month ago, or a year ago had no bearing on treatment decisions.

rebecka: on being hospitalized

Despite the terror I felt at leaving my family and friends behind, I was relieved that I would be in a safe, secure place where I couldn't hurt myself. It was unfamiliar and lonely, but they did a good job of making us feel protected and as comfortable as we could be given the situation.

The staff tried to teach us lessons about coping that I initially rejected and scoffed at—much like everyone else did. Now, however, some of those lessons help me in everyday life.

While Rebecka was in the hospital, the attending psychiatrist put her on Risperdal in addition to her antidepressant. Risperdal is an antipsychotic prescribed to treat symptoms of mental illnesses such as schizophrenia. There are a host of possible side effects, but one really disturbing side effect in children is what's called Parkinsonism. The Mayo Clinic website provides the following definition of this condition:

> Parkinsonism is any condition that causes a combination of the movement abnormalities seen in Parkinson's disease—such as tremor, slow movement, impaired speech or muscle stiffness—especially resulting from the loss of dopamine-containing nerve cells (neurons).[1]

Because this is a known side effect of antipsychotics in children, the doctor also subscribed benztropine to stave off muscle stiffness and other symptoms of Parkinsonism.

Medication Facts: Risperidone (Risperdal)

» Risperidone is a potent antipsychotic in the atypical antipsychotic class.

» Janssen-Cilag brought Risperdal (trade name) to market in 1994. Generic versions are available.

» The Risperdal label indicates that it may be used to treat schizophrenia in adults and teens, bipolar mania in children, teens, and adults, and irritability associated with autistic disorder in children and teens.

» Warnings include increased mortality in elderly patients with dementia-related psychosis, neuroleptic malignant syndrome (potentially fatal), tardive dyskinesia (potentially irreversible, involuntary movements), hyperglycemia and diabetes mellitus, dyslipidemia, weight gain, and seizures.

» There is a long list of "adverse events," including Parkinsonism (which affected between 16 percent and 28 percent of participants in a trial of pediatric patients with schizophrenia). Please see FDA label for full list.

» Regarding pediatric use, the label states: "Safety and effectiveness of RISPERDAL® in children less than 13 years of age with schizophrenia have not been established.... Safety and effectiveness of RISPERDAL® in children less than 10 years of age with bipolar disorder have not been established."

» Risperdal was the fourteenth-most-prescribed psychiatric drug in 2011, with about 12 million prescriptions (up 14 percent since 2009).

Sources: US Food and Drug Administration, PsychCentral

We were baffled by this concept of prescribing medication to treat symptoms of another medication, but we went along with it. The psychiatrist was likable and seemed competent, and we trusted that he had our daughter's best interest in mind, which to this day I do not doubt. We wanted to trust his treatment plan.

Rebecka stayed at Sanders for six days. She participated in various types of therapy,* learned relaxation techniques, and even got to go out on the lake. It was almost camp-like. The only other tenant on the unit was a much younger boy with severe OCD. He was visibly in much worse shape than Rebecka (hallucinations and all), and Todd and I questioned if she really belonged in this type of clinical setting.

When we arrived for our family meeting prior to Rebecka's discharge on August 18, we got to visit with a therapist, who explained that she had been working with Rebecka to manage the hallucinations. We also met with the psychiatrist, who suggested that we check in with Rebecka once a day to ask about hallucinations, depression, eating, and cutting. Not more frequently than that. "We don't want to make a big deal about it," he said.

I thought it was kind of a big deal, but I understood where he was coming from.

The hospital staff sent us home with a referral to a Sanders outpatient eating disorder program at a different facility closer to home, and instructions to make a "happy box" with Rebecka. This box would contain items that relaxed her and made her happy. Today I know these would be considered "coping strategies." At the time, all I knew was that this happy box was supposed to help Rebecka feel better.

"Oh, and it would probably be a good idea to hide the kitchen knives and other sharp objects," the therapist suggested while Rebecka was out of the room.

This was getting to be way too real.

We welcomed Rebecka home with pomp and circumstance. We were proud of her recovery and so glad to have her home again. There were purple streamers in the living room, a cake for Todd's birthday (one day late), and a brand new Wii Fit.†

We were excited about getting help with the disordered eating. Finally!

---

* We believe these therapies would have benefited Rebecka much more—and sooner—had she not been under the influence of powerful psychotropic medications.

† Rebecka had told me that it was a really fun game—in hindsight, she was probably looking for innocent-seeming ways to fuel her eating disorder.

Maybe this would be the turning point in this so-far horrific experience.

The following Monday, I drove Rebecka to the suburban campus of Sanders Psychiatric Hospital. This facility was not nearly as nicely situated as the picturesque hospital Rebecka had just left, but it didn't matter. I was so thrilled that Rebecka was out of the hospital and getting help with the eating issues. We were on the road to recovery!

But there were bumps in the road ahead.

On the evening of the second day of the outpatient treatment, Rebecka attended an end-of-summer party at a friend's house. She called to be picked up early because she wasn't feeling well.

Hospitalization #2

Later that evening, while Todd and I were hanging out in the living room, Rebecka came out of her bathroom looking shaken, and asked to speak to me in private. I gave Todd a worried look, got off the couch, and ushered her into the master bedroom, closing the door behind us.

"What's wrong, sweetie?" I asked.

"When I was in the bathtub, I had a really strong urge to put my head under the water and drown myself," she answered with a shaky voice. "Mom, I'm scared."

I felt my heart rate quicken and stomach tighten. *Noooooo! I can't handle this*, I screamed inside.

But instead of losing it, I called Sanders (it was all we knew to do) and explained the situation. Whenever there are suicidal thoughts involved, it's pretty much a ticket to get admitted, assuming there are available beds, so I sent Rebecka to her room to pack her bag. Todd drove us to the hospital in the dark.

The admissions process this time was a lot more involved. We signed dozens of papers and were asked an equally large number of questions. Everything was painstakingly entered into an ancient computer. The intake nurse asked us about current medications, medical history (all the way from pregnancy), family history, and what we hoped to get out of the hospital visit (no more thoughts of drowning in the bathtub…?).

Once Rebecka was admitted and ushered to her room, the attending psychiatrist, Dr. H, sat down with Todd and me for quite a while. Not used to this amount of attention from doctors, we poured our hearts out and tried to formulate our thoughts on what had been going on. Throughout the summer,

Todd's and my conversations with each other had become more and more centered on Rebecka's health. We questioned our past actions, her choice of friends, wondered about mental illness genes, and tried our best to "figure it out." We were not used to problems we couldn't solve. So it was nice to have another person to talk to about these things.

Dr. H homed in on the fact that Todd once responded well to an antidepressant called Remeron (mirtazapine). Todd had taken this during a bout of situational anxiety and depression during his PhD studies (apparently, getting depressed during one's graduate studies is pretty common). Dr. H said that children respond very quickly to antidepressants, so we should know within a couple of days if it was working or not.

Medication Facts: Mirtazapine (Remeron)

» Mirtazapine is an antidepressant in the tetracyclic antidepressant class.

» Organon USA (a division of Merck & Co.) brought Remeron (trade name) to market in 1996.

» The Remeron label indicates that it may be used to treat major depressive disorder in adults.

» Warnings include clinical worsening, suicide risk, serotonin syndrome, and the possibility that some patients will develop bipolar disorder.

» There is a long list of "adverse events," including dizziness, weight gain, and elevated triglycerides. Please see FDA label for full list.

» Regarding pediatric use, the label states: "Safety and effectiveness of mirtazapine in the pediatric population have not been established." (Yikes!)

» Remeron was not among the twenty-five most prescribed psychiatric medications of 2011.

Sources: National Library of Medicine, US Food and Drug Administration, PsychCentral

Todd and I looked at each other. We had encountered the first contradiction related to Rebecka's treatment. Her pediatrician had said it could take weeks for her to respond to the antidepressant. This psychiatrist was saying it should only take days. We decided to trust the psychiatrist. With our consent, he switched Rebecka from Prozac to Remeron. He also took her off the antipsychotic medication. Nice. We liked this doctor.

A structured environment and life without electronics turned Rebecka into a well-adjusted, pleasant child within days. One day when we came to visit during the rather limited visiting hours, she told us that we were "awesome parents." She'd heard some horror stories from the other kids on the unit, and she'd started to realize that her parents were pretty decent in comparison. It felt good to be appreciated.

Since she seemed to be doing so well, and since Todd was about to move back to Decorah for the fall semester, we convinced Dr. H to discharge her after five days in the hospital. Rebecka wanted to go home, and we wanted her at home with us. The doctor was completely onboard with this. It was a Sunday, so the regular staff wasn't around. Hence, there was no proper follow-up plan defined at our rather hasty departure. They would let us know in a couple of days, they said.

The following day, August 30, Todd left for Decorah. Rebecka and I did some back-to-school shopping, and in the evening we went down to the school to set up Rebecka's locker. I was relieved that she would be able to start eighth grade with the rest of her friends. Rebecka wasn't overly excited, but seemed to be doing okay. On August 31, she hung out with a couple of her friends.

Hospitalization #3

rebecka: on hospitalization #3

> *A lot of very intimate details of my life are in this book. My third hospitalization is one of the most painful memories I have and not something I wish to go into full detail about. When we were writing this section, I ultimately decided to narrate the first part of it myself.*
>
> *The night after I was with my friends, I was seized by suicidal urges that I had never felt before, and experienced some of my strongest hallucinations. My mother, with the help of a good friend, was able to help me calm down long enough to call the hospital and check for availability.*

I don't remember much, but I do remember my mother singing Swedish lullabies to me—a big comfort whenever I got scared as a child.

When we got to the hospital, Dr. H was again the attending psychiatrist. No surprise, he did not expect me back so soon. He decided to consult the neurologist and get scans of my brain to make sure nothing was physically ailing me. Nothing ever came up.

A few days into the hospitalization, I started going into these deep psychoses for fifteen to thirty minutes at a time. I was apparently unreachable from the outside world for this time and had to come back to reality on my own terms. I don't remember a lot about where I thought I was or what was happening during these episodes.

On September 3, Dr. H decided to take Rebecka off Remeron and put her on Seroquel (quetiapine fumarate). Seroquel is an antipsychotic prescribed to treat schizophrenia in adults and children who are at least thirteen years old. Like all of the psychotropic medications, Seroquel has a list of frightening side effects, many serious enough to warrant the immediate discontinuation of the medication, for example "jerky muscle movements you cannot control, trouble swallowing, [and] problems with speech."[2] Dr. H hoped this medication would help with the psychotic episodes.

Todd and I got to witness one of these episodes during a visit. We were sitting with Rebecka in her room when all of a sudden she got up from her bed with a glazed look on her face. She walked out the door and wandered down the hallway as if we were not in the room with her and she couldn't hear us. Nervous and not sure what to do, I followed Rebecka into the stark hallway, my eyes searching for a hospital attendant.

"Excuse me," I asked the first person I could find, a nurse who I'd seen interacting with Rebecka when we arrived. "What . . . ?" I didn't even have the vocabulary to ask a question. I just pointed to Rebecka.

The nurse gently steered Rebecka back to the room and sat her down on the bed.

"Try to keep her on the bed until this passes," she said casually as if we were simply waiting for the rain to stop. "That way she won't injure herself by bumping into things."

Medication Facts: Quetiapine Fumarate (Seroquel)

» Quentiapine fumarate is an atypical (second-generation) antipsychotic.

» AstraZeneca brought Seroquel (trade name) to market. The FDA originally approved it in 1997. Now, several generic versions are available.

» The Seroquel label indicates that it may be used to treat schizophrenia in people age thirteen and older, bipolar I disorder in adults, and manic episodes associated with bipolar I disorder in children ages ten to seventeen.

» Warnings include risk of death in the elderly with dementia, risk of suicidal thoughts or actions, high blood sugar (diabetes), increased cholesterol and triglycerides, and weight gain.

» There is a long list of possible side effects, including neuroleptic malignant syndrome (can cause death), tardive dyskinesia, and seizures. Please see FDA label for full list.

» Seroquel was the tenth-most-prescribed psychiatric drug in 2011 with about 14 million prescriptions.

Sources: US Food and Drug Administration, PsychCentral

As soon as the nurse left, Rebecka tried to get off the bed and struggled as we attempted to keep her safe. As the episode went on, she became increasingly frustrated.

I sang to her the songs that had soothed her as a young child. Todd tried to coax her out of her trance. We cried and wondered, is this it? Have we lost our little girl forever? Is she going to be institutionalized for the rest of her life?

It was possibly the most terrifying experience of our lives.

Todd and I spent a lot of brainpower trying to figure out what might be causing these psychotic episodes. We could not accept that Rebecka's mental health could go downhill so quickly. How could she go from melancholy—but otherwise fully functional—to extremely psychotic in a few short months? We analyzed the past and the present. We looked for patterns. But we couldn't figure it out. All we knew was that once she started "treatment," she declined rapidly. And during that visit, recovery felt out of reach.

rebecka: on the side effects of seroquel

A side effect of one of my medications was twitching. There were a few days where I would have convulsions in my neck, shoulders, arms, and hands, and I was powerless to stop it. I was usually conscious when these happened so I remember well the accompanying embarrassment of not being able to control my movements.

We came back later that day for the evening visiting hours, hoping we wouldn't have to witness another episode. We didn't know if we could take it. When we entered her room, Rebecka was sitting on her bed talking to her roommate. Our beautiful daughter was convulsing with involuntary movements of all the major muscles in her upper body.

What? It's worse? We were petrified, but tried not to show it.

Rebecka attempted to be lighthearted about her new affliction (clearly a side effect of the medication, though we didn't know it at the time), but she also expressed a lot of anxiety about what was happening to her and worried about her future. We spent our visit comforting her, and reassuring her that we would figure it out and that we would always be there to take care of her.

By the time we left an hour later, the involuntary movements had subsided a good bit, so we thought maybe they were anxiety-induced and that our reassurance had helped ease the anxiety some.

The next day, Dr. H added Remeron back into the mix. I can't recall the reason, but my guess is that it was for anxiety. What surprises me when I think back on this time is that he didn't immediately take Rebecka off Seroquel, considering the severe side effects she was experiencing.

At this point, our belief in medications as treatment for Rebecka's emotional distress had been shaken to the point that I asked Dr. H to take her off all the psychiatric medications the following day. They clearly weren't working. In fact, she was getting worse—exponentially worse. Dr. H completely agreed.

The deep psychoses stopped. And over the next few days, Rebecka reported that the hallucinations disappeared completely.

Is It Contagious?

(September 7, 2010–October 14, 2010)

A few mental illnesses identified and popularized in the United States—
depression, post-traumatic stress disorder, and anorexia among them—
now appear to be spreading across cultural boundaries and
around the world with the speed of contagious diseases.

—Ethan Watters, *Crazy Like Us*

The excitement I felt over the withdrawal of Rebecka's medications was soon tempered. The same evening, I received a phone call explaining that I needed to come to the hospital. Rebecka wanted to talk to me.

I dashed over to the hospital, heart pounding, to learn that she had started experiencing flashbacks of a traumatic event that had occurred in her past. During these flashbacks, Rebecka had significant involuntary movements and was "out of it" for a few minutes. These episodes also included screaming and protesting. She worried it would happen when she went back to school and what her friends would think.

Rebecka also told us that her roommate suffered from flashbacks. It made us wonder if she was actually picking up psychiatric behaviors in the hospital, perhaps as a way unconsciously to empathize with those around her. After all, this whole ordeal had gotten kicked off by Rebecka losing weight—just like her friends at school. And there *is* evidence that eating disorders may be contagious.[1] I also had suspicions that she had picked up cutting from another one of her friends. This is not often discussed, but as Dr. Norman Berlinger writes in *Rescuing Your Child from Depression*, "Emotional contagion is real. It is not a statistical quirk or a fortuitous clustering of tragedies."[2]

At this point, Dr. H was feeling like he was in over his head and decided to take Rebecka's case to his team's weekly staff meeting. He indicated he would like a more senior psychiatrist to assess the case.

I was torn between relief that more help was coming and sorrow that our daughter's case required more advanced assistance. We also didn't want to lose Dr. H, because he was easy to talk to and seemed to listen to our concerns, even if he, too, was embedded in the medication discourse.

We never found out what came out of that meeting, but a day or so later, Rebecka was released from the hospital—still off psychotropic medications— with prescriptions for a number of other medications including Pepcid for her stomach and Singulair for suspected allergies. She was to go to school during the morning hours and attend day treatment at Sanders Psychiatric Hospital in the afternoon.

On September 10, Rebecka went back to school for the first half of the day and attended the day program the second half. She was resolved to find meaningful activities and made plans to try out for a vocal ensemble. I signed her up for a hip-hop dance class and started looking into community choirs so she could pick up choral singing again.

She was motivated and said she was ready to "focus on school and have a good year." I was hopeful this would come true, now that she was off medication and home with us.

It went well for a couple of weeks. During this time, her beloved aunt and uncle came to visit, and she started getting back into socializing with her friends. We also make a trip to Decorah to visit Todd. She felt so good that we dared to leave her alone in the apartment for a few hours. It seemed like everything was going to be okay.

However, as soon as we returned to Brookfield, Rebecka admitted that she had started cutting again.

Devastation.

I responded by signing us up for a beginning yoga class. But it would be months before we made it there.

Hospitalization #4

The very next day, I got a call from the school to say that Rebecka wasn't feeling well. She wasn't "feeling safe." I took her to the day program that afternoon, and before I knew it, she was admitted to the hospital due to the expression of suicidal thoughts with a plan.

She was now under the care of the director of the hospital, Dr. Z. He caught up with me in the hallway as I was headed to my car after bringing a bag of clothes, toiletries, slippers, and schoolwork during evening visiting hours.

"I met with Rebecka this evening," he said. "She is very bright, but she doesn't know what she wants." He proceeded to describe Rebecka and what was going on with her in a most perceptive manner, throwing the word 'comorbidity' around as if I was supposed to know what that meant. Overall, I was impressed by his assessment of the situation. However, I was dejected when I got home and looked up 'comorbidity' online to find that it meant multiple disorders co-occurring in a patient. I realized that Rebecka's situation was complex, but this sounded insurmountable.

At least she's off medication, I thought.

The following evening, after I'd already gone to bed, I got a call from Dr. Z's nurse. She was asking for verbal consent to put Rebecka back on Prozac and an antianxiety medication called Klonopin (clonazepam). I was so tired I just said yes. No time for research or discussion. Put on the spot. But I did remind the nurse that the last time Rebecka was on antidepressants, she started hallucinating.

"Okay," she said.

I put the phone down and laid my head back on the pillow. More medicine. More hospitalizations. Would it ever end?

I cried myself to sleep.

Medication Facts: Clonazepam (Klonopin)

» Clonazepam is a benzodiazepine (the same class of drugs as Librium and Valium).

» Hoffmann-La Roche brought Klonopin (trade name) to the US market. The FDA originally approved it in 1975. Now, many generic versions are available.

» The Klonopin label indicates that it may be used to treat seizure disorders and panic disorder.

» Warnings include interference with cognitive and motor performance, suicidal behavior and ideation, and withdrawal symptoms.

» There is a long list of adverse reactions, including depression and reduced intellectual ability. Please see FDA label for full list.

» Regarding pediatric use, the label states: "Safety and effectiveness in pediatric patients with panic disorder below the age of 18 have not been established."

» Klonopin was not among the twenty-five most prescribed psychiatric medications of 2011.

Sources: National Library of Medicine, US Food and Drug Administration, PsychCentral

Rebecka stayed at the hospital for several days. Eventually, she started feeling safe again.

Her social workers told me she was displaying early signs of borderline personality disorder and suggested a therapy called dialectical behavior therapy (DBT).

I went online to research DBT and liked what I found. DBT is like a cross between cognitive behavioral therapy and Eastern philosophy. Over the past several years, I had become interested in Buddhism and the power of mindfulness. I was happy to see that mindfulness was one of the four modules in DBT.

I approved.

Treatment Facts: Dialectical Behavior Therapy (DBT)

» Dr. Marsha Linehan, professor at the University of Washington, developed DBT to treat people suffering from borderline personality disorder, or more generally speaking, people with self-harm behaviors.

» DBT is a type of cognitive behavioral therapy with the important distinction of possessing these additional therapy strategies:
  › Validation strategies (acceptance-based interventions)
  › Dialectical strategies (balancing acceptance and change)

» Several clinical trials have demonstrated that DBT is more effective than treatment as usual in treatment of BPD.

» For more details on DBT, see chapter 15.

Source: Behavioral Tech, LLC

When Rebecka was finally discharged from the hospital on Tuesday, October 5, she was still on the Prozac/Klonopin cocktail. The follow-up plan called for her to attend the day program, participate in a DBT skills group, and go to an eating disorder support group.

I felt a little better about this plan than previous plans, because it included the DBT. But we never got that far.

I was at work over the weekend, overseeing the deployment of a major software release when Rebecka called me to ask if she could come to the office because she was bored. It was not a good time, so I told her no. Instead, she turned to reading about multiple personality disorder in her psychology book. I got home late, exhausted and running on Red Bull and Milk Duds.

The following day, Rebecka went off to school without any problem. By mid-morning, I got the dreaded call from her school. Rebecka's hallucinations were back. And she was hearing voices.

I left my corner office and drove over to the school. The principal was sitting with Rebecka, encouraging her to draw pictures. Rebecka was able to speak coherently about her summer vacation, but something was off. She had taken on a new "ditzy" personality (speaking in a lilting, silly voice and appearing to be "out of it"). I know my daughter. She is anything but ditzy. Over time, we started referring to this new personality as "blonde Rebecka." Once again, I had no framework for responding to the situation. As I look at this event in the rearview mirror, I wonder how much of this new personality was linked to Rebecka's study of multiple personality disorder the day before. Was reading about mental disorders another source of "contagion"?

Rebecka's desperation to fit a diagnosis demonstrates the power of the prevalent discourses on mental illness. A diagnosis would make her problems real—it would validate and explain her struggle. This complicated the situation. If "mental illness" had been kept out of the equation from the start and the professionals had taken a more holistic approach to easing Rebecka's distress, I am sure we would have had a completely different experience. Rebecka was unconsciously trying to fit into the box that is modern psychiatry. In this box, mental distress means something is "wrong" with your brain, and based on how you behave and feel, there are different names (diagnoses) for the brain disease. There is no room for the ups and downs of the human experience—such as coming of age in the digital era in a split home with an uncertain future.

The school psychologist met with me and said they couldn't keep Rebecka at school in her current state. I didn't blame them.

So I brought her home for a couple of hours until it was time for her to go to the day program.

Nobody Will Listen

(October 15, 2010–November 1, 2010)

If psychiatrists listened to their patients about how the drugs were affecting them, we would have only a few patients on them long-term.

—Dr. David Healy, quoted in *Anatomy of an Epidemic*

Hospitalization #5

Those few hours at home with blonde Rebecka were like a psychedelic nightmare. Questions swirled through my head. Where was our child? What was this medication doing to her? Was she making it all up to get attention? Or was being at school just so stressful that she couldn't cope?

My brain worked in overdrive in search for answers to these questions. But there were no answers to be found.

After lunch, I took Rebecka to the day program, where Dr. Z saw her and admitted her back into full hospitalization. I had started to lose track of how many times she had been hospitalized and the different discharge plans started running together.

Will this vicious circle of inpatient/outpatient/inpatient/outpatient ever end? I wondered. *It clearly isn't working.*

Visiting Rebecka during this hospitalization was painful. How could our very normal teenager—as of just a few short months ago—be so far removed from us, mentally? It didn't compute in my head.

A couple of days into her hospitalization, Rebecka started complaining about hearing voices that would not go away. The staff let her sit in the "quiet room" (basically a padded room where it's impossible to get hurt and the patient can't disturb the other patients) and scream at the voices.

Rebecka was extremely worried that she wouldn't be able to come back home and go to school with all these voices shouting in her head. "What will the neighbors think when I start screaming at the voices to stop?" she asked. I told her not to worry about it. But she was worried. And I was worried.

How I even functioned is a mystery to me now.

Rebecka started to think that the only solution was to go to a residential program—one of those programs where you're locked away from the world for months on end. "It worked really well for one of my friends," she said. Todd and I worried that sending her off to this type of setting would make it even harder for her to re-enter the real world later.

When I visited that evening, I got to speak to Dr. Z one-on-one. He sat me down and said that if this were twenty years ago, he would diagnose Rebecka with bipolar disorder. The reason being that she responded to the antidepressant with mania, which is how he was interpreting the "blonde" state. This didn't make sense to me at all.

But it did make sense when, months later, Todd and I read in *Anatomy of an Epidemic*, by Robert Whitaker, about a 1982 study in which the researchers indicated that antidepressants could be used as a diagnostic tool to uncover bipolar illness.[1] However, Whitaker argues that rather than unmasking the illness, antidepressants and stimulants are actually *creating* it: "A child who may be hyperactive or depressed is treated with a drug that triggers a manic episode or some degree of emotional instability," he writes, "and then the child is put on a drug cocktail that leads to a lifetime of disability."[2]

Dr. Z explained that there are a couple of different medication options to address the symptoms of bipolar disorder (or, in this case, symptoms of the antidepressant?). One is a mood stabilizer (e.g. lithium), and the other is an antipsychotic (e.g. Zyprexa). He said the mood stabilizer is pretty high-maintenance, because it has to be monitored closely with lab tests. The antipsychotic has a side effect of weight gain, which would be good in Rebecka's case, as she was restricting her food intake off and on throughout all these hospitalizations. I agreed to switch her to Zyprexa. I was tired of hallucinations and screaming Rebecka. I was tired of the quiet room. And I wanted Rebecka to feel better. Whatever it took.

Medication Facts: Olanzapine (Zyprexa)

» Olanzapine is an atypical antipsychotic.

» Eli Lilly brought Zyprexa (trade name) to the US
   market. The FDA originally approved it in 1996.
   Now, generic versions are available.

» The Zyprexa label indicates that it may be used to
   treat seizure disorders and panic disorder.

» Warnings include suicide, neuroleptic malignant syndrome,
   hyperglycemia, weight gain, and tardive dyskinesia.

» There is a long list of adverse reactions, including
   sedation, increased appetite, and fatigue in
   adolescents. Please see FDA label for full list.

» Regarding pediatric use, the label states: "Safety and
   effectiveness of ZYPREXA in children <13 years of age
   have not been established. Safety and effectiveness
   of ZYPREXA and fluoxetine in combination in children
   <10 years of age have not been established."

» Zyprexa was the twenty-second-most-prescribed psychiatric
   drug in 2011, with about 4.5 million prescriptions.

Sources: US Food and Drug Administration, PsychCentral

One huge point that didn't come through in the conversation with Dr. Z was that the antipsychotic would be *in addition* to the two medications Rebecka was already taking. I didn't realize this until she was released from the hospital and I received the prescription sheet along with the other discharge papers. These conversations with Dr. Z were confusing and cryptic, to say the least. And not once were the possible side effects of the medications, except weight gain, brought to our attention.

Todd came home on Friday night, October 15, after a long week of teaching. We went straight to the hospital so as to not miss the very small window of opportunity to see our daughter during the brief visiting hours. We had our hopes up that Rebecka would be feeling better. That she would be able to talk to us and tell us funny stories about the staff.

Hopes are good, but they don't always materialize.

When we arrived, Rebecka was sitting in the quiet room, rocking back and forth, asking the voices to stop. Our hearts sunk all the way through our feet and landed with a soft thud on the carpeted floor.

But we had a sense that she had some control over her behavior, that she could be "normal" if she needed to (though it was hard work). So we told her, firmly, that we were here to visit with her, and if she was just going to be talking to the voices in her head, we might as well go home.

This may sound harsh, but we had learned that sometimes we needed to be harsh toward this madness that had taken hold of our child.

It worked. She ignored the voices and became "normal" and responsive. At this time, Dr. Z entered the quiet room, and before we knew it, we were having a family therapy session on the floor—in the quiet room. Dr. Z had built some kind of relationship with Rebecka, and apparently he had learned that we are not perfect parents.

(Yes, we were a bit defensive.)

Rebecka told us that her anxiety stemmed from having to be "perfect" and "happy" all the time. She had been feeling this pressure since early elementary school, when we both were very busy—me with my career, and Todd with his PhD.

(Slap in face.)

We tried to explain that we didn't have unrealistic expectations of her. We just wanted her to do her best. We knew she was more than capable of doing great work. I made a comment along the lines of, "I never see you study, so I don't know if you're trying your hardest."

(That was not the right thing to say.)

"Don't you dare tell me I'm not trying my hardest," Rebecka lashed out at me. The fury in her voice scared me. I had never heard her talk to me like this before.

I backed off. "Okay. If you say you're trying your hardest, I believe you."

She was sobbing by this time, and I was so upset, I just started shutting down. She continued to say that we never listen to her. We never think about what's best for her. She brought up the impending move for the first time since

that Fourth of July picnic, and said she didn't want to move. And the only reason we were moving was so Daddy could continue with the career he loves.
We were not taking her happiness into consideration. She was tired of making
everybody else happy.

I reflected later that this was the third major crying episode Rebecka had
had in the last several months. They were all related to the thought of moving
again. We definitely recognized that the move was a big deal for her, but at
the same time, Todd and I also had lives to live and dreams to realize, and
Brookfield just didn't feel like home. We had already spent countless hours
talking about different scenarios, keeping financial realities in mind. There
was no ideal solution.

After the session in the quiet room, Todd and I also spent increased conversation time and spare mental energy looking for clues from the past. Did
we miss something? Should we have seen this coming?

I thought back to the summer before Rebecka's fourth grade year, when the
company I worked for acquired the business in Wisconsin. I was designated to
help with integration of the two companies and started traveling on Midwest
Airlines up to Milwaukee on an almost-weekly basis.

At the time, Todd was still in his PhD program and had a fairly flexible
schedule. I didn't worry much about leaving Rebecka, because Todd was
home, and he is a great dad. It turns out that Rebecka didn't care much for the
arrangement, though—and she was also anxious about our post-PhD plans. In
fifth grade, she worked with the guidance counselor at school to formulate the
following questions for us:

Mom,

Why do you have to go all the time?

Could you spend more time at home?

What does your boss tell you about when to go, what to do there?

How do you feel about going on all these business trips all the time?

How do you think Dad, Sophie & I feel about this?

Dad,

*If you take a job anywhere, what am I going to do every day when I come
home? I don't like being in the house alone for a long period of time.*

Who would take care of me if you found someone to look after me?

What if I'm alone in the morning too?
What is going to happen to Sophie? What if we don't have a backyard?
How is the whole Sophie thing going to work out?
How are we going to move with her?

This should have been a wake-up call for us to take a look at our lifestyle and our future plans, and how they were impacting Rebecka. I was working sixty to sixty-five hours per week and completely absorbed in my work. Due to my demanding job, I had even quit my children's choir director responsibilities at church, despite Rebecka's pleas for me to continue. But we continued openly to discuss Todd's future teaching plans and the difficult job market, I continued to travel and to work insane hours, and Rebecka and Todd (and Sophie) continued to make do without me.

Based on Rebecka's statements in the quiet room, perhaps all this had contributed to her mental distress. If that was the case, how was medication supposed to help?

A couple of days later, on October 18, Dr. Z released Rebecka from the hospital with a lengthy follow-up plan: day program, dialectical behavior therapy (DBT) assessment, eating disorder support group, and a psychological evaluation. She was now on a cocktail of Prozac, Klonopin, and Zyprexa to be administered morning and evening.

However, I'd also had conversations with the hospital social worker assigned to Rebecka's case, and she was not onboard with the doctor's follow-up plan. She thought Rebecka should be in school full-time, because the day program didn't seem to be helping her. It concerned me that the treatment team was not on the same page regarding Rebecka's follow-up care.

The same day, Rebecka and I drove to the Valentin Clinic to meet a psychotherapist named Marla Clark, to see if Rebecka would be a good candidate for DBT. As Marla explained the ins and outs of DBT, I sat on the comfy couch, nodding my head in agreement. Everything about this approach felt right.

Rebecka, on the other hand, was sitting in the corner of the couch, eyes darting around the room like she was seeing things we could not see. When Marla and Rebecka talked alone, Rebecka told Marla that she was having hallucinations. She was not able to focus. She was also worried about having an "episode" with other kids around.

Marla said no to DBT for Rebecka for the time being. Rebecka was going to need to be able to focus better than she was right now. Get the hallucinations and episodes under control.

I was discouraged, to say the least. I had so much hope for DBT—that it would be the magic bullet that would make our daughter all better, or at least help her function in the real world.

I was mad at Rebecka's darting eyes. I was mad at Marla for not giving us a chance. And I was mad at Dr. Z and his staff for not knowing how to make all the problems go away—and for not being on the same page.

I was torn between family responsibilities and work responsibilities. I felt like I wasn't doing a good job in either sphere of my life. I didn't have enough time to take a step back, do research, call around, and find appropriate care for Rebecka. And leaving work every day to drive her to the hospital and other appointments was making me feel like I wasn't able to give my work proper attention.

Something would have to give.

That day, when I was back in the office, I asked my boss, the CEO of our company, if we could have a quick meeting. He came over to my office. A minute into the meeting, I was sobbing uncontrollably. My boss sat and waited patiently while I composed myself.

"So it's that bad," he said.

I nodded.

I asked for a leave of absence through the end of the year, which would amount to about ten weeks. He didn't miss a beat in responding in the affirmative to my request.

"So you mean like starting tomorrow?" he asked.

"No, no," I said, "starting next week." I didn't want to leave without having a proper plan in place during my absence.

I was so relieved. Now I could focus completely on finding appropriate care for my daughter and helping her get back to her old self. I left the office that evening with renewed pep in my step.

But I also thought about all the other parents in the world who were going through the same thing—parents who didn't have the financial means to take ten weeks off to care for their struggling children. My heart ached for them (and still does).

Since the start of school that year, we had been telling Rebecka not to worry about schoolwork, but rather to focus on feeling better. She wasn't in high school, so we weren't overly concerned about grades. But Rebecka wasn't quite able to make the shift to "not worrying about school." She had missed a lot of class time.

We made an appointment to meet with the school counselor and principal to go over her schedule. Since school was a huge stressor, we decided to try to ease her into the school day with an easy first hour. The second hour, she would work independently in the office, followed by math tutoring the third hour. She would wrap up the morning with "the important subjects": math and language arts.

The principal reiterated to Rebecka that her top priority should be her health. I don't know that it sunk in, but I was thankful for the support of the school administration. It's always good when caring adults are on the same page.

Later that morning, October 19, my phone rang. It was the school. Over the course of the school year, both Todd and I had come to dread looking at our phones for fear of seeing the school's phone number. It was never good news.

"Rebecka had an episode," they said. "She's in the office." That meant they wanted me to come talk to her. I drove over to the school and found Rebecka in the guidance office. She was coherent and told me she'd had a flashback during class. She was exhausted and wanted to go home.

I hated to take her away from school yet again, but I was exhausted too. We walked out to the car together. On the way home, she asked if we could stop at Panera Bread, the national deli chain. Since Rebecka's eating was still spotty, I jumped at the opportunity to feed her.

At Panera, Rebecka ate a big cookie and drank a smoothie. Then she went out to the car to retrieve her lunch box and ate most of its contents as well. I was happy to see her hearty appetite.

After lunch, we decided to go to the mall. I felt a little guilty taking Rebecka out of school and going to the mall, but somehow it felt like the right thing to do. We bought a pair of shoes (Rebecka *loves* shoes) and browsed Barnes & Noble. While at the mall, Rebecka acted completely fine. *Maybe we should move her classes to the mall*, I mused.

The following morning, Rebecka felt well enough to take the bus to school. I was so relieved. Were things finally starting to get back to normal? Was the medicine finally working? Or was the day program actually helping?

When you're walking through mental illness hell with your child, you cling onto each little ray of light that promises a normal future. A bus ride to school means everything will be all right. Your child can function, can be like other children.

Because you see all these signs of hope, every setback is so much worse. "But," you say, "she was doing so well. We went to the mall. She rode the damned bus to school."

That doesn't mean you won't get a call from school the same day. "Rebecka has been sleeping the past forty minutes," they say. "Should we wake her up?"

I suspected the medication was making her sleepy, and said "Yes, please wake her up." So they did and called back saying Rebecka had a headache. Could I please bring some medicine?

For the gazillionth time, I sent a quick note to my team saying I needed to run an errand. I got my coat, purse, and keys—and laptop, just to be safe—and headed out the door.

I had to swing by our apartment first to pick up the Motrin. *Why don't I just keep a bottle at school?* I chided myself. My head was fuzzy. What was happening to my little girl? Why couldn't I help her?

Then I remembered: just three more days. Then I would have all the time in the world to help her. I couldn't wait for my leave of absence to start. I was determined to do everything in my power to get our daughter back.

I took Rebecka's medicine to school and worked from home until it was time to pick her up. She had slept all her precious school time away. And her head was hurting so badly she decided to stay home from the day program.

That night, Todd came home for fall break and all of a sudden, life was just a little bit better.

Thursday came along, and with it another call from the school. This was a new one. Rebecka didn't know where she was. She was also hallucinating. When Todd and I arrived at the school, we found her playing cards with the school counselor and the principal. I felt a huge amount of appreciation toward these busy school administrators for taking time out of their busy schedules to calm my child.

When we sat down to chat, Rebecka echoed the message from the school, indicating that she didn't know where she was. She knew she was in a school, but it wasn't her school. (But she recognized us, so that was good.)

We knew she couldn't sit there all day playing cards, so Todd took Rebecka home, and I stayed to talk to the counselor about downplaying her hallucinations. Feeding into them wasn't effective. In fact, it seemed like the more we focused on them, the worse they got. We also talked about this new state of confusion. Now there was one more thing to figure out . . .

Later in the afternoon, I called Rebecka's social worker at the day program to tell him about the day's events. I also requested a phone call from Dr. Z to ask him about a neurology lab appointment that had been scheduled for the following day. We were confused, since Rebecka had already had an EEG.

When Dr. Z called back, he wanted to talk about medication. Rebecka had told him that I was not one hundred percent on board with the medication, or rather, didn't want her to be medicated at all. I tried to explain my concerns, but it felt like talking to a wall. We went in circles and didn't end up anywhere different. And related to the neurology appointment, he didn't know the purpose of it. It was as if the medical professionals who held Rebecka's life and sanity in their hands were not communicating at all. It troubled me deeply.

During our conversation, Dr. Z also mentioned homeschooling as an option for Rebecka, since school seemed to be such a stressor. To me, it seemed like giving up. Wasn't the goal of treatment to enable her to face her stressors, to function in the real world? Rebecka, of course, was excited by the idea. No more getting up early and getting on the bus. No more worrying about having "an episode" at school.

The following day, Todd took Rebecka to the neurology lab appointment to find that it was indeed another EEG. They went through with it, and Rebecka actually fell asleep like you're supposed to. But this experience increased our concern that Rebecka's health care providers were not communicating. I called the hospital again to try to figure out what was going on—to no avail.

Later in the day, Rebecka started running a fever (something I have since learned is a symptom of anxiety), so we picked her up early from the day program.

That evening, around eleven o'clock, Rebecka came into our bedroom and woke us up. She seemed somewhat incoherent and kept asking, "what's happening to me?" She said she was having trouble breathing and needed help. Could we please help her? Could we take her to the ER?

It was heartbreaking. I had often wondered why the trauma she was experiencing didn't seem to faze her. She was clearly strong and brave. But in the dead of night, the fear set in and it made her wild with anxiety.

We assured her that she was safe. We watched some *Glee* (her favorite show at the time) to distract her, but it didn't work. She kept saying we weren't listening to her. She needed help.

I knew in my heart that she was having an anxiety attack, but my own anxiety took over and I started wondering if maybe the safe thing to do would be to take her to the ER.

Rebecka was complaining that our voices were distant and everything was blurry. The blurry vision scared me. It sounded dangerous.

But Todd was calm. He always kept a cool head in these types of situations. He was the one who held me back when we were training six-month-old Rebecka to fall asleep in her own bed, so I wouldn't burst into her room and pick her up when she cried that first night. And that night, he did it again. I was frustrated, but he was right.

Rebecka didn't need to go to the ER. She needed to sleep. And eventually, that's what she chose to do. "I'm going to sleep it off," she said. I slept in the bed with her, mostly for my own sake.

As I think about this time, there is a certain amount of irony related to the feeling of not being heard. Todd and I felt like Dr. Z wasn't hearing us. Rebecka felt like we weren't hearing her. And Dr. Z probably felt like we weren't hearing him. Clearly, there were deep communication issues on all levels, making the situation even worse than it should have been.

The following weekend was about as normal as they come. Rebecka was complaining of a sore throat, but mentally, she seemed well. She was still hallucinating and hearing voices, but she told us it wasn't bothering her. Rebecka was clearly doing better at home than at school. She felt safer at home, she said. But she still did not think the medication was helping her depression.

I had a hard time understanding this depression. I thought depression that was bad enough to necessitate medication was debilitating to the point that the person could not function socially. I imagined people lying on their beds in the fetal position or rocking back and forth in a dark living room in an empty house. This was not Rebecka. Of course, that doesn't mean it wasn't real to her, but I really questioned the use of medication—especially since it didn't make her feel better, but worse!

The following Facebook message to a friend exemplifies my sentiments at the time:

> Saw your question about the family in your blog comment.
> Rebecka has been struggling with some mental health issues for
> several months and it's quickly going downhill. I think the cycles
> of experimentation with medications & hospitalizations has been
> making it worse, so I'm taking some time to focus 100% on
> Project Rebecka* and get her health back on track. Talking to

---

* My loving term for the task of finding appropriate care for Rebecka and helping her ease back into normal life.

the Dr. tomorrow! I wish medications were always a *last* resort . . .

On Sunday evening, despite feeling under the weather with a sore throat and a fever, Rebecka suggested that we have a family game night. We played Whoonu, Life, and Scattergories. She didn't flinch when she lost, and she didn't stress out over Scattergories, which she sometimes did. It was a good evening.

Of course, we did have to throw in a visit to the urgent care because Rebecka's sore throat was really bothering her. The doctor prescribed an antibiotic after ruling out mono. Rebecka's weight was 110 pounds. This was the highest weight since her eating problems started. She didn't say anything about it.

Sigh of relief.

On Zyprexa and Weight Gain

One of the reasons Dr. Z wanted to put Rebecka on Zyprexa over other medications was because it stimulated appetite. Indeed, since Rebecka had started on Zyprexa, she'd been eating like there was no tomorrow. Initially I was glad, because she needed to gain weight. However, one afternoon, I witnessed her eat three individual packages of Pop-Tarts for a total of 1,200 calories. That scared me. I didn't want her to become dangerously overweight! I didn't know it at the time, but Zyprexa can cause patients to gain so much weight that it becomes a medical concern![3] In *Anatomy of an Epidemic*, Robert Whitaker provides the following illustration of the ill effects of Zyprexa:

> Imagine that a virus suddenly appears in our society that makes people sleep twelve, fourteen hours a day. Those infected with it move about somewhat slowly and seem emotionally disengaged. Many gain huge amounts of weight—twenty, forty, sixty, and even one hundred pounds. Often, their blood sugar levels soar, and so do their cholesterol levels. A number of those struck by the mysterious illness—including young children and teenagers—become diabetic in fairly short order. Reports of patients occasionally dying from pancreatitis appear in the medical literature. Newspapers and magazines fill their pages with accounts of this new scourge, which is dubbed metabolic dysfunction illness, and parents are in a panic over the thought that their children might contract this horrible disease. The federal government gives hundreds of millions of dollars to scientists at the best universities to decipher the inner workings of this virus, and they report that the reason it causes such global dysfunction is that it blocks a multitude of neurotransmitter receptors in the brain—dopaminergic, serotoninergic, muscarinic, adrenergic, and histaminergic. All

of those neuronal pathways in the brain are compromised. Meanwhile, MRI studies find that over a period of several years, the virus shrinks the cerebral cortex, and this shrinkage is tied to cognitive decline. A terrified public clamors for a cure.

Now such an illness has in fact hit millions of American children and adults. We have just described the effects of Eli Lilly's best-selling antipsychotic, Zyprexa.[4]

That weekend also marked the transition from my role as software product manager to full-time manager of "Project Rebecka," the project to get to the bottom of what was happening to our daughter and to do whatever it took to help her feel better. My first action was to create a "Rebecka Chron" spreadsheet (a chron file is a project-management organizational tool) detailing Rebecka's journey through the mental health system so far. I hoped this would improve our communication with her current and future health care providers and help tell Rebecka's story in a way that communicated just how quickly all of her severe mental health symptoms had manifested.

I went back through all of her medical records from the current year, noting visits to the doctor, prescribed medications, changes in dosage, and hospitalizations. I also noted everyday events that seemed relevant to what was happening to her, including absences from school related to fevers and other ailments. I ended up with about one hundred entries.

Monday arrived and Rebecka complained of a sore throat, so we kept her home from school. The fact that she was missing so much school worried us. While we weren't worried about her performance, exactly, we also didn't want her to have to repeat eighth grade. I had started to set up meetings with her teachers to learn how I could best support her at home.

To illustrate this effort, here is an email I sent to the guidance counselor that very morning:

Hi Margo,

I hope you had a great weekend. You've probably figured this out by now, but Rebecka is home from school today. She was sick all weekend and needed one more day to recover (she's on antibiotics now). I left a voice mail for the absentee reporting line and also informed Mrs. Martino when I came to meet with Mrs. Camden.

Mrs. Camden and I had a good meeting, and I feel good about working with Rebecka on her math now. I think if she feels like she's on top of it, it will really reduce her anxiety. It would be great to do a similar meeting with her language arts teacher either tomorrow or Wed, if possible. Let me know.

I'm hoping Rebecka will feel up for school tomorrow and if you don't hear from me, please assume that she is coming and I'll encourage her to stop by and check in before classes start.

Thanks, Tabita

That morning, Rebecka surprised me by doing the dishes—without being asked. (If you have teenagers, you know this doesn't happen.) I praised her for helping out. It felt so good that she was showing consideration and willingness to help. I could see the proverbial "light at the end of the tunnel."

I'm not sure if helping with the dishes was a way to butter me up, but the conversation eventually turned to homeschooling. Rebecka *really* wanted to be homeschooled. I explained that her therapists felt that she really should be living as normally as possible and that going to school was part of normal. Also, how would we know if she was getting better if she avoided things that caused anxiety? I conceded that we could consider it if all else failed. That was good enough for Rebecka.

Later that evening, we went out for dinner and had a really fun time. I had cleared my brain of work-related concerns and—ironically, given the circumstances—was relaxed in a way that I had not experienced in years. When we returned home, I remember walking through the underground parking garage on our way up to the apartment, laughing and teasing. As I pushed open the secured door to the building, Rebecka said, "This mom is fun to hang out with! Work mom is icky."

I had made the right decision. But there was still a lot of work ahead for Project Rebecka to be a success.

We got through the rest of the week without frightening hallucinations or major episodes. In fact, Rebecka was even able to hang out with friends and attend a Halloween sleepover. We worried about it, but decided to let her go. She came back in good spirits, but very tired.

On Halloween Day, Rebecka went trick-or-treating with friends, without incident.

However, I believe something that day or the previous evening stirred up difficult emotions with which Rebecka was unable to cope.

Because later that Halloween evening, Rebecka came into our bedroom and said there was somebody in her room telling her to hurt herself.

My heart sank. *Not again . . .*

If this had been just a few weeks ago when I was still working, we probably would have called the hospital. However, we had gotten to the point where we did whatever it took to keep Rebecka out of the hospital. In fact, we were starting to think she was developing an addiction to being in the hospital.

Instead, I ended up crawling into her white IKEA bed for yet another night of listening to her heavy breathing and hoping that she would sleep soundly. This closeness made her feel better, and she was able to sleep through the night.

However, the next morning, I didn't hear my alarm, so we overslept. Rebecka does not like to rush, but she made it to school on time. By 8:30 a.m. I got a call from the school. Rebecka wasn't feeling safe. She wanted to talk to me.

I drove down to the school and picked her up. It felt so good not to have to worry about work and to be able to be fully present with Rebecka. We stayed home until it was time for her to go to the day program.

Rebecka was not a happy camper when I picked her up from Sanders. She wanted to be admitted to the hospital because she wasn't "feeling safe" and felt like nobody was listening to her. She expressed feelings of worthlessness and said she saw no reason to go on living.

Her treatment team thought she should use the coping skills she'd acquired at the day program and stay out of the hospital and live her life. I agreed. Plus, the whole point of my leave of absence was to free up time to help turn things around. A hospital visit was just more of the same—the opposite of progress.

Hospitalization #6

But here's one thing about Rebecka. She is very persuasive. Even though I knew it wasn't the right thing to do, I called the intake number at the hospital and told them the situation. Again, because she was feeling suicidal and may have been a threat to herself, they admitted her.

Once Rebecka was situated on the unit (after signing the equivalent of one large tree's worth of paper), I had a chance to talk to Dr. Z. We had an extended conversation about my concerns about medication and Rebecka's rapid decline.

This was one of the most frustrating conversations I've ever had. All the doubts that had been nagging in my mind about Rebecka's medication and if it really was making things worse bubbled up to the surface. I asked him point blank if there was any chance that the medication was making Rebecka feel suicidal and have hallucinations, since I had read online that these were known side effects.

Dr. Z didn't stop for even one second to consider that this *might* be the case. He dismissed my doubts as quickly as they left my mouth.

"No, no, no," he said.

"But she was fine just six months ago," I tried. "I don't understand how things have gotten so bad so quickly."

He looked condescendingly at me and replied, "it is normal for things to get worse before they get better. This is not out of the ordinary."

This didn't make any sense to me. At this point I was ninety-five percent sure that the medication was causing some, if not all, of these problems, and I wanted to be heard. However, Dr. Z, a highly regarded psychiatrist, was so embedded in the discourse that says that medication is the *solution* that he could not fathom that medication could be the *problem*. And he could not hear that before medication, Rebecka had none of these symptoms and was able to function quite well.

I had recently watched the documentary *Food Matters*, which discusses the use of therapeutic doses of niacin to treat severe depression. In addition, Andrew W. Saul, PhD and therapeutic nutrition specialist, claims in the film that "two handfuls of cashews give you the therapeutic equivalent of a prescription dose of Prozac."[5] So why couldn't I just feed Rebecka cashews and be done with it?

I asked Dr. Z for his thoughts about supplements, trying to sound intelligent talking about niacin and depression. He quickly responded that there is nothing in the literature (i.e. clinical studies published in peer-reviewed journals) that indicates that it works. He said that we were welcome to try, but that he couldn't help us with it. "But I'll be here when it doesn't work and you want to come back," he offered.

I was frustrated and disappointed. How could this man call himself a doctor and be so limited in his methods to help my daughter?

But he was not done talking. "The reason you're not seeing results with the medication is because Rebecka knows you're against it. As long as there is disagreement over the effectiveness of the treatment, it's not going to work."

It took a little while for this to sink in. He was accusing Todd and me of being the problem, because we asked questions about known side effects and possible alternatives to dangerous, mind-altering drugs for our thirteen-year-old.

I felt the tears start to well up and promptly ended the conversation.

I couldn't take it anymore, not without Todd there by my side to counteract the large bundle of patronizing testosterone sitting on the other side of the table.

As I've thought about this conversation over the years since that evening in the hospital, I have realized that Dr. Z indirectly admitted that medication doesn't work any better than a placebo—and many unpublished research studies indicate as much.[6] You have to believe in it for it to work. Unfortunately, studies with "negative" results often don't get published, so patients—or physicians, for that matter—don't get the full story. Harvard Medical School's Irving Kirsch and Glen I. Spielmans of the University of Wisconsin–Madison explain:

> The FDA's framework for evaluating clinical trials allows drugs with minimal efficacy in terms of symptomatic improvement—and no benefit in terms of quality of life or social functioning—to enter the marketplace as approved treatments. The published medical literature inflates the apparent efficacy of antidepressants (and other psychiatric drugs) while downplaying or altogether hiding adverse events.[7]

It was a sad drive home through the dark. I was discouraged that even while on a leave of absence, I had not been able to keep Rebecka out of the hospital. I was also disappointed because my youngest sister, Miriam, was arriving from Sweden the following day—specifically to spend time with Rebecka. Everything felt so hopeless.

Thank God for new days.

The follow morning, I woke up with a new resolve to turn things around. After my morning run and chores, I walked over to the library to see if I could find any useful reading materials to help with my quest.

I admit I felt a bit self-conscious perusing the "mental health" section of the library. What would people think if they saw me? That I had "issues"? I pushed these thoughts aside and quickly homed in on a book called *Rescuing Your Teenager from Depression* by Dr. Norman T. Berlinger, whose son had suffered from depression.

Just reading the title made me feel brave and strong. The fact that it also had "10 Parental Partnership Strategies" made me feel even more excited about it. This was it. I was going to read this book and rescue my teenager from depression, just as Dr. Berlinger had done.

If only it were that simple...

I checked out the book, returned to our apartment, and started reading. I had trouble identifying with the story in the book for a variety reasons, but primarily because Dr. Berlinger's son seemed to be in much worse shape than Rebecka was when she started taking medication—like he was suffering from a different level of depression.

But I kept reading, because I knew I would learn something from it. I brought the book with me when I went to pick up my sister in Chicago and remember reading a big chunk of it right there in the airport. At one point in the story, the family turned to medication to treat the depression. All of a sudden, I didn't like this book quite as much, but at the same time, it also made me wonder if maybe I was wrong about the medication. Indeed, Dr. Berlinger makes the following statement:

> One of the biggest mistakes made with antidepressants is to stop them too soon. Don't worry about long-term side effects of long-term therapy. Over the past fifteen years, literally millions of prescriptions for SSRIs have been written. These drugs have proved to be remarkably free of adverse effects on the function of any organ or physiological system.[8]

This was a doctor who definitely had his son's best interest in mind. He was smart, educated, and mindful. I had come to respect him while reading his book. And the antidepressant seemed to help his kid. There was a happy ending.

The message in this book swayed me toward trying to accept that medication might be the right way to go. Perhaps Dr. Z was right. Maybe it does get worse before it gets better.

When my sister finally arrived, there were many hugs and tears and smiles. It felt so good to have family around, and I realized just how much I missed the support that family can provide. Miriam was eager to see Rebecka, and we drove straight to the hospital so they could meet before visiting hours ended.

Rebecka was back to her normal self when we found her in her hospital room. She was excited to see her Swedish aunt, and realized she didn't want to be in the hospital. She would much rather be home with Miriam!

And sure enough, the following day, she was released from the hospital after just two days. One good thing that came out of the visit was that Dr. Z took her off Klonopin. I had started to worry about Rebecka being on that medication for too long, as it is highly habit-forming (oh, and may increase thoughts of suicide).

Dr. Z recommended continued day treatment and DBT, but I decided (supported by the social worker) that we'd had enough of day treatment. It was time for a different approach.

While Miriam engaged Rebecka with creative art activities and songs on the guitar, I started exploring the possibility of temporary homeschooling. Rebecka seemed to do fine when we were together, so Todd and I decided that it would be worth exploring homeschooling for a while until she stabilized. Looking back, I think Rebecka simply needed time with her mom, who had been absent—mentally, and often physically—for so many years.

I worked with the school's eighth grade guidance counselor and the school psychologist to figure out the best route to keeping Rebecka at home. They suggested applying for special education and homebound instruction. It was all pretty confusing, but the good news was that Rebecka was able to continue her schooling at home.

We enjoyed nine days with my sister, including a visit to the Discovery World Museum in Milwaukee. Rebecka seemed moderately interested during this visit, and I noticed she tired quickly. But she ate a hearty snack, so I felt good about that.

Indeed, she had gained at least fifteen pounds since starting on Zyprexa. She didn't say anything about it, and I didn't either. I hoped the weight gain would speed up her recovery.

Misinformation

(November 2, 2010–May 10, 2011)

*Pharma spends twice as much money ($60 billion) on promotion
as on research, and too often they fund the wrong kind of
clinical research, done in the wrong way, and with the wrong
motives—avoiding lines of inquiry that might actually teach us
something important, in favor of surefire 'experimercials' that
are mostly intended to promote marketing, not discovery.*

—Dr. Allen Frances, *Saving Normal*

Aside from arranging home schooling, my other big task as manager of Project Rebecka was to assemble a team of providers to treat Rebecka on an outpatient basis.

We started with Marla at the DBT clinic, who said she was willing to give Rebecka another shot. After one session, Marla recommended that Rebecka attend the eating disorder program at Sanders. Rebecka was still struggling with restricting and bingeing (a common cycle). Marla said she would call in a referral. So still no DBT. The eating disorder program evaluation ended up recommending a therapist who specialized in eating disorders, and a dietitian. (I felt like a hot potato being passed from provider to provider.)

I also needed to find a psychiatrist to "manage her medication." The first doctor we met, Dr. V, zeroed in on an offhand comment by Rebecka that she had been feeling paranoid, and started talking about Rebecka having schizophrenia-like symptoms, which could be caused by stress. I was quite dismayed that she said this in front of Rebecka, knowing how sensitive she was to this type of information.

To Rebecka's previous doctors' credit, none of them had attempted to give Rebecka a formal diagnosis. Her symptoms were all over the board, so the best thing they could say was that she had "comorbid illnesses." In the past several months, we had heard suggested diagnoses ranging from generalized anxiety disorder to borderline personality disorder to bipolar disorder. Her doctors were also leery of giving her a diagnosis for future insurance purposes, which we appreciated.*

However, Rebecka desperately wanted to know what was wrong with her, so she clung on to any clues as to what might be ailing her and started exhibiting more of the symptoms that might result in a diagnosis. After the session with Dr. V, her paranoia grew exponentially and her visual hallucinations returned.

She wanted to take a pillow in the car to protect her head in case we were in a car accident. She almost refused to cross a walking bridge in case it would collapse. She didn't want to walk outside in the rain because we might be struck by lightning. She even started to stutter and had trouble concentrating.

Rebecka also started seeing a female hallucination that exerted an extreme level of control over her. For example, we had to ask the woman where to have lunch. Turns out the woman didn't like me (probably because I was saying we should ignore her).

The onslaught of these symptoms was so sudden, it was very clear to me that they were being caused by anxiety about a potential schizophrenia diagnosis and not knowing what was happening to her, but there was no point in trying to have a rational conversation with Rebecka in her current state.

Just two days prior, she had been mostly "fine." These sudden shifts in behavior were perhaps the hardest aspect to deal with. As soon as we thought things were getting better, something like this would happen. Enervating doesn't even start to describe this experience. I can't imagine what Rebecka was feeling.

I decided to give Dr. V a call to see if she could calm Rebecka down.

---

* With the Affordable Care Act, which was introduced the same year (2010), people with pre-existing conditions cannot be denied coverage, but Rebecka's doctors were clearly still operating with the old rules in mind.

I explained the situation and Dr. V agreed that it was probably anxiety. She had not meant to indicate that Rebecka had schizophrenia; just that she had schizophrenia-like symptoms.

Once I explained this to Rebecka, she went back to "normal."

How powerful the mind is.

The following week, we went to a studio photographer for a family portrait. You would never have known that Rebecka had "issues." She looked beautiful and the photographer asked if Rebecka had considered modeling. (She had, but we had said no, because of her disordered eating.) We also celebrated Thanksgiving and Rebecka thoroughly enjoyed the meal, including the "happy" (humanely-raised, heirloom) turkey.

After Thanksgiving, Rebecka declared that she was ready to go back to school. However, we had just barely gotten started with the tutor, and the guidance counselor strongly suggested we continue the homebound instruction until the end of the calendar year. Rebecka was disappointed, but she got over it after a couple of days.

Based on the "too-much-information" experience with Dr. V, I made an appointment with a different psychiatrist, Dr. E, who had been recommended to us. We met with him in early December, and I liked him immediately.

He asked all the right questions: Did Rebecka exercise? Was she sleeping well? What was she eating?

Finally! A doctor who asked about things other than which medications we wanted. However, in the very same session, he told us he would never take anybody off Prozac. "It only does good things for your brain," he said. He proceeded to explain that Prozac helps the brain create new nerve cells and connect these nerve cells. It sounded good. I nodded and smiled. (Another point for pills—at least antidepressants.)

He also said that since everything seemed to be going fairly well, he didn't want to mess with the medication at this time. But we should consider getting Rebecka off Zyprexa eventually.

Overall, I was happy with Dr. E and checked "psychiatrist" off the "Find Outpatient Providers" list.

But that was just the first step. I had not heard back from the therapist who specialized in eating disorders (she was clearly very popular, which seemed like a good thing). Also, I needed to find a dietitian. And I definitely wanted to convince Marla Clark to let Rebecka into the DBT adolescent group.

I managed to keep Rebecka out of the hospital for over a month while I worked on assembling the dream team that would accompany Rebecka on the road back to normal.

During this time, we definitely had our ups and downs. We participated in the beginning yoga class I had signed up for in a moment of despair, and Rebecka met with her tutor and tried her best to keep up with her schoolwork. However, she was sick frequently and one evening in the middle of December, I walked into the living room to find Rebecka sitting on the floor covering her ears, screaming.

The auditory hallucinations had returned (or gotten worse), and Rebecka was screaming at them to go away. It scared me. Again, I had visions of an adult Rebecka sitting in a psychiatric institution, rocking back and forth.

Rebecka said that the voices were telling her to hurt herself. She didn't feel safe. She wanted to go to the hospital. Per our new philosophy, I convinced her that she would be safe at home. She didn't need to go to the hospital.

Rebecka eventually calmed down and spent the night at home. However, this calm was short-lived.

Hospitalization #7

The following day, I called Todd to talk about Rebecka—she was about all we ever talked about. Beyond the mental health symptoms, we were trying to figure out why Rebecka was getting sick all the time. I had called her pediatrician and she had referred Rebecka to an ear, nose, and throat specialist.

While we were on the phone, Rebecka came into the bedroom. I quickly realized that she was in blonde mode, the ditzy personality she slipped into occasionally. This always seemed to happen when I was on the phone or otherwise unavailable.

I said a hasty goodbye to Todd and got off the phone. Rebecka told me that Alice had come in through the bedroom window and was telling her to hurt herself.

No! Not Alice again!

To show that she was serious about this, she walked over to the safe where we kept all the medications and knives and attempted to open it. When that didn't work, she tried to explain to me that she didn't feel safe and wanted to go to the hospital.

I really, really didn't want Rebecka to go to the hospital. I felt like the hospital visits only perpetuated the problem. So I negotiated. I told her that we could call Dr. E in the morning if she was still feeling unsafe. Rebecka agreed and spent another night at home.

The following morning, things were not better. At one point, Rebecka tried to break a glass ornament to use it to cut herself. I had to physically restrain her to prevent her from running out the back door. It took everything I had to remain composed and rational, because on the inside, I was an emotional wreck.

When Rebecka realized that I was not going to let her hurt herself, she stopped resisting my grip and broke down crying. "Help me. Please help me," she pleaded between sobs. It was one of the saddest moments of my life. Mostly, I was sad for Rebecka that she had to go through all this. But I was also dejected that despite my most valiant efforts, I still hadn't been able to help my child escape these horrible symptoms.

I kept my promise and called Dr. E. He recommended that we come in for an evaluation. This was our first trip to Porter Psychiatric Hospital. While we waited to see Dr. E, Rebecka started feeling better. It was as if she just needed assurance that we *would* let her go to the hospital if she really needed to.

I hoped that Dr. E would say that she was okay to go home, but since she was expressing suicidal thoughts, he admitted her. I felt like an utter failure. I had expended so much effort to help Rebecka turn a corner. How was it that I still didn't have her dream team in place? Playing the role of care coordinator was more difficult than I ever imagined it would be.

Rebecka was ready to leave the hospital the following day. She was bored and didn't enjoy the programming at the hospital. And her fellow patients were no fun.

Dr. E, however, decided to keep Rebecka for another day for three reasons.

1. He was giving her a new medication, clonidine, to help with her sleep, and wanted to monitor her overnight. Clonidine is a medication generally used to treat high blood pressure, but it is also administered to children with attention deficit/hyperactivity disorder (ADHD) because it helps them relax.

2. Rebecka didn't eat breakfast; that is, she was back to restricting her food intake.

3. He wanted to reinforce with Rebecka that you can't jump in and out of the hospital on a whim.

When Rebecka was released from the hospital the following day, she was excited to be back home, reporting that the hallucinations where gone. The only problems over the next couple of weeks were complaints of abdominal pain and headaches (both side effects of clonidine, incidentally).

Right before Christmas, Todd received some good news. Luther College had decided to convert his temporary contract into a permanent tenure-track faculty position. This rarely happens, so it was certainly a testimony to his skill in the classroom and beyond.

Todd and I were so excited. We could finally settle down! Todd would be able to continue to live his passion, and I could become involved in a wonderfully progressive community.

But our excitement was dampened by the fact that we would have to tell Rebecka. We hadn't uttered a word about moving or anything related to moving since Rebecka's meltdown in the family therapy session on the floor in the quiet room.

It was with great trepidation that I approached Rebecka about the subject. "Daddy got a tenure-track job at Luther," I started.

"Does that mean we get to move to Decorah?" she asked.

"Well, yes it does." I replied. "Are you okay with that?"

She responded in the affirmative. Oddly enough, she seemed almost excited about it. We were shocked that she took it so well, but in hindsight, it made sense. She no longer had to worry about where we would be moving. And now that she was feeling better and finally out of the inpatient/outpatient cycle, it felt like a new beginning—a place to start over.

In fact, she wanted to move right away. But she wasn't back in school yet, and Todd would be home in January to help with that transition, so we told her we needed to see how things went at school in Brookfield before we could make any decisions about moving dates. I planned to keep my job at least through the summer, so I wasn't in a great hurry to move.

The week between Christmas and New Year's Day, we took a quick trip to Decorah to look at houses. It was exciting! We looked at lots of homes, but there was only one that fit the bill. It was a fairly new house with hardwood floors and a gorgeous kitchen in an old neighborhood close to Decorah's quaint downtown. Complete with a workout room in the basement, it was as if it was built for us.

We didn't wait long to place an offer on our dream home and within days, we were able to come to an agreement with the owners.

Things seemed to be falling into place. By the time I returned to work at the beginning of January, 2011, I had assembled a treatment team for Rebecka including Dr. E, an eating disorder therapist (whom Rebecka actually liked), and a dietitian. In early January, Rebecka had her tonsils out to help with the recurring illnesses. By February, Rebecka was back in school and attending

Marla's DBT adolescent group. And soon we would all be together in one magical town. The future looked bright!

On February 28, we closed on our house and spent the weekend moving the contents of Todd's apartment into the house. On Saturday morning, Rebecka came and sat down next to me on the bed. She asked me to help her zip up one of her cute little black dresses. I couldn't do it. She was too big. In fact, she had gained close to fifty pounds since Dr. Z put her on Zyprexa. She wasn't fat, but I was also quite certain that this was not her "ideal" weight.

She tried to be brave when I told her the dress no longer fit, but I could see that she was fighting back tears. "I'm sorry," I said. "This must be so hard." She cried then. I held her, whispering words of reassurance, and silently cursed the medication that hurt my baby so.

rebecka: on gaining weight on zyprexa

Honestly, I didn't know it was happening until I saw it on the scale, and my once loose clothes became tight. Once I did notice, I was fifty pounds gone. As someone who would restrict calories to almost nothing, to suddenly be eating copious amounts and to no longer be able to see my hip bones and collarbones was petrifying. The weight gain definitely set off my next bout of disordered eating.

The move to Iowa meant that we had to find a new treatment team for Rebecka. We decided to go with a minimalist approach, since she seemed to be doing so much better (and the options were limited in our small town). We found a therapist and signed up with a psychiatrist in town, Dr. X.

On the first visit with Dr. X in early March, he increased the dose of Prozac to thirty milligrams (higher than the recommended dose for children aged eight to eighteen years, which is ten to twenty milligrams). When Todd asked if he thought there would be a time when we could take Rebecka off medication, he responded, "I don't know." He was exceedingly pessimistic about Rebecka's prognosis. We were sad to hear that there was no exit strategy, but at least Rebecka was functioning, so we tried not to let it bother us too much.

On Rebecka's second visit to Dr. X's office, he took her off Zyprexa and prescribed Abilify, another atypical antipsychotic with similar effects, but typically without the weight gain. I was relieved. Perhaps now Rebecka could have a fighting chance to get her weight back to normal.

Medication Facts: Aripiprazole (Abilify)

» Aripiprazole is an atypical antipsychotic with additional antidepressant properties.

» A Japanese company, Otsuka, brought Abilify (trade name) to the US market jointly with Bristol-Myers Squibb. The FDA originally approved it in 2002.

» The Abilify label indicates that it may be used to treat schizophrenia in adults and teens, bipolar I disorder in adults and children ten and over, major depressive disorder in adults, and irritability associated with autistic disorder in children ages six to seventeen years.

» Warnings include suicide, tardive dyskinesia, metabolic changes, and potential for cognitive and motor impairment.

» There is a long list of adverse reactions, including dizziness, blurry vision, and fatigue in adolescents. Please see FDA label for full list.

» Regarding pediatric use, the label states: "Safety and effectiveness in pediatric patients with major depressive disorder or agitation associated with schizophrenia or bipolar mania have not been established."

» Abilify was the sixteenth-most-prescribed psychiatric drug in 2011, with close to 9 million prescriptions.

Sources: US Food and Drug Administration, PsychCentral

Unlike Dr. E, who tried not to mess with the medication if things were going okay, Dr. X seemed to be treating our daughter as an interesting science experiment. On one level, we liked this, because maybe, just maybe, Dr. X would find the magic formula that would allow Rebecka to become completely well. On another level, we really just wanted her off these mind-numbing medications. We missed our spirited, engaging girl.

A few days later, it was Rebecka's birthday. She had planned to have a birthday party, but as the big day grew closer, more and more regrets arrived. In the end, Rebecka decided to cancel her party. She was really sad about it, and we tried to explain that it's hard when you're new in town to try to have an event like this. And kids have a lot going on...

Rebecka interpreted: "And you're not at the top of their priority list."

I realize now that this seemingly benign event started a domino effect that made the rest of the spring, well, hellish.

rebecka: on moving to decorah

The moved initially helped. I was overjoyed to move somewhere where no one knew I was sick. Looking back, however, I think it would've been best to wait until the next school year to move, instead of moving in the middle of the year. My illnesses were not gone, just temporarily masked while I adjusted and tried to make friends.

Rebecka immediately started to accumulate lots of sick days. So many, in fact, that Dr. X decided to run a bunch of blood tests and also refer Rebecka to an infectious disease specialist at the Mayo Clinic in Rochester, Minnesota. All the labs from both visits were normal.

Then one day in early April, we had to pick Rebecka up from school because she had cut her wrist—only superficially, but it was enough for the school to realize something was up. This led to an aide being assigned to (discretely) monitor Rebecka between classes.

Not an ideal way of "starting over."

At the next visit with Dr. X, he decided to up the Prozac dose to thirty-five milligrams. He also took Rebecka off of clonodine. The increased dosage of Prozac did not go well. Rebecka slipped back into her blonde mode and had to be picked up from school just a week later. As soon as we went back to the thirty-milligram dose, she was back to "normal."

This made me realize just how powerful these medications are. That five milligrams could make such a huge difference blew my mind.

Another week passed, and again Rebecka took a turn for the worse. By the time May rolled around, the hallucinations were back and she exhibited a number of odd symptoms. She had a very realistic hallucinatory episode that scared her to the point that she ended up talking to the guidance counselor and principal about the event as if it really happened. Not until I prompted her a few times did she consider that perhaps the event was really a hallucination.

She was also feeling suicidal and felt as if we were not taking her seriously, even though we assured her that we were. We felt like we were walking on extremely fragile eggshells. One wrong word or action could set her off. Every day was a never-ending drama with extreme ups and downs. At night, I lay awake worrying that medicated Rebecka would harm herself—or us! We were all exhausted and edgy. And there was no longer a light at the end of the tunnel—only darkness.

Part 2

Breaking Free

The Turning Point

(May 11, 2011–October 4, 2011)

When I look back on the kids that stayed on the drugs and those who got off, it is the ones that are off that are the successes.... The thing is, if you get off the drugs, you start building these coping mechanisms. You learn internal controls. You start building these strengths.

—Interview with a foster mother in *Anatomy of an Epidemic*

On the morning of May 11, I returned from my workout to my friend's house (where I stayed when I was in Wisconsin for work) and found several missed calls and a text from Todd to call him. I felt the anxiety coming on as I dialed Todd's number.

He told me that Rebecka had felt so worried about harming herself that she had been admitted to the local hospital. *Not again!* I could hear the exhaustion and frustration in his voice. I told him I would get on the road as soon as I showered and packed up.

I arrived at the hospital four hours later. Once again, I felt like I was living a nightmare. Was this really happening? Was my sweet fourteen-year-old daughter really in the hospital again? When I stepped into her room, all I could do was give her a big hug. I think she expected us to be mad at her. But how could we be mad when we were so relieved that she was okay? This was clearly a cry for help.

My personal coping strategy was to speed-read a book that a friend had recommended several months earlier: *It's Not Mental* by Jeanie Wolfson, a parent who had refused to accept her two daughters' psychiatric-like symptoms being caused by brain disorders.

Reading this book gave me hope that perhaps Rebecka's problems *didn't* stem from a broken brain. Maybe we would find an underlying physical disorder that manifested itself in the symptoms that Rebecka was exhibiting. I decided we needed to find a new primary care physician to help us figure this out.

Hospitalization #8

Per the protocol for suicidal intent, Rebecka had to be admitted to a psychiatric hospital before she could come home. The treatment team at the local hospital recommended a treatment center in Mason City, Iowa, but said it might be hard to get a bed. But it turned out they did have beds available. Public service staff transported Rebecka the ninety or so miles to Mason City. Todd and I drove together in our car.

It was a long drive, but we "entertained" ourselves by reading the book *Anatomy of an Epidemic* by Robert Whitaker, which explores the astonishing rise of mental illness in America and won the Investigative Reporters and Editors Award for the best investigative journalism book of 2010. One of Todd's colleagues had lent it to us when he learned what was going on with Rebecka. We were able to relate to this book every step of the way. We nodded in recognition of the various stories we read and were horrified to learn the dark secret of psychiatry: that the big pharmaceutical companies are in total control. Indeed, this book was possibly one of the most influential of my life—a true game changer.

We read *Anatomy of an Epidemic* on all of our trips back and forth to Mason City and at home as well. And we were soon convinced that as Rebecka's parents, it was our duty to protect her from these drugs that were clearly causing so much harm.

During a phone conversation with Rebecka, we found out that the attending physician had prescribed at least one medication, Risperdal, without our consent. This was the same drug the psychiatrist had prescribed during her first hospitalization. Had we come full circle?

Todd put a call in to the doctor the very same evening to discuss the matter of medication. The doctor was not available, but the staff assured us that we would be able to speak to him the following day.

In preparation for the call, we compiled a list of problems that we believed to be side effects of the medication:

- Fatigue
- Difficulty concentrating
- Jumping from activity to activity
- Loss of interest in everything (except Facebook and friends)
- No energy
- Heavy breathing
- Hallucinations
- Lack of empathy for others
- Some antisocial behavior

For some reason, "suicidal thoughts" was not on our list, but I firmly believe that Rebecka's intentions to hurt herself were also a side effect of the medication.

Armed with this list, Todd was ready to fight for our daughter's right to receive treatment without medication, all senses on high alert. But when the phone call came, there was no fight. "That sounds reasonable," was the doctor's response to our request. It was almost a little anticlimactic. Nevertheless, we were thrilled. No more medication! And this time, we would not go back, no matter what.

Dr. X, being fully embedded in the mainstream discourses on mental illness, was not as easily convinced. When Todd and Rebecka went to see him for a follow-up after the hospitalization, he vehemently opposed our decision to discontinue the medication. Todd told him that we were going to try some alternative treatment options, such as DBT. Dr. X responded sternly that there is no evidence that DBT works (except, there is).[1] He also said that if we decided to go back to medication, he would be available to work with Rebecka. Without medication, there was nothing he could do. Todd later reflected on this conversation:

> He made it clear that we were making a big mistake. And I remember thinking how difficult it was to make such a decision when so many experts and psychiatrists were telling you that this was wrong. We trusted our instincts, and our experience and knowledge, even when the psychiatric establishment opposed us at almost every step. In retrospect, this was one of our most courageous moments.

The following day, we received the good news that Rebecka was ready to be released from the hospital after only four days. As part of the discharge process, a therapist reviewed with us the grim results of a psychological evaluation they had conducted with Rebecka. The report stated:

> Rebecka's test results reveal a very serious acute psychiatric disturbance and also raise concern about the presence of problematic personality traits and relationship behaviors.
> She seems to be both very depressed and highly anxious.
> . . . She seems to ruminate about her many perceived faults and failures. She offers that she hates herself and may believe that she is deserving of punishment.

The report also noted that Rebecka expressed in a test that the future "looks bleak."

In a subsequent paragraph, the author of the report wrote, "Rebecka's test results are consistent with the presence of an eating disorder."

At least now we now had a diagnosis of sorts, something around which to anchor the treatment. The discharge team recommended that Rebecka see an eating disorder specialist and participate in a DBT group (sound familiar?).

I kicked myself for having thought that Rebecka no longer needed treatment for disordered eating. It all made sense now. This had been the underlying constant from the beginning. The weight-loss. The bingeing. The purging. The self-loathing. The self-harm. And now, Rebecka had decided that if we would not let her hurt herself by other means, she would simply starve herself to death.

Once home, Rebecka stuck with her resolution and refused to eat for the most part. Per the therapist's instructions, we ignored the behavior. The theory was that eventually she would eat.

At least she wasn't hallucinating.

She tried to use the restricting behavior as a reason not to go to school, saying she was worried she might faint from lack of food. But we insisted she follow her normal routine. The first day back at school, she lasted until 10:45 a.m. I picked her up and took her to her favorite coffee shop for a PB&J. She ate the whole thing. I tried not to seem too excited.

The same day, we met with her regular therapist, who refined the instructions for how to respond to Rebecka's erratic eating, asking us to provide food at every meal (to show we cared), but to not push the issue of eating. She also agreed that DBT would be great for Rebecka and offered to refer Rebecka to the Mayo Clinic for an eating disorder program evaluation.

The next couple of days were tough. Rebecka was trying so hard to restrict, and we responded by taking away phone and Internet privileges. Her therapist had instructed us not to reward undesirable behavior, so when they called from school and said that Rebecka had collapsed and was in the nurse's office, I went to the school with the intention of staying with Rebecka until the end of the school day. I brought my laptop so I could work and some food for Rebecka so she could eat.

The principal found an empty conference room for us, where we sat for a while in silence. Eventually, Rebecka started nibbling at the food I had brought. Then she said, "I want my privileges back. I'm going to start eating again." And she ate all the food and went back to class.

Progress!

Over the next couple of weeks, Rebecka's eating and mood improved. From May 21 to June 1, the only entry I have in my spreadsheet is "Good day!" Rebecka had started seeing a dietitian in a nearby town and was receiving acupuncture treatments, which helped her relax. Rebecka had also started seeing a therapist in town who specialized in eating disorders, so we canceled our appointment at the Mayo Clinic. We were already traveling seventy miles to Rochester every week so Rebecka could attend an adolescent DBT group, and it was difficult to think about adding yet another treatment modality to the mix.

Summer travel centered around visiting family—first in Mobile, Alabama, and then in Sweden. Rebecka was doing okay for a while, but then the eating disorder prevailed. She confessed that she was purging, and at one point got really worried when she noticed that there was blood mixed in with the vomit.

Based on the fact that Rebecka had so many different appointments every week, we agreed that I needed to be more available when school started and Todd went back to teaching. Considering how stressful my job was, I felt this would also contribute to my own mental health. Thus, I quit my job of nine years and started an Internet consulting business so I could work from home and have a more flexible schedule.*

By the time she started ninth grade, Rebecka was restricting her intake to nine hundred calories per day. Todd and I were against the idea of hospitalization again and were determined to keep her home with us. We were done

---

* This is not to say that moms should stay home. This arrangement made most sense for our family. In other families, Dad might need to be around more and hence cut down on work. You do what you need to do to help your child feel better.

with hospitals and medications. We had hope that between DBT, therapy, dietary counseling, acupuncture, dietary supplements, and a stable home life, Rebecka would turn a corner and beat this illness that had taken over our lives.

I encouraged her to take advantage of the 24/7 phone support that was part of the DBT program and call her DBT therapist before she purged. But Rebecka didn't call. It was as if she were clinging on to this disorder as part of her identity.

Throughout the summer, I had been working with her primary care physician to eliminate any physiological problems that could be making things worse. The doctor ran all of the tests I requested, but everything looked good. She eventually referred us to the Mayo Clinic to see a GI specialist, since this seemed to be the area that was troubling Rebecka the most (not surprising, considering her eating patterns).

At the end of August, we made the trek up to Rochester to see a Dr. Tung. I was amazed by the amount of time the doctor spent with us. She ordered allergy testing and an ultrasound and also referred us to the Mayo Clinic eating disorder program with an appointment set for October 5.

Lifesaving Help

(October 5, 2011–January 31, 2012)

Antidepressants, particularly selective serotonin reuptake inhibitors (SSRIs), have not been found to be beneficial in the treatment of women with anorexia nervosa or in the treatment of women with anorexia nervosa and comorbid depression.

—Pouneh Fazeli, et. al., "Psychotropic Medication Use in Anorexia Nervosa between 1997 and 2009," *The International Journal of Eating Disorders*

While Todd and I were relieved that all of the medication-induced psychiatric symptoms had abated, we were becoming increasingly frustrated that we were not getting more direction from Rebecka's treatment team regarding how we should respond to Rebecka's eating disorder. Intuitively, we knew that taking away privileges worked, but we were not sure if this was an appropriate way to handle the issue at hand. We were also unsure about how forceful we should be regarding getting Rebecka to eat. And should we be doing something to try to prevent the purging other than pleading with her to stop?

In search of answers, I read books such as *Help Your Teenager Beat an Eating Disorder* and *The Parent's Guide to Eating Disorders: Supporting Self-Esteem, Healthy Eating, and Positive Body Image at Home.* I learned that per the Maudsley approach, a family-based eating disorder treatment methodology, parents are not viewed as the problem, but rather as "the best resource in treatment."[1] To date, we had definitely felt more like the problem and for the most part didn't feel like we were being considered part of the treatment team.

Tensions grew at home as Rebecka continued to refuse to eat, despite promises made during therapy sessions. One morning in early September, I got up early to make Rebecka a delicious fruit smoothie. (She had agreed in therapy that she would drink a smoothie for breakfast.) When breakfast time rolled around, Rebecka sat down at the table, took a couple of sips, and announced that she was done. I totally lost it. By the time Todd came into the kitchen, I was in a pile on the floor, sobbing, and Rebecka was sitting at the table looking guilty. (You could say it was a low point.) I was ashamed that I hadn't been able to hold it together and so angry at this disorder that had taken my daughter hostage.

When we talked it through later, Rebecka explained, "I feel like a failure when I'm not restricting." My response was, "I feel like a failure when you *are* restricting." Somehow, this brief exchange helped both of us understand where the other was coming from. It felt like a breakthrough. I had finally told her point-blank how I felt (hear the eggshells crunch), but I also got a glimpse into her mind and her struggles.

Reading about the Maudsley approach convinced me that it was the way to go, but we didn't have anybody to guide us through the process. In fact, some of Rebecka's providers didn't think this approach would work, due to all the tension at home. To me, this didn't make sense at all. The tension came from not knowing how we were supposed to handle feeding our child, and Rebecka not feeling that like we were doing anything to help her (despite multiple visits to see various therapists and other health professionals every week). I couldn't wait for that Mayo Clinic appointment!

When Rebecka went in for her next dietitian appointment in late September, we learned that Rebecka had lost almost twenty pounds since May (in addition to the weight she had already lost by coming off Zyprexa). Her dietitian did not see this downward trend stopping and recommended immediate hospitalization. After a conference call with Rebecka's primary doctor and therapist, we determined that this would be the best course of action. I reminded them that we had an appointment coming up on October 5, and they agreed we could wait for that.

On Wednesday, October 5, 2011, we got up before the crack of dawn to make the 7:45 a.m. check-in at the Mayo Clinic Generose building on the St. Mary's campus. The staff showed us to a meeting room where they left us to fill out paperwork. Eventually, a friendly and extremely peppy woman about my age entered the room. She introduced herself as Dr. Leslie Sim, director of the eating disorder program.

Dr. Sim talked to Rebecka and me for a while to understand what was going on and explained their treatment approach to us. It was based on the Maudsley approach, but modified to include specific calorie minimums for each meal and snack. Dr. Sim explained that she had found that this relieved some stress on the part of the eating disorder patients, but also removed any ambiguity related to portion sizes. It seemed logical to me.

Once we understood the basics of the program and the level of commitment required by the family—which you can't fully grasp until you're in the middle of the program—it was time to tour the facilities.

They were impressive. There seemed to be a lower patient-to-staff ratio, and the nurses and other staff we saw looked happier and less stressed than in previous hospitals. Dr. Sim showed us the kitchen where the eating disorder patients ate their meals, the timer used to time the meals, and measuring devices to count out the exact amount of calories.

During our tour, I asked the question that had been on my mind since we got in the car early that morning, the answer to which would make or break the deal.

"Are you going to push medication?"

"Oh no," Dr. Sim responded. "I'm a psychologist, so I like to treat without medication if at all possible." I breathed a sigh of relief. Everything felt right about this place, from Dr. Sim to the staff to the details of the program. This would be a good place for Rebecka.

Now we just had to get it cleared with the health insurance company, because there was no way we could pay for this treatment out-of-pocket at over $2,000 per day. (Yep, you read that right!) Dr. Sim was going to work on that.

Hospitalization #9

Dr. Sim made it happen. Five days later, we were back at the Mayo Clinic to drop Rebecka off at the Psychiatry and Psychology Treatment Center. Rebecka seemed relieved finally to be getting the help she needed. Todd and I felt a certain amount of relief as well. At least for a little while, getting Rebecka to eat would be somebody else's problem. We needed a break!

Dr. Sim started Rebecka off at three thousand calories per day. This is a lot of food for somebody who has been trying to live on around a thousand calories per day for a long time. Rebecka hated it, but it was what we had signed up for. The goal was to get Rebecka's weight up to a healthy level that she could maintain. Rebecka quickly discovered that milkshakes were a great way to consume lots of calories with minimal effort. But it was still a challenge to meet the daily calorie requirements.

The hospital therapy program relied heavily on rewards and removal of privileges to manage eating behavior. Everything from phone calls to parents to access to the Internet depended on successful completion of meals at the prescribed calorie levels. It worked. Soon Rebecka had earned enough "points" to call us and receive visits. As her weight increased, the daily calorie requirements went down, and she gained more freedom.

As part of the process of moving from Level 1 (hospitalization) to Level 2 (close monitoring at home), Todd and I were required to monitor some of Rebecka's meals at the hospital and also take her out for three successful meals at restaurants. (The attention to detail of this program amazed me.) Before heading out to the restaurant, Rebecka had to do research online to find menus with calorie counts and compose her meal. Each time, we brought the printout with us to the restaurant. And every meal was successful. She didn't like how much she had to eat, but she would rather eat than lose her privileges. And she was ready to come home and get on with her life!

rebecka: on the mayo clinic eating disorder program

Initially I saw a lot of flaws that ended up being the characteristics that made the program so unique and helpful. For example, it was not its own unit, but a program within the regular adolescent mental health program. We socialized with, lived amongst, and had lessons with patients who had a variety of behavioral problems. The only thing the eating disorder patients did separately was eating.

I thought this was odd. How were we supposed to recover if we only learned lessons pertaining to general mental disorders? Where were the lessons about diet and health? I realized later on the way they did this was very beneficial. There was less time for the eating disorder patients to sneakily collaborate on ways to restrict and whine amongst themselves about the copious amounts of food. Instead, we socialized with people who had no disordered eating.

After four weeks of hospitalization, we got the good news that Rebecka could come home. Unlike all the other hospitalizations, this one had been transformational. Rebecka emerged more mature and with a sense of purpose. She had a life to live, fun to be had, and an education to pursue.

As I met with Dr. Sim for a chat as part of the discharge process, she said something that gave me immense hope for the future and validated Todd's and my belief that Rebecka's psychiatric symptoms were not caused by a genetic, unavoidable, life-long illness. "Rebecka is not a psych patient," she said. "She's more like my medical students." (This was a reference to Rebecka's intellect and ambition.) Dr. Sim went on to talk about how bright Rebecka was and what a great future she had ahead of her. Indeed, she saw the child *we* knew, the child that Rebecka's former psychiatrists could not (and would not) see. I nodded and smiled and tried to hold back the tears of joy and relief that threatened to spill over. I wanted to give Dr. Sim a big hug. At that moment I knew that despite what all the doctors said and despite what the awful psychological testing results said, Rebecka was fine. We would all be fine.

But we had a lot of work ahead of us. With Rebecka released from the hospital and back home with us, the true meaning of family-based therapy kicked in. Rebecka had to devise meal plans for each day using, at a minimum, the calorie counts assigned to each meal and snack. At every meal, Rebecka had

Another initially perceived flaw was the way we picked food. Typically, eating disorder programs set food in front of you and tell you to eat it. This is designed so the patients are forced not to focus on the calories and fat grams. Mayo did things much differently. We picked our own meals using a large menu with the calorie, fat, and protein amounts listed. At first, this panicked me.

The daily calories we consumed increased almost every day. Once I hit four thousand calories per day, it actually became a comfort to know that I was in control over the way I could take that in. People with eating disorders crave control above all. By letting us choose our food, I think they were trying to give us control in a healthy way.

❦

to assemble her food while one of us monitored her. We recorded the amounts on a daily eating chart that we kept in a green binder. Then we had to set the timer for thirty minutes and watch her eat every bite and drink every drop. We noted successful meals with a sticker or a smiley face. At school, the nurse monitored her meals and sent a note home indicating success or failure. And after every meal, we had to watch Rebecka for an hour to make sure she didn't throw up her food.

Rebecka had regular appointments with Dr. Sim, which she cherished. She also continued to attend the adolescent DBT group. We tried to coordinate the appointments so that we didn't have to make the trip to Rochester more than once per week. Rebecka had already missed so much school, and we didn't want her to miss any more than absolutely necessary, primarily to avoid additional stress and anxiety over getting behind in her classes.

Sometimes I tried to imagine how we would have managed during this time if I had still been working full-time outside the home. We probably would have found a way, but it would have been extremely difficult and stressful. I felt grateful to be in a position to focus on supporting Rebecka during her journey of healing.

As Rebecka continued to have a solid track record of successful meals and maintaining her weight, we gradually allowed her more and more freedom. Dr. Sim coached us through this process. First, we reduced the monitoring time after meals to thirty minutes. Then we eliminated the after-meal monitoring all together. As Dr. Sim frequently pointed out, the scale was the ultimate purging detector, so we would quickly find out if she slipped back into those behaviors. Eventually, we also agreed that we could stop the lunch monitoring. This was a relief for Rebecka. Now she could join her friends for lunch again. Life was slowly getting back to normal.

We were still holding our breaths, though.

By the end of 2011, Rebecka was doing so well, that—with Dr. Sim's blessing—we agreed to let her go by herself on the train to Wisconsin to visit her best friend. We were worried about it, but we also wanted to reward her for all her hard work of sticking with her eating plan and staying healthy. It was wonderful that Rebecka was participating in life again, and we wanted to encourage that.

She returned safely from her trip without incident. The following day, she had an appointment to see Dr. Sim. During the routine weigh-in, Dr. Sim noted that she had lost a couple of pounds. She didn't worry too much about it since Rebecka had been out of town and probably too busy to focus much on eating.

However, she did ask me to monitor her weight every other day to make sure she wasn't losing any more.

My gut instinct told me that I should also start monitoring her meals again, but it was so nice not to have to do all that weighing and measuring and recording and monitoring. So I ignored my intuition (never a good thing). I did monitor Rebecka's weight, however, and it was not dropping any further, so that was good.

As someone who grew up singing in choirs and participating in musicals, I was so excited that Rebecka had decided to sign up to be part of the Madrigal Dinner put on by the high school every January. We had invited her aunt and uncle and baby cousin from Virginia to come visit and had tickets for the dinner.

Days before the big event, I took Rebecka to see her local therapist. Halfway through the session, her therapist came to the waiting room and asked me to join them. She looked serious. *Oh, no.* I sat down next to Rebecka, whose eyes were fixed on her shoes, and waited for the therapist to say something.

"Rebecka has something to tell you," she said, looking encouragingly at Rebecka.

Rebecka glanced sideways at me. "Don't be mad at me, but I've been restricting again," she said with a small voice.

"But your weight," I responded. "You haven't lost any..."

With that, she blurted out what had been going on the past week. Ever since she found out she had lost weight; she couldn't stop obsessing about losing more. So she stopped eating lunch and tried to minimize her intake at the other meals by eating in the basement as much as possible and putting her food down the garbage disposal. "I'm sorry for wasting food," she said. I appreciated how well she knew me (I don't like wasting anything), but wasting food was the least of my concerns. I still didn't understand why her weight hadn't changed.

"I drank a bunch of water before our weigh-ins," she eventually admitted. "So it wouldn't look like I was losing weight." This child never ceased to amaze me with her ability to make weight loss happen.

I was trying to remain calm, but on the inside a thousand thoughts whirled through my head. *I should've continued to monitor her meals. I should've weighed her at random times. I should've...*

Getting myself back into the conversation, I went into problem-solving mode. "Okay," I said. "We're going back to full monitoring. You'll need to make up the calories you've missed today so far by the end of tomorrow. Otherwise, you'll be on alert."

Being on "alert" was a part of Dr. Sim's process and happened if Rebecka didn't meet her calorie minimum on any given day. Going on alert meant that Dr. Sim would get a call, and we would schedule an appointment for the following day. If Rebecka was able to make up the calories the following day, we canceled the appointment. If not, we went up to the Mayo Clinic with a six-pack of Ensure (flavor of your choice), and Rebecka had to stay there until she made up the calories by drinking the Ensure. If she wasn't able to make up the calories, she would go back to Level 1—hospitalization. To date, Rebecka had never been on alert.

The next twenty-four hours were dreadful. We prepared meals for Rebecka with the specific calorie counts, but she wouldn't eat. I pleaded, threatened, and basically behaved in all the different ways you're not supposed to behave when trying to parent a child with an eating disorder. Selfishly, the thing I fretted most about was that she would miss her performance. That performance was supposed to be the ultimate sign that Rebecka was all better—that she was back among the living and had hobbies that did not revolve around disordered eating.

Needless to say, Rebecka went on alert.

The following day, we made the drive up to Rochester, carrying with us a six-pack of chocolate-flavored Ensure. The staff ushered us into a conference room where they asked us to wait for Dr. Sim. She appeared quite a while later, expressed her concern that Rebecka wasn't eating, and explained that Rebecka had an hour to make up her calories by drinking a specified amount of Ensure. In the meantime, Dr. Sim and I would visit.

Dr. Sim's tactic here was to not reward Rebecka's restricting behavior with a therapy session. Rebecka was furious. She was expecting a good heart-to-heart with Dr. Sim, and instead she was left alone to drink meal-replacement drinks, which she detested. Rebecka would have none of that. By the time I returned an hour later, she had drunk exactly zero ounces of Ensure. My heart sank, but at this point, I had resigned myself to the fact that she would most likely miss her aunt and uncle's visit, and worse, the Madrigal Dinner.

They didn't have any beds available on the adolescent unit for the upcoming night, so they sent us home with the promise that Rebecka could avoid hospitalization if she got back on track with her calories. At this point, however, the eating disorder had taken full control, and Rebecka was in a fast downward spiral. I marveled at how quickly things had taken a turn for the worse.

Hospitalization #10

Three days later, on January 16, 2012 (my thirty-eighth birthday), Rebecka was readmitted to the Mayo Clinic Psychiatry and Psychology Treatment Center. It was a sad day. Rebecka was definitely going to miss her aunt and uncle's visit and the performance. On the other hand, I was glad that Dr. Sim's program was set up in such a way that we wouldn't have to wait weeks and months for her to get help. It was all about nipping relapses in the bud.

During this second round of Mayo Clinic eating disorder programming, Rebecka got to experience what happens if you don't eat during your hospitalization. After refusing to eat breakfast and lunch one day, Dr. Sim ordered that she change out of her regular clothes into a hospital gown and stay in bed. The staff removed everything except the bed from her room, so she literally had nothing to do but stare at the ceiling. "Since you're not eating enough calories, we can't allow you to expend any calories," Dr. Sim explained. Brilliant. By the time dinner rolled around, Rebecka was ready to eat. And she continued to eat all her calories at every meal.

rebecka: on the not so glamorous aspects of ed treatment

There were lots of annoying things, like locked bathrooms, measured urine, having a nurse follow us everywhere, and the (valid) suspicion that we were always trying to restrict or purge.

For example, one time I was simply washing my face and hands, and my nurse thought I was purging in the sink and told my "team" (an attending psychiatrist, a resident psychiatrist, an attending general physician, a dietitian, a med student, a psychologist, and my nurse— quite a crowd for my small hospital room) about her suspicions. They gravely lectured me and said this might cost me an extra week. I was furious and stormed out of the room feeling betrayed and belittled.

So, yes, it's a very demanding and cautious environment, completely focused on making you gain weight and maintain mental stability. But it worked for me.

❧

This hospitalization was shorter and lasted only two weeks. The experience was night-and-day compared to her many other hospitalizations, especially those outside the Mayo system. While the first eight hospitalizations were haphazard and focused on stabilization and medication management, the last two were well-organized and focused on recovery and viewing the child and the family holistically—an integrative approach to treatment.

As we drove home through snow-covered fields, Rebecka and I agreed: no more hospitalizations. Time to move on and let the eating disorder bite the dust. And that's what happened! We continued to monitor her calorie intake, starting off at 3,900 calories per day and dropping three hundred calories every two to three days until she was at a normal 2,100 calories. Eventually, she was able to get to Level 3, self-monitoring.

What a relief!

That spring, Rebecka had a small part in a local production of *The Merchant of Venice*. I finally had my performance. She finally had her life back.

At the time of this writing, three years have passed. Rebecka has not been hospitalized again or experienced any other symptoms of mental illness. She maintains a healthy weight and eats what she wants. She loves to order nachos with friends at the local Mexican restaurant or indulge in a soft serve ice cream at the Whippy Dip during the summer months. And every now and then, she even eats Pop-Tarts—in moderation, of course. She participates in school clubs and choir, recently spent a semester studying in Sweden, and can't wait to start college and spread her wings. In other words, she is a remarkable but very normal teenager. And that's the way we like it!

Breaking Free Factors

Medicines don't treat the entire patient.

—Dr. Henry Emmons, quoted in *Rescuing Your Teenager from Depression*

Looking back at our treacherous journey through the mental health care system, I can point to a specific set of factors that allowed Rebecka to break free from the hell that was closing in around her, making her incapable of living a normal teenage life.

A Medication-Free Brain

We view the moment we took Rebecka off psychiatric medications as the turning point in her journey toward recovery. Once the medications were out of her system, the hallucinations vanished, her suicidal ideations stopped, her brain fog cleared, and we were able to focus on the real problem at hand, her eating disorder.

We had to fight hard to get to this point. By the time Rebecka was hospitalized the first time, she was a completely different person. The doctors who treated her didn't know bright, funny, intuitive Rebecka. They just knew listless, cynical, medicated Rebecka: a psych patient in need of more and more medication. But we knew and felt in our guts that medicating Rebecka was not the right thing to do. Reading other people's stories, understanding better the history of psychiatry, and discovering research studies that raised questions about the effectiveness of medication helped us muster the courage to stand up to the system and request the removal of all psychotropic medications from our daughter's prescription list.

In doing so, we deviated from the discourse that says that medication is the best way to treat mental distress. While the doctor on call complied when we asked him to take Rebecka off psychiatric medications, her regular psychiatrist told us in so many words that we were making a bad decision. Battling the established beliefs about mental illness and appropriate treatment was lonely, and we felt completely unsupported by the system until we met Dr. Sim—a psychologist—at the Mayo Clinic.

A Stable Home Environment

Rebecka was not able to start healing until our family was together in one place with no plans to move. Our family spent five years living apart for portions of most weeks starting the summer before Rebecka's fourth grade year and continuing until the summer before she started ninth grade. This put an extreme strain on our family—as Rebecka well expressed in her questions to us all those years ago. Being together again helped us all heal.

It also helped that I was able to work from home and be available to cook nourishing food, help with homework, and be a listening ear at the end of a long day at school.

Being together and following our passions allowed Todd and me to be happier at home. Parents' moods and struggles rub off on their kids. According to Marilyn Wedge, a family therapist and the author of *Suffer the Children: The Case against Labeling and Medicating and an Effective Alternative*, you should not share your adult problems with your children. Rather, you should talk about what's going well, because it makes kids feel safe. In a powerful case study about eleven-year-old Laura, who was taking eight different medications, performing poorly in school, and had recently threatened to commit suicide, Wedge instructs Laura's mother (after the mother admits that she talks about her problems in front of her daughter):

> I want you to tell Laura every day what a good day you had at work. I would like you to tell her every morning that you are looking forward to your day (you make up the reason why) and tell her every evening why you enjoyed your day. You'll have to arrange lunches with friends, workouts at the gym, or whatever, so you'll be telling her the truth.[1]

Now we know.

Professional Help for Disordered Eating

The eating disorder was real. No doubt about it. But the doctors ignored this problem in favor of the severe symptoms resulting from her medication, such as hallucinations and suicidal ideation. The eating disorder was also masked by giving Rebecka the antipsychotic Zyprexa to help with weight gain, but not addressing any of the underlying issues such as distorted body image or anxiety.

Anorexia has the highest mortality rate of all psychiatric illnesses. In fact, 6 to 10 percent of patients suffering from this devastating disorder die.[2] Recent studies confirm that medication is not an effective method in treating patients with anorexia. Dr. Pouneh G. Fazeli and colleagues write, "antidepressants, particularly selective serotonin reuptake inhibitors (SSRIs), have not been found to be beneficial in the treatment of women with anorexia nervosa or in the treatment of women with anorexia nervosa and comorbid depression." Yet close to 50 percent of Fazeli's study participants reported being on an antidepressant.[3] Other studies show that the family-based treatment approach is highly effective in treating eating disorders. For example, a one-year study conducted by the Maudsley group reported that 90 percent of patients receiving family-based treatment had a good outcome compared to only 18 percent of patients receiving individual therapy. A follow-up study showed that the family-based treatment group continued to do well five years later. It is the best long-term approach.[4]

This was our experience as well. Once Rebecka got appropriate care, she was able to recover fully.

Coping Strategies

Life is not easy. Not for kids, teens, or adults. There will always be difficult breakups, hurtful comments, deaths of loved ones, family tensions, bullying, and disappointments. It happens to everybody. The key to surviving life's difficulties is the ability to cope with, and accept, unpleasant feelings.

Rebecka was fortunate enough to learn lots of coping skills and strategies during her hospitalizations, in therapy, and as part of the DBT skills group program. She learned that listening to music helped her relax and that watching sitcoms helped cheer her up if she was feeling down. I wish I had learned some coping strategies when I was a teenager!

Our story has a happy ending. However, there are many other stories that do not end well. In fact, 250 children are disabled by mental illness *every day*.[5] The most commonly prescribed type of drug for kids and teens ages twelve to nineteen is central nervous system stimulants such as Ritalin. I find this shocking and completely unacceptable. It is a wake-up call that something is amiss in our society and with the environment in which we raise our kids.

Thus, the rest of this book will be dedicated to exploring the disturbing truth about the current state of psychiatry, proposing alternatives to medication for treating kids and teens who display symptoms of mental disorders, and, most importantly, discussing what we can do to boost—or *optimize*—the mental health of our children and stop the cycle of mental distress.

Part 3

What We Learned
About Psychiatry

In parts 1 and 2 of this book, Rebecka and I shared our story with you, not to get sympathy or to be sensational, but rather to raise awareness about the potential dangers of psychiatric medications, especially when administered to children and teens. Further, I wanted to highlight the misinformed and backward approach many psychiatrists and general practitioners take in responding to young patients exhibiting symptoms of mental illness—because they are embedded in the dominant discourses on mental health. These discourses consider mental illnesses as disorders of the brain, which are treated best with medication—and don't know what to make of cases like Rebecka's when the medication makes things worse.

However, as our story illustrates, it is not all doom and gloom. My goal is to provide hope to desperate parents and caregivers that medication doesn't always have to be the answer. There are other ways to address sadness, worry, attention problems, aggression, and disordered eating.

However, before we move on to alternative treatment options and how we can optimize the mental health of our children, I will share what we've learned about the current state of psychiatry, the pharmaceutical industry, the brain-disease theory, expanding diagnoses, and the problem with treating kids with drugs designed for adults.

I will also show that Rebecka's case is not a one-off. Families everywhere are struggling to find integrated care. And children's mental distress—presenting as depression, anxiety, obsession, violence, withdrawal, and a host of other symptoms—is often treated with medication as a first resort, sometimes with horrific side effects. We are indeed witnessing a mental health crisis.

From Psychotherapy to Psychotropics

*The psychopharmacology revolution was born from one
part science and two parts wishful thinking.*

—Robert Whitaker, *Anatomy of an Epidemic*

In a powerful 2011 *New York Times* article, "Talk Doesn't Pay, So Psychiatry
Turns Instead to Drug Therapy" by Gardiner Harris, psychiatrist Donald Levin
describes the transformation of psychiatry over the course of his career. When
he started practicing psychiatry in the early 1970s, he saw a manageable number of patients for forty-five-minute talk-therapy sessions. Now, he sees 1,200
patients for fifteen-minute visits—all focused on prescribing and managing
medication.

Why this change? The main reason is that insurance companies won't reimburse forty-five minutes of talk therapy at the psychiatrist's office now that
there are social workers and psychologists offering talk therapy at lower rates.
So psychiatrists wanting to maintain their current level of income are stuck
diagnosing mental disorders, and prescribing and monitoring medication.

"Nobody wants to go backwards, moneywise, in their career," says Levin.
"Would you?"[1]

This is only one of many examples of how psychiatry has changed over the
last sixty years. The most important changes I cover in this chapter relate to
the rise of using medication to treat mental illness.

Before Psychotropic Drugs

Using medication to treat mentally ill people is a relatively new phenomenon. Prior to the 1950s, the most common treatments for the mentally ill were institutionalization, frontal lobotomy (a surgery that severs most of the connections to and from the prefrontal cortex), electroshock therapy, and psychotherapy.[2]

Institutionalization was possible because of the relatively low number of people who had been diagnosed as severely mentally ill (that is, people who were disabled by their illness). For example, in 1955, there were 355,000 people with psychiatric diagnoses in our country's mental hospitals. That's 1 in 468. By contrast, in 2007, 1 in every 76 Americans was disabled by mental illness—over 500,000 of those being children.[3]

And with the advent of humane mental institutions, such as the Friends Asylum for the Relief of Persons Deprived of the Use of Their Reason (now Friends Hospital), founded by the Quakers in 1813, some severely mentally ill people had a safe place to go to heal.[4] However, many mental institutions were not quite as humane, as described by Albert Deutsch in his 1948 book *The Shame of the States*.

Frontal lobotomy was the frightening precursor to psychotropic medications in that it messed with the brain and often left patients incapacitated. Its temporary popularity is highlighted by the fact that the inventor of the lobotomy, António Egas Moniz, actually received the Nobel Prize for Physiology or Medicine in 1949. Today, most view lobotomy as a major error of judgment best suited for the history books.

Electroshock therapy, also called electroconvulsive therapy, worked by inducing a seizure in the patient, which was supposed to eliminate psychotic thoughts. This technique is still used today in severe, medication-resistant cases of depression and other mental illnesses.

Psychotherapy was popularized by Sigmund Freud at the turn of the twentieth century and has evolved and expanded significantly since the middle of the twentieth century.[5] It is a noninvasive treatment option that looks at the whole person and his or her environment (including the past) to help relieve the symptoms of mental distress. This may include learning coping skills to deal with unpleasant thoughts and training one's brain to use new patterns of thinking. Research shows that psychotherapy is just as effective as drugs in treating patients with mild to moderate symptoms. It may just take a little longer to experience relief, because humans are complex beings. Psychiatrists used psychotherapy extensively as recently as the 1990s.[6] Social workers and psychologists still use psychotherapy extensively, often in conjunction with drug therapy.

The First Psychotropic Medications Were Accidental

In the normal course of developing medication, scientists identify the cause of the illness and then develop a drug to counteract the cause.[7] However, this is not how the first psychotropic drugs were developed. Rather, they were completely accidental.

The first psychiatric drug, Thorazine (generic name chlorpromazine), grew out of research at a pharmaceutical company in France to find a cure for malaria. This particular research didn't work out, but in 1946, the researchers found that one of the compounds they had been testing might be useful to prevent histamine responses during surgery. In 1949, a French surgeon, Henri Laborit, started using this compound with some of his patients and discovered that it calmed them down. Based on this, he suggested that a "cocktail" including this compound might be useful as an anesthetic as well.

Thus a new drug, chlorpromazine, was born. As expected, it worked well as an anesthetic, but Laborit also suggested that it might be helpful in treating people with mental illness. He said it "produced a veritable medicinal lobotomy."[8] By 1955, the drug had made it to the United States, where it was marketed as Thorazine and classified as a "major tranquilizer."

I was surprised to learn that psychiatrists realized at the time that they were not treating diseases with this drug. Rather, it was purely meant to calm, or tranquilize, institutionalized psychiatric patients.[9]

Around the same time, a researcher in London, Frank Berger, who was trying to find a drug to treat respiratory, urinary, and gastrointestinal illnesses, "stumbled on a potent muscle-relaxing agent." He found that when administered in small doses, it made mice display tranquility without paralysis. By 1955, Berger had moved to the United States to work for Wallace Laboratories and developed a drug to treat anxiety. Wallace marketed it as Miltown, a "minor tranquilizer."[10]

The point here is that the first generation of psychiatric drugs was not originally developed to treat the causes of mental illness, because we still don't know the exact causes of mental illness. Rather, researchers accidentally discovered that these drugs calmed, sedated, and tamed mice and humans, and pharmaceutical companies and psychiatrists embraced the new drugs in "treating" the mentally ill. According to David Healy, an Irish psychiatrist and author of several books on the history of psychiatry, psychiatrists especially enjoyed the new drugs because they allowed them to become real *medical* doctors. As Whitaker explains, "doctors in internal medicine had their antibiotics, and now psychiatrists could have their 'anti-disease' pills too."[11]

The development and administration of these drugs was not based on any known physical cause or brain disorder, but rather simply to address symptoms exhibited by a range of individuals from institutionalized "lunatics" to anxious housewives.

And tragically, this started the movement of psychiatry away from treating patients and the causes of their symptoms with psychotherapy to treating just the symptoms with medication (and often creating more symptoms in the process) in fifteen-minute sessions.

The Development of SSRIs and Atypical Antipsychotics to Treat a Theory

Everybody knows that mental illness stems from chemical imbalances in the brain, right? That's what we've heard over and over, both from our doctors and from the pharmaceutical companies. For example, a pamphlet on teens and antidepressants from the Mayo Clinic states: "Sometimes, your level of neurotransmitters may be low, or they may be reabsorbed too soon.... As a result, there is not good communication between brain cells. This can cause you to be depressed."[12] An early TV ad for Zoloft explains: "While the cause is unknown, depression may be related to an imbalance of natural chemicals between nerve cells in the brain. Prescription Zoloft works to correct this imbalance."[13]

It is a nice explanation, allowing people to think of mental illness as a disease, like diabetes, that can be managed solely with medication. At the same time, a diagnosis of major depressive disorder or bipolar disorder becomes a lifetime sentence, because according to this explanation, there's no cure—it's a chronic problem with your brain.

Guess what I learned about chemical imbalances (including low levels of neurotransmitters such as serotonin and dopamine) in my research? Their role in mental illness is an unsupported theory.[14] Nothing more. There is not one shred of evidence that low serotonin *causes* depression or that low dopamine *causes* schizophrenia. Even the National Institute of Health doesn't claim to know for sure what causes depression:

> Most likely, depression is caused by a combination of genetic,
> biological, environmental, and psychological factors. Depressive
> illnesses are disorders of the brain. Longstanding theories
> about depression suggest that neurotransmitters—chemicals
> the brain cells use to communicate—are out of balance
> in depression. But it has been difficult to prove this.[15]

However, this hasn't stopped the pharmaceutical companies from developing a class of antidepressants called selective serotonin reuptake inhibitors (SSRIs) that specifically change the balance of serotonin to boost mood. You've probably heard of them: Prozac, Zoloft, Celexa, Paxil, and Lexapro. Antidepressants are now the number one most prescribed medications in the United States for adults ages twenty to fifty-nine,[16] with sales totaling $11.6 billion in the United States in 2010.[17]

Atypical antipsychotics are the other rising stars in the world of psychiatric medications. These medications are marketed based on the theory that symptoms of schizophrenia, such as psychosis, are caused by dopamine imbalances (a.k.a. "the dopamine hypothesis of schizophrenia"). They are also used to treat symptoms of bipolar disorder and other mental disorders. These medications are called "atypical" because they were initially touted as having fewer and less-severe side effects than earlier antipsychotics such as Thorazine. However, as you've learned throughout this book, even atypical antipsychotics have their fair share of unpleasant (and dangerous) side effects. The most common atypical antipsychotics are Seroquel, Risperdal, Abilify, and Zyprexa. They have been fully embraced by psychiatrists and primary care physicians alike: US sales of antipsychotics totaled $16.1 billion in 2010.[18]

So while many of the popular psychiatric medications target a specific chemical, we know that mental illness is much more complex than a chemical imbalance. A Harvard Medical School article on the causes of depression explains:

> It's often said that depression results from a chemical imbalance,
> but that figure of speech doesn't capture how complex the disease
> is. Research suggests that depression doesn't spring from
> simply having too much or too little of certain brain chemicals.
> Rather, depression has many possible causes, including faulty
> mood regulation by the brain, genetic vulnerability, stressful life
> events, medications, and medical problems. It's believed that
> several of these forces interact to bring on depression.[19]

This is why medication must be considered *one of many* treatment options in an individualized, integrated approach to help people recover from mental illness. There is no one-size-fits-all treatment plan. And when we're talking about kids, medication should be a last resort.

Amphetamines for Our Absentminded and Rowdy Kids

Leaders of corporations are generally charged with maximizing profits for the shareholders. One way to increase profits is to expand your market. When the adult market is saturated, you turn to the children. We've seen this happen in other industries, such as fast food, with the McDonald's Happy Meal, and fashion, with stores such as Gap Kids and Limited Too (now called Justice). This is one of the main reasons why the use of psychotropic drugs has spread to children as young as toddlers.[20]

As I mentioned above, the most commonly prescribed drugs for tweens and teens ages twelve to nineteen are central nervous system stimulants, which are used to treat ADHD. The diagnosis of attention deficit disorder was first introduced in the *Diagnostic and Statistical Manual of Mental Disorders* (*DSM*),* third edition (*DSM-III*) in 1980. It was expanded in *DSM-III-R* in 1987 to include the hyperactivity component in the name of the disorder.

When I read the diagnostic criteria for ADHD, I can't help but think of kids who when I was growing up would have been labeled as "absentminded" or "active" or "rowdy." Now they are labeled as "mentally ill" and prescribed medication that acts like cocaine.[21]

Not only are psychiatric labels devastating for kids and parents alike, but the medications are also known to cause psychosis, often leading to a diagnosis of bipolar disorder.[22]

These medications, like antidepressants and atypical antipsychotics, are prescribed to treat symptoms of a disorder of which we do not know the cause. When I typed in the search term "What causes ADHD?" Google responded with three top excerpts (I added the emphasis):

1. "*Scientists are not sure what causes ADHD*, although many studies suggest that genes play a large role. Like many other illnesses, ADHD probably results from a ..."[23]

2. "*The exact cause of ADHD isn't known.* Experts do know that there are changes in the brains of people with the condition.

---

* The DSM is psychiatry's "Bible," which I discuss in more detail in chapter 12.

It is not caused by home or school . . . "[24]

3. "*While the exact cause of ADHD is not clear*, research efforts continue. Multiple factors have been implicated in the development of ADHD. It can run in families . . . "[25]

So instead of trying to figure out why so many kids are inattentive and squirmy (that is, instead of looking beyond the chemical imbalance theory), doctors label, medicate, and kick-start the downward spiral toward a life of mental health issues. And the kids who really need help often fall through the cracks.[26]

Treating Drug-Induced Symptoms with More Medication

Remember how Prozac "unmasked" manic symptoms in Rebecka, causing her doctor to consider a bipolar diagnosis and add Zyprexa to her psychotropic cocktail? Even when the doctor initially explained this to me, it didn't make logical sense. Why would you give a diagnosis based on symptoms caused by a medication? In my research, I discovered that making diagnoses based on drug-induced symptoms and treating these symptoms with more drugs is not uncommon. Rather, it's a great marketing strategy. My favorite example is how Eli Lilly, the maker of Prozac and Zyprexa actually conducted studies to show that Zyprexa could help with the manic symptoms caused by Prozac. Brilliant![27]

Judith Warner, author of *We've Got Issues*, a book about the problems with our current mental health care system, especially as it relates to children who really need help, writes, "the multiple use of medications, many child psychiatrists agree, is one of the worst developments to have come out of the managed care-driven health system we have today."[28]

Instead of considering the possibility that drugs might be causing the symptoms, well-meaning doctors frequently prescribe a second and third medication to deal with the symptoms caused by the first medication (e.g. sleeplessness, anxiety, and depression). In 2007–2008, 4.6 percent of children ages 0-11 had used two or more drugs (including non-psychiatric drugs) in the last month. For the age group 12-19, this number was 6.9 percent.[29] These drug interactions have not necessarily been studied—especially in children—and it's scary to think about the potential long-term effects on our children's brains of all those chemicals running through their bodies.

Medication as a First-Line Treatment

We would not be writing this book if psychotropic drugs were used only in extreme situations for the treatment of severe cases of mental illness where all other forms of intervention and treatment have failed: a nurturing, accepting environment; nutritional therapy; exercise; meditation; mindfulness; coping skills; behavioral therapy; etc.

However, in the United States and other parts of the "developed" world, this is not the current scenario. On the contrary, medication is recommended, and often used, as a first-line treatment for mental illness.

There are a few reasons why doctors are so quick to prescribe medication to treat symptoms of depression, anxiety, restlessness, etc.:

1. **It's quick and easy.** We are a fast food nation. We want quick fixes without having to work too hard. Medication promises a quick fix. However, there is little reliable evidence that medication is more effective than other treatment methods, especially for depression.[30] In fact, if Whitaker is right, the drugs may be *causing* our mental health epidemic. He points to the fact that mental illness disability rates have increased dramatically since the introduction of psychotropic medications—and especially since the launch of Prozac and similar drugs. Whitaker laments, "Most disturbing of all, this modern-day plague has now spread to the nation's children."[31]

2. **It's cheap.** Compared to psychotherapy, which requires significant time with a trained mental health counselor or psychologist, medication is inexpensive. The insurance companies' bottom line is dictating kids' mental health care, explains Warner. This results in a lack of comprehensive care and a focus on medication as the primary treatment option. The devastating consequence of this is that children often end up on multiple medications, because, as we saw in Rebecka's case, side effects from the first medication are treated with additional medications.[32]

3. **It's hyped up.** As I will discuss in chapter 11, pharmaceutical companies continuously train doctors on the supposed benefits of medication. They do this by hiring well-known medical researchers to speak at conferences, and by sponsoring other continuing education opportunities for health professionals. In addition, they have sales representatives who visit doctors' offices on a regular basis, handing out free samples of the

drug they're pushing—in addition to providing fancy lunches and other perks for the prescribing physicians.

4. **It's being advertised.** When I talk to my doctor friends about this issue, their number one complaint is that patients are demanding specific medications. Patients hear about Cymbalta or Celexa during the commercial breaks of the evening news and show up at the doctor's office self-diagnosed and self-prescribed. One friend said, "It's like they don't think they're getting their money's worth unless they leave my office with a prescription." That's the power of marketing—and discourse.

Ultimately, the transition from psychotherapy to psychotropic drugs is mostly about money and convenience. Insurance companies would rather pay for pills than for psychotherapy; psychiatrists make more money prescribing pills than performing psychotherapy; many patients would rather pop a pill than visit a therapist; and pharmaceutical companies encourage this behavior through direct-to-consumer advertising of brand-name medications, by expanding their markets to include kids and teens, and by hiding the studies that show that psychotropic drugs aren't really as effective as they're made out to be.[33]

11

❧

Under the Influence of Big Pharma

Those who took the most money from makers of [atypical antipsychotics]
tended to prescribe the drugs to children the most often, the data suggest.

—from "Psychiatrists, Children and Drug Industry's Role,"
The New York Times, May 10, 2007

I am by nature fairly naïve—or trusting, to put a positive spin on it. My friends and family know that it doesn't take much to fool me into believing something that isn't true. So it's not surprising that for most of my life, I assumed that pharmaceutical companies had people's best interest in mind and worked toward the common good by providing medicine to cure us of everything from cankers to cancer. I didn't really even think of pharmaceutical companies as for-profit businesses, because wouldn't it be kind of unethical to try to make money off of people who are sick?

Not until I read Robert Whitaker's *Anatomy of an Epidemic* during those trying weeks in the late spring of 2011 did I even begin to realize the enormous influence "Big Pharma" exerts over the mental health care field. And the more I researched, the more dismayed I became. *How is this allowed to go on?* I wondered. And then I realized: it's all about the money. Like most other problems in our society, it's about big profits and the related concepts of power and greed.

In this chapter, I'd like to share with you just a few of the facts I learned about how the pharmaceutical industry influences psychiatry in our country.

This is not new news, but I've met enough people who are not aware of what's going on that I feel compelled to summarize the basics below.

Pharmaceutical Companies Are For-Profit Corporations

Yes, this is an obvious statement, but it's still worth a brief discussion. As I've mentioned before, leaders of corporations are generally hired to maximize profits for shareholders. Some corporate leaders are able to do this while participating in some form of corporate social responsibility, but ultimately, their mission boils down to profit—or maintaining the infamous bottom line.

As such, pharmaceutical companies are driven to expand their product lines and markets, which includes conducting research studies that attempt to demonstrate the safety of adult medications in children, and marketing psychiatric illness beyond US borders.

The chief marketing officers of these companies do whatever it takes to get free samples of the latest wonder drug into the hands of as many physicians as possible. That's why there were close to 95,000 pharmaceutical drug reps in the United States in 2007. That's one rep for every 2.5–7 physicians, depending on how you crunch the numbers. Free samples constituted 58 percent of the overall $29.9 billion spent by the pharmaceutical industry on marketing in 2005. That makes sense, since studies indicate that free samples do influence doctors' prescribing habits. And guess which type of drug was marketed the most. You got it, antidepressants.[1]

Big Pharma-Funded Research

In order for new medications to be approved by the FDA, pharmaceutical companies must demonstrate their efficacy and safety in the populations for which they are to be used. Pharmaceutical companies do this by conducting double-blind, placebo-controlled, randomized clinical trials. For example, language from the Zyprexa label regarding the indication for the acute treatment of manic or mixed episodes associated with bipolar I disorder and maintenance treatment of bipolar I disorder states that:

> Efficacy was established in one 3-week trial in patients with
> manic or mixed episodes associated with bipolar I disorder
> (14.2).* The increased potential (in adolescents compared

---

* The numbers in parentheses refer to the sections of the label that include further details about the specific topic.

with adults) for weight gain and hyperlipidemia may lead clinicians to consider prescribing other drugs first in adolescents.[2]

Did you notice the duration of the clinical trial? Three weeks. And if you scroll down to section 14.2, you'll find the total number of participants in the study: 161. So the efficacy of this blockbuster drug for use in acutely manic adolescents was determined in three weeks with 161 participants. The label admits that "there is no body of evidence available to answer the question of how long the adolescent patient treated with ZYPREXA should be maintained."[3] Rebecka was on Zyprexa for over five months.

Moreover, researchers at pharmaceutical companies have been known to hide clinical trials that do not support the efficacy or safety of their drugs, and to design biased trials to get the results they want. Whitaker provides many examples of this, calling the literature "hopelessly poisoned."[4]

One troubling example of the lack of scientific evidence and biased trial design is the revelation that only three of the fifteen pediatric antidepressant trials reviewed by the FDA prior to 2004 showed positive results. In fact, the FDA rejected applications from six pharmaceutical companies looking to sell antidepressants to children. Prozac was the only antidepressant approved for pediatric use, and that was only because the researchers at Eli Lilly used biased trial designs to achieve "positive" results.[5]

As I started looking at various studies regarding the efficacy and safety of drug therapies for the treatment of various mental illnesses, I quickly realized that I couldn't trust anything I read. It is extremely difficult to determine whose money is behind any given study. As Warner points out, "we need answers regarding best practices, and we need to trust that those answers come to us from researchers and clinicians whom we can trust to have formed their opinions *independently of the drug companies.*"[6] Maybe one day…

Big Pharma Educates Psychiatrists

Not only do the pharmaceutical companies sponsor research studies that are designed to demonstrate the efficacy of their products, they have also, for a number of years, been paying for a significant portion of the continuing education that psychiatrists and other physicians receive. As Warner explains, "continuing medical education is increasingly provided and paid for by the pharmaceutical industry. In 2008, half of all continuing medical education in the United States was funded by drug companies."[7] While this might seem like a noble thing to do, the reason pharmaceutical companies sponsor continuing education is to increase brand recognition (so doctors will be more likely to prescribe their drugs versus those of their competitors) and blatantly to promote their drugs as the best treatment option for a given ailment.

How do the pharmaceutical companies get away with this? Here's how it works. The big drug companies such as Eli Lilly, Johnson & Johnson, and AstraZeneca, have so-called "speakers bureaus," which consist of a group of highly respected psychiatrists at major research universities (think Harvard and Yale) who receive consulting fees to speak at conferences and write journal articles to promote various aspects of pharmacology.

In 2009, *The Boston Globe* reported that about sixty doctors in Massachusetts had collectively earned over half a million dollars that year in speaking fees from Eli Lilly, the maker of Prozac, "including two Boston Medical Center physicians whose participation is being reviewed for possible violation of a hospital policy against marketing activities by its doctors."[8] When I discovered the magnitude of this practice, it really shed some light on the statement Dr. E had made about Prozac and how it "only does good things for the brain." These words almost sound as if they came straight out of an Eli Lilly pamphlet or seminar.

Now that this questionable practice has been uncovered, the leaders of the pharmaceutical companies are forced to become more transparent about how they spend their money. With the 2013 Physician Payments Sunshine Act, pharmaceutical companies must report publicly on payments to physicians and teaching hospitals.[9] However, much of this data is already available for the past few years, thanks to additional policies and regulations. Eli Lilly's Physician Payment Registry is available online; so is a list of Janssen's payments to physicians, and the details of AstraZeneca's "physician engagement" program.[10] Of course, this accountability doesn't stop the companies from paying large sums of money to psychiatrists to provide drug-promoting lectures and testimonials to their colleagues. It just provides more visibility.

During my research, I was pleased to learn that the Mayo Clinic does not allow their physicians to participate in speakers bureaus.[11] One step in the right direction would be for all universities and teaching hospitals to institute similar policies.

Big Pharma Is Always Looking for New Markets

In *Crazy Like Us*, a book about how we are "Americanizing the world's understanding of the human mind," Ethan Watters tells the story of Laurence Kirmayer, an expert on cross-cultural psychiatry, who in 2000 was invited to attend a conference in Japan, where GlaxoSmithKline was about to launch its antidepressant Paxil. Watters writes, "[Kirmayer's] first inkling that this wasn't a run-of-the-mill academic conference came when the airline ticket arrived in the mail. This ticket was for a seat in the front of the plane and cost nearly $10,000."[12] Kirmayer eventually realized that he had been invited to shed light on "how cultures shape the illness experience." The GlaxoSmithKline people wanted to understand how to create a market for antidepressants in Japan. And they were willing to pay big bucks for it.[13]

The GlaxoSmithKline marketers ended up running a successful marketing campaign that framed depression as "*kokoro no kaze*, like 'a cold of the soul'"— and, consequently, antidepressants as cold medicine for the psyche.[14]

Allen Frances, a high-profile psychiatrist and the author of *Saving Normal*, confirms Big Pharma's approach: "The business model of the pharmaceutical industry depends on extending the realm of illness—using creative marketing to expand the pool of customers by convincing the probably well that they are at least mildly sick."[15] Now our children are the targets of this expansion.

As I mentioned above, Prozac is the only drug approved by the FDA for use in treating depression in children ages eight and older.[16] Yet doctors prescribed several different antidepressants during Rebecka's year of taking psychotropic drugs. This practice is called off-label prescribing, and it is extremely common, especially among pediatricians. In fact, 50 to 75 percent of medications prescribed by pediatricians are off-label. Why? Clinical drug trials are expensive and most medications are initially developed for adults.[17] Often, pharmaceutical companies choose not to conduct clinical trials with children because of the cost involved—and why would they spend the extra money when this loophole exists? The practice of off-label prescribing is driven in part by a desire by the pediatrician to help her patients, but it is certainly exaggerated by the free drug samples, books such as *Child and Adolescent Psychopharmacology Made Simple* by psychiatrist John O'Neal (which claims that medical treatment promotes normal brain development),[18] and continuing education sponsored by pharmaceutical companies that teaches pediatricians how to use specific drugs to treat newly discovered disorders.[19] This is problematic, because children are not miniature versions of adults and cannot be treated as such.[20]

In a chapter titled "The Epidemic Spreads to Children," Whitaker describes in detail the shift from hardly medicating children for psychiatric illness at all before 1980, to our current situation where ADHD medication is the most prescribed drug for older children and adolescents. He covers ADHD, depression, and juvenile bipolar disorder. I highly recommend reading this chapter for all the details, but here are just a couple of the sobering consequences of medicating our young kids:

- The number of preschool-aged children on mental health disability tripled between 2000 and 2007, when it became more common to prescribe psychotropic drugs to two- and three-year-olds.[21]

- According to a US Government Accountability Office report from 2008 "one in every fifteen young adults, eighteen to twenty-six years old, is now 'seriously mentally ill.'"[22]

Based on this data, it is easy to draw the same conclusion as Whitaker: that medication as first-line treatment for kids and teens is making things worse. And while the pharmaceutical companies cannot legally market drugs for off-label use, it is clear that the pediatric market is the new frontier.[23]

We should be outraged that pharmaceutical companies are peddling their adult drugs to our pediatricians, without proper evidence of long-term efficacy, just so they can expand their market.

Big Pharma's Cozy Relationships

When I started my research for this book, I was really excited to learn about an organization called the National Alliance on Mental Illness (NAMI). On the "About" page of its website, the organization is described as follows:

> NAMI is the National Alliance on Mental Illness, the nation's largest grassroots mental health organization dedicated to building better lives for the millions of Americans affected by mental illness. NAMI advocates for access to services, treatment, supports and research and is steadfast in its commitment to raise awareness and build a community for hope for all of those in need.

I liked the way that sounded. Grassroots. Building better lives and a community of hope.

Then I read another piece of information on the website that made me think I should probably look at the sponsors list to see who was behind the organization. On the "Treatments and Services" page, medications are listed at the top with the following blurb: "Mental health medications do not cure mental illness. However, they can often significantly improve symptoms and help promote recovery and are recognized as first-line treatment for most individuals."

Recognized as first-line treatment for most individuals . . . recognized by whom? Who makes the decision that medications should be the first-line treatment in our culture?

I had to use a Google search and a bit of detective work to find the "Major Foundation and Corporate Support" page on NAMI's site.[24]

Here are some of NAMI's corporate supporters from the first two quarters of 2013:

- Eli Lilly (Prozac, Zyprexa): $120,000
- GlaxoSmithKline (Paxil): $20,000
- Janssen (Concerta, Risperdal): $185,000
- Jazz Pharmaceuticals (Luvox, FazaClo): $50,000
- Novartis (Clozaril): $25,000
- Otsuka (Abilify): $450,000
- Pharmaceutical Research and Manufacturers of America (PhRMA): $80,000
- Shire (Adderall): $235,000

That's at least $1,165,000 from pharmaceutical companies. So much for being able to trust the information on www.nami.org.*

When I looked up NAMI in the *Anatomy of an Epidemic* index, I found that the group is one of four players in the questionable partnership between the pharmaceutical companies and other organizations that further the mission of these corporations: to sell more drugs—all the time.

In a section called "Four-Part Harmony," Whitaker tells the story of how a partnership emerged in the 1980s between the American Psychiatric Association (APA) and the pharmaceutical industry. Prior to the 1980s, pharmaceutical companies were not allowed to present "scientific" talks at the APA's annual meeting. However, in 1980, the APA changed that rule, and that was the start of the "speakers bureaus" we discussed earlier in this chapter.[25] The pharmaceutical industry contributed over $5 million to the APA in 2012.[26]

---

* Please note that local NAMI chapters may be more or less married to the medical model of mental health and don't necessarily have any ties to the pharmaceutical industry.

The names of the majority of the APA's research fellowships also reflect the partnership with Big Pharma:[27]

- Lilly Resident Research Award
- APA/Pfizer MD/PhD Psychiatric Research Fellowship
- APA/Lilly Psychiatric Research Fellowship
- APA/Merck Early Academic Career Research Award*

In addition to the relationships with NAMI and the APA, the pharmaceutical industry also got cozy with the National Institute for Mental Health (NIMH). NIMH's hopeful vision statement reads: "NIMH envisions a world in which mental illnesses are prevented and cured."[28] However, in direct contradiction to its vision, NIMH promotes the broken brain theory of depression and other mental health illnesses, which in turn promotes the use of medication to treat the symptoms of mental illness—not to prevent or cure it. For example, if you go to the NIMH website to read about depression, you will learn the following about its "cause":

> Depressive illnesses are disorders of the brain. Brain-imaging technologies, such as magnetic resonance imaging (MRI), have shown that the brains of people who have depression look different than those of people without depression. The parts of the brain involved in mood, thinking, sleep, appetite, and behavior appear different. But these images do not reveal why the depression has occurred. They also cannot be used to diagnose depression.[29]

Notice the last two important sentences. Even NIMH admits that MRIs can't tell us *why* depression happens. *There is no biology-based diagnostic tool.* Rather, diagnosis is based on observing symptoms and referencing the "Bible of Psychiatry," the DSM, which classifies and describes the disorders that the pharmaceutical industry promotes heavily.

The close relationship between NIMH and the pharmaceutical industry is further illustrated in the "Mental Health Medications" section of the website. NIMH answers the question "What are psychiatric medications?" as follows:

> Psychiatric medications treat mental disorders. Sometimes called psychotropic or psychotherapeutic medications, they have changed the lives of people with mental disorders for the better.

---

* The webpage where I found this information now redirects to the page "Research Training and Career Distinction Awards," which denotes grants, fellowships, and awards supported by a pharmaceutical company with an asterisk, per the Sunshine Act.

> Many people with mental disorders live fulfilling lives with the help of these medications. Without them, people with mental disorders might suffer serious and disabling symptoms.[30]

This may be true for some people, but definitely not for all, and especially not for children. If these medications actually worked, psychiatric disability rates for children and youth under eighteen wouldn't have skyrocketed in the twenty years between 1987 (when Prozac was launched) and 2007 from 16,200 to 561,569.[31] True, as critics of *Anatomy of an Epidemic* point out, medication isn't necessarily the only *cause* of the mental health epidemic,[32] but it certainly isn't helping in many cases, especially in the long run.

12

Expanding the Definition of
Mental Illness

*The greater the number of mental health clinicians, the greater the
number of life conditions that work their way into becoming disorders.
Only six disorders were listed in the initial census of mental patients
in the mid-nineteenth century; now there are close to two hundred.*

—Dr. Allen Frances, *Saving Normal*

In the previous two chapters, I made brief references to the *Diagnostic and
Statistical Manual of Mental Disorders (DSM)*. Unless you've been in the mental health system or studied psychology, it's likely you've never heard of this
book—and I'm sure you won't be buying it, since the latest edition, the *DSM-5,*
released in May, 2013, has a list price of $199. However, it is impossible to talk
about psychiatry today without understanding the vast influence of this publication on the field.*

The American Psychiatric Association Committee on Nomenclature and
Statistics published the first version of the DSM in 1952. Not surprisingly, this
timing coincided with the initial launch of psychiatric medications. The purpose of the *DSM* was to classify mental disorders and to be the official manual
of mental disorders to be used in clinical settings.[1] Psychiatrists needed a set of
definitions to aid in the diagnosis of mental illnesses so that they would know

---

* As of this writing, the *DSM-5* is number ten on the "Amazon Best Sellers of 2014" list—quite the
cash cow for the American Psychiatry Association.

123

how to treat their patients.

In this chapter, we'll explore some of the problems with defining mental disorders and take a look at why we have so many diagnoses—and so many people being diagnosed. But first, let's dive into a brief history of mental illness and acknowledge the voices that have questioned—and still question—the motivation behind psychiatric diagnoses and the legitimacy of confining and treating people with unusual or deranged behavior.

Mental Illness as a Social Construct

French philosopher Michel Foucault discusses the evolution of Western society's treatment of "the mad" in his seminal 1964 book *History of Madness*. He writes that toward the end of the Middle Ages, the mad took the place of the lepers at the outskirts of town. As long as they stayed out of the way of "normal" people, everything was okay. While the mad were the new "no-beings," they were not considered ill. Rather, they were "lumped in with the poor and indigent as a basic threat to the social values on which a mercantile economy rested."[2]

Not until the end of the eighteenth century did madness become the object of scientific study and considered a disease. For Foucault, "the modern medical positivism which developed from the end of the eighteenth century is based on an attempt at objectifying madness which, when looked at in detail, in particular in the institutions it accompanies, is a new mode of social control."[3] As Neel Burton explains in a 2012 *Psychology Today article*, "According to Foucault, 'madness' is a social construct dating back to the [E]nlightenment, and its 'treatment' is nothing more than a disguised form of punishment for deviating from social norms."[4]

The late Thomas Szasz, psychiatrist and author of over thirty books, including *The Myth of Mental Illness*, had similar views. He did not believe that mental disorders were medical in nature. Rather, he believed that mental diagnoses, especially schizophrenia, were labels created to control unacceptable social behavior.[5] Szasz did believe it was valid to treat people who suffered from unusual behavior or thought patterns, but treatment should be educational rather than medical in nature[6] and should only take place between consenting adults.[7]

These sentiments, sometimes labeled as "anti-psychiatry," are clearly controversial. However, I think it's important to explore the *possibility* that at least some mental disorders are social constructs—subjective medical diagnoses for problems that are more cultural or situational in nature.[8] This does *not* mean the suffering is an illusion—that the symptoms of depression and ADHD and anorexia are not devastating. We've experienced this suffering! But we cannot close our eyes to the negative effects of medicalizing deviant behavior and should think about constructing alternative beliefs about emotional and behavioral problems.

For example, in the article "The Social Construction and Reframing of Attention-Deficit/Hyperactivity Disorder," management consultant Barbara A. Mather urges us to reframe ADHD "from a disease to that of a positive difference." She notes that the stigma and negative social interactions associated with the ADHD diagnosis can have detrimental effects on children's self-esteem and self-confidence. Rather than think of ADHD as a disorder, can we focus on the strengths of people with symptoms of ADHD, such as creativity and imagination, to *build* self-esteem and self-confidence?[9] Constructing ADHD this way seems like a much more positive approach than pathologizing and medicating.

There are many examples of social constructs that categorize and stereotype people. For instance, my husband Todd teaches, writes, and speaks on the topic of Islamophobia. He frequently discusses the social construct of Muslims in the West, where young Muslim men are constructed as violent and evil terrorists. Who benefits from this? The media? The military? The government? We certainly don't hear a whole lot of news stories about young Muslim men doing great things in mainstream media.

We must question social constructs that create stereotypes, allow some people to exert power over others, and increase stigma. In the case of mental illness, the social construct allows and encourages the institutionalization and medication of people who exhibit abnormal behavior. Who benefits from this? Caregivers? Doctors? Hospitals? Pharmaceutical companies? There are a whole lot of people who may benefit more from this than the person with the unacceptable social behavior.

Social constructs are very real, but not necessarily constructed consciously. We need to be aware of them and consider how they affect our view of eccentric, difficult, and "unstable" people and what role they play in the ever-expanding definition of mental illness.

☙

The Problem with Defining Mental Disorders

While there are established laboratory tests to diagnose medical illnesses such as cancer and diabetes, there are no biological tests to diagnose any of the close to two hundred disorders listed in the *DSM-5*. Rather, diagnosis is based on the patient's description of symptoms, the training and experience of the doctor, the criteria listed in the *DSM* for specific disorders, and, occasionally, psychological testing. In other words, mental disorder diagnoses are *subjective* and depend largely on the patient's symptoms and the doctor's interpretation of said symptoms, using the *DSM* as a guide.

Additionally, the fact that these diagnoses are available in printed form and accessible to physicians increases the likelihood that they will be used. In *Crazy Like Us*, Watters tells the disturbing story of how the American version of anorexia infiltrated Hong Kong, based on interviews with Sing Lee, anorexia researcher and clinician:

> Over a short period of time the presentation of anorexia in Hong Kong changed. The symptom cluster that was unique to [Lee's] Hong Kong patients began to disappear. What was once a rare disorder was replaced by an American version of the disease that became much more widespread.[10]

Until the *DSM* became the global standard for diagnosis and the Hong Kong media jumped on the bandwagon, eating disorders were extremely rare in Hong Kong. And patients didn't even have the same symptoms. Whereas the *DSM* criteria require distorted body image, the Hong Kong "anorexics" viewed themselves as thin and came to Dr. Lee for help to gain weight. The naming and acceptance of the disorder as described in the *DSM* enabled the traditional Western anorexia symptoms to become part of the Hong Kong symptom pool.[11]

The lesson from this story is twofold: naming a disorder increases the likelihood of diagnosis, and symptoms of distress take different forms in different cultures. However, if exposed enough to a given set of symptoms, some people will start exhibiting those symptoms.

If anybody knows the *DSM*, it's Allen Frances. He chaired the *DSM-IV* Task Force and was part of the leadership group for *DSM-III* and *DSM-III-R*, making him one of the most influential psychiatrists in the world. Even he has come to the conclusion that there are no useful definitions of mental disorder: "I have reviewed dozens of definitions of mental disorder (and have written one myself in *DSM-IV*) and find none of them the slightest bit helpful either in determining which conditions should be considered mental disorders and which not, or in deciding who is sick and who is not."[12]

As you can see, mental disorder diagnoses are complex, subjective, and there is plenty of room for error. Yet, more Americans, including children, are being diagnosed with mental disorders than ever, often after just one visit to the doctor.

Diagnostic Inflation

Going back to the history of the *DSM*, we find that the original *DSM-I*, published in 1952, included definitions of 106 disorders. That's quite the expansion from the seven categories included in the 1900 census: "mania, melancholia, monomania, paresis, dementia, dipsomania and epilepsy."[13]

And with each subsequent edition of the *DSM*, the American Psychiatric Association has added definitions of new disorders. The *DSM-5* includes fifteen new disorders including "Disruptive Mood Dysregulation Disorder" (for over-the-top temper tantrums) and "Hoarding Disorder." While it may be reasonable to think that this increase in defined disorders is purely related to scientific advancement, this is not the whole story.

In *Saving Normal*, Dr. Frances discusses what he calls "out-of-control psychiatric diagnosis." He writes about the influence of the various versions of the *DSM* on diagnostic inflation. For example: "Diagnostic inflation has been the worst consequence of *DSM-III*. Part of the fault lies in how *DSM-III* was written, much of it in how it has been misused, particularly under the influence of drug company disease mongering."[14] And regarding *DSM-III-R:* "Prozac and *DSM-III-R* were both introduced in 1987. Prozac's sales took off at least in part because the *DSM* definition of major depressive disorder was so loose."[15]

Most interesting is Dr. Frances's story about *DSM-IV*, published in 1994. He indicates that he and the other authors of the *DSM-IV* didn't view it as a bible, but rather as a guidebook—"a collection of temporarily useful diagnostic constructs, not a catalog of 'real' diseases."[16]

Yet, *DSM-IV* didn't save normal—quite the opposite. Dr. Frances highlights that one of the major problems (not anticipated by the *DSM-IV* Task Force) was that three years after the publication of *DSM-IV*, the United States started allowing direct-to-consumer advertising of pharmaceuticals:

> Pretty soon the airwaves and print were filled with glowingly misleading representations that everyday problems were in fact unrecognized psychiatric disorder. DSM-IV turned out

to be a very weak dike unable to block the flood of false demand instigated by the aggressive and devilishly clever drug company push. Although we had consistently rejected suggestions that would have benefited drug companies, we failed to predict that even our conservative manual could provide such easy fodder for advertising gold. Within a few years, it was clear the drug companies had won and we had lost.[17]

Dr. Frances outlines a number of causes of psychiatric diagnostic inflation. I will list some of them here and briefly explain the concepts.

- **Copying Preventive Medicine:** Preventive medicine was a good idea, but unfortunately it was hijacked by companies making money off of expensive screenings and laboratory tests. Psychiatry has ended up with the same problems as the rest of medicine: "the combination of harmful excess for some, combined with heartless neglect for others."[18]

- **Societal Trends:** Our society has less and less tolerance for people who are different. People who don't follow social norms are considered mentally ill. In addition, we believe that our lives must be perfect at all times, otherwise we are depressed or anxious.[19]

- **Psychiatric Fads:** Created by defining specific diagnoses in the *DSM* and then having the media and pharmaceutical companies hype them up.[20]

- **Insurance Requirements:** Health insurance companies often won't reimburse visits that don't result in a diagnosis. Therefore, physicians are forced to give clients a quick diagnosis, often on the first visit.[21]

- **Easy-to-Take Pills:** The second generation of psychotropic medications, starting with Librium and Valium, had fewer (known) serious side effects. As a result, physicians became more liberal in prescribing them. But as Dr. Frances points out, "the paradox is that dangerous drugs capable of causing massive obesity, diabetes, heart disease, and a shortened life span now account for $18 billion a year in sales."[22]

- **Big Pharma Sells Illness:** I was shocked to learn that pharmaceutical companies spend twice as much on marketing as they do on research. And most of their "research" is focused on expanding markets. They use marketing dollars to buy politicians, influence the media, provide doctors with product samples, and of course, advertise directly to consumers. They are very good at creating demand: "The pitch to customers is that life is perfectible, if only they will take the simple brain-toning steps to perfect it." And as I mentioned earlier, Big Pharma didn't stop with the adults. Rather, when the adult market was saturated, they turned their attention to children. Dr. Frances writes, "it is not by accident that all the recent epidemics of psychiatric disorder have occurred in kids."[23]

- **The Placebo Effect:** People who would normally get better on their own with time and resilience are the ones who often benefit the most from the placebo effect. The drug companies obviously want good results, so they encourage physicians to diagnose and prescribe broadly and market to normal people to convince them that they are sick.[24]

These are just some of the causes of diagnostic inflation. Let's take a look at the alarming results:

- Half of all Americans qualify for a mental disorder diagnosis at some point in their lives.[25]
- Seven percent of Americans are addicted to a legal psychiatric drug.[26]
- Childhood bipolar disorder increased fortyfold in the last fifteen years.
- Autism increased twentyfold in the last fifteen years.
- ADHD tripled in the last fifteen years.[27]

There are countless stories of children being diagnosed with every disorder under the sun, only to find that the problem was physical (e.g. needing glasses), related to maturity (younger kids are more likely to be diagnosed with ADHD),[28] or some other underlying problem that eventually worked itself out.[29] And in Rebecka's case, the cause was likely a combination of going through puberty, an unstable home situation, peer influence, and medication—*not* a chemical imbalance. Yet her doctors suggested a number of different diagnoses, depending on her behavior du jour. None of them were helpful and, thankfully, none of them stuck.

Diagnostic inflation is truly out of control. The owners and leaders of pharmaceutical companies play a big role, but so do government officials, physicians, teachers, and consumers. Whereas we had a handful of categories of mental illness just over one hundred years ago, now we have hundreds of diagnoses ranging in severity from schizophrenia to caffeine withdrawal. It's the diagnoses that target well people and promote drugs as a first-line treatment that concern me the most. I don't want other kids and parents to go through what we went through.

We have a big problem on our hands. The big players (Big Pharma, NIMH, NAMI, and the APA) continue to promote the theory that mental illness is caused by a chemical imbalance, best treated with drugs. Thousands of well-meaning psychiatrists and general practitioners, who have been educated by the pharmaceutical companies, make quick diagnoses and prescribe dangerous medication to distressed—but healthy—children, teens, and adults. Eight hundred fifty adults and 250 children are disabled by (supposed) mental illness and accompanying drugs every day.[30] And the people who really need help often don't get it and end up on the streets or in prisons.

That is what we learned about psychiatry in the United States.

Part 4

Alternative Treatment Options

It's infuriating that the pharmaceutical industry has so much power over our collective health and well-being. And it's disappointing that medication is touted as the primary treatment option, often without mention of other alternative or complementary approaches.

In my research I've found that many physicians, therapists, and concerned citizens agree that medication is too often used as a first-line treatment of symptoms associated with mental disorders. This is especially true when it comes to our children and teens. In addition, there are significant ethical problems with prescribing dangerous drugs to children and teens, since they are not making the decision to take the medication. Yet, as we discovered in chapter 11, many pediatricians, general practitioners, and psychiatrists prescribe psychiatric medications, often off-label, to children and teens.

When we began to seek help for Rebecka's feelings of depression and rapid weight loss, the two treatment options presented to us were talk therapy *or* psychiatry, essentially the opposite of an integrated approach to mental health care. Nobody sat down with us and went through the full list of treatment options available. They didn't tell us that exercise is just as effective as medication for people with mild to moderate depression.[1] They didn't tell us that diet affects a person's mood.[2] They didn't tell us that drugs are not effective for treating anorexia.[3] They *did* tell us about family therapy, but not why it might be very beneficial for our family. And they didn't tell us that time and resilience often heal depression if you let it run its course.

While doing the research for this part of the book, I was reminded how daunting it is to sift through all the information out there and figure out whom you can trust and who is just trying to make a buck or two with their latest fad diet to cure fill-in-the-blank ailment.

I have done my best primarily to include alternative treatments that have scientific backing, while acknowledging that this can in itself be limiting. For example, Rebecka's psychiatrist refused to attempt any kind of nutritional supplement treatment because he claimed there was nothing in the literature that supported, for example, treating symptoms of mental illness with therapeutic doses of vitamin B12. In fact, Dr. Z was flat out wrong. There are several studies that demonstrate a linkage between vitamin B12 and depression.[4] I have no idea whether Dr. Z had never read these studies or if he simply did not think there were *enough* studies to consider this type of treatment. What I do know is that he didn't even acknowledge the existence of such studies in my conversations with him.

The main reason why there is not as much research on "alternative" treatment approaches is that there is often no money to be made. Nobody is going to make big bucks demonstrating that it's best to eat real food and walk or bike to school. Researcher James Sallis's explanation for why he hasn't conducted any research on how children use unstructured natural sites is telling: "Because it's free, there's no major economic interest involved. Who's going to fund the research? If kids are out there riding their bikes or walking, they're not burning fossil fuel, they're nobody's captive audience, they're not making money for anybody.... Follow the money."[5]

If you are a parent or caregiver, I want you to keep this in mind when you're doing your own research and wading through the endless websites of information on the Internet about how to help your child. Just because there isn't a double-blind, placebo-controlled clinical trial supporting a specific treatment option doesn't mean it may not help your situation. As long as there are no possible negative side effects, it may be worth talking to your doctor about it.

13

Taking Care of Physical Needs

*Taking care of your body is a powerful first step towards mental
and emotional health. The mind and the body are linked.
When you improve your physical health, you'll automatically
experience greater mental and emotional well-being.*

—Melinda Smith, et. al. "Improving Emotional Health," *Helpguide.org*

I started exercising regularly shortly after Rebecka was born. Initially, I was mostly interested in losing the "baby fat," but eventually—especially once I started running—it became kind of addicting. I noticed that on days I didn't exercise, I felt sluggish and slightly depressed. In fact, I'd often warn people if I hadn't exercised on a given morning that I might be cranky, like a coffee drinker warning people not to talk to him until he's had his morning coffee.

Exercise affects mood. There is no doubt about it. Our bodies were built to move. We have joints and muscles and a heart that can handle a decent amount of strain, assuming you condition it on a regular basis. It is natural for our bodies to move daily.

But exercise isn't the only thing that affects mood. So does food, altruism, stress, and the amount of sunlight we get, to mention a few factors. Emotional health is complicated and every human being is unique. What works for one person doesn't necessarily work for the next person. But there are some common factors that generally set us up to be as emotionally healthy as we can be. They have to do with taking care of our basic physical needs in the best way possible.

When I write and speak about wellness, I often talk about "doing what's natural." There is so much in our world that isn't natural (for example, eating highly processed foods, sitting in front of a computer all day, interacting mostly through social media, and avoiding physical exercise by driving everywhere), and I believe that if we concentrate on doing things that *are* natural and taking care of our basic physical needs, wellness will follow.

In this chapter I will address four basic physical needs that contribute greatly to physical, emotional, *and* mental health:

- Natural movement
- Whole food nutrition
- Rest and sleep
- Being in nature

Natural Movement

We all know that moving our bodies—or "exercise"—is good for us. It keeps our hearts healthy and burns calories so that we can maintain a healthy weight. It can also prevent osteoporosis, type 2 diabetes, certain types of cancer, and even the common cold.[1] We know that we should exercise at least 150 minutes per week, and that it can be done in increments as small as ten minutes.[2]

We are also learning that a sedentary lifestyle is a health risk. In fact, the 150 minutes of exercise per week doesn't make up for sitting on the couch or in front of the computer the rest of the time (somebody who does this is called an "active couch potato"). We need to move and stretch throughout the day to avoid physical health problems and premature death.[3] Unfortunately, we've engineered natural movement out of our lives. We drive instead of walk. We use riding lawnmowers instead of push mowers. We have machines to wash our dishes and clothes (for which I am thankful!). We have desk jobs instead of farm jobs. We don't even have to get up from the couch to switch the channel or put in a movie. We have to consciously make an effort to move our bodies throughout the day by choosing to walk or bike to work, going for walking breaks while others take coffee breaks, and setting reminders to get out of the chair every hour to walk around or do some office yoga.

In *The Blue Zones*, National Geographic Explorer Dan Buettner visits five areas around the world where people live for a long time.* He and his team interview elders and scientists in these areas and try to find common factors

---

* These areas are called "Blue Zones" because the researcher who first identified them circled them with blue ink on a map.

that may contribute to longevity. One of the stories I remember well from the book is about a seventy-five-year old shepherd who still watches his sheep. In the process, he walks at least five miles per day. Exercise is built into his everyday life. This is indeed a common factor in all the Blue Zones: daily, natural movement keeps the seventy-, eighty-, ninety- and hundred-year-olds healthy and alive![1]

So yes, we know that exercise is good for our bodies. But there is also increasing evidence demonstrating that exercise may be even more important for our *brains*. Neuropsychiatrist John J. Ratey covers this topic extensively in his book *Spark: The Revolutionary Science of Exercise and the Brain*. In the book's introduction, he states, "I often tell my patients that the point of exercise is to build and condition the brain."[5] I learned from Dr. Ratey that because of our hunter-gatherer biological history, "the relationship between food, physical activity, and learning is hardwired into the brain's circuitry."[6] Our brain requires our body to move to function optimally.

Ratey describes how exercise can help with everything from stress to anxiety to depression to ADHD. He points to research that supports his claims, including a 2000 study from Duke University showing that exercise is better than Zoloft at treating depression over the long term. In fact, it's even better than treating depression with both medicine *and* exercise.[7] Another study from Chile showed that adolescents had a significant decrease in anxiety after participating in a school-based physical activity program.[8] And these are just examples. The literature speaks for itself: exercise works.

So why is exercise not widely accepted as a first-line treatment for depression, anxiety, and ADHD? Well, actually, in Britain it is. Over twenty percent of general practitioners in the UK write prescriptions for exercise and hand to their depressed patients.[9] This happens in other countries as well, including Sweden.[10] I have a number of hypotheses about why most US doctors do not consider exercise as a first-line treatment:

1. There are no sales reps pushing exercise.
2. Doctors are embedded in the pills-as-first-resort discourse. Only when pills don't work do they start looking for alternatives.
3. Exercise is hard and takes time.
4. Doctors don't think there is enough evidence that exercise works.

But here's the thing: exercise is free and has no negative side effects (unless you do too much too soon). So why not try it first? Especially for kids and teens? Exercise lays a foundation for ongoing mental and physical health while antidepressants simply mask the symptoms. As Ratey writes, "Yes, exercise is an antidepressant. But it is also much more."[11]

What would a prescription for exercise look like? Well, according to the Centers for Disease Control and Prevention, all kids should get at least sixty minutes of aerobic exercise every day. And on at least three of those days, they should increase the intensity (for example, run).[12] The prescription would likely last for at least sixteen weeks, but, of course, we should never stop moving our bodies.

Our bodies were designed to move. Our brains developed to support this movement. We must move to survive—physically and mentally.

Whole Food Nutrition

We are what we eat. No other activity is as intimately connected to our being as eating. What we put into our mouths becomes part of who we are. It fuels our body and, equally importantly, our brain.

It's not surprising then that there are thousands of books about what to eat and what not to eat. Every decade the powers that be change their minds about what we should be eating. The food pyramid turns into MyPlate. Low-fat is replaced by low-carb. And in the grocery store, we are faced with thousands of packaged, processed "foods" that are just *so* tasty and convenient. Eating well has become exceedingly complicated and, frankly, stressful.

I have read a lot of books about nutrition—from *The China Study* (animal protein is bad) to *The Paleo Diet* (grain, sugar, dairy, etc. are bad) to *The World Peace Diet* (go vegan or else!) and everything in between. And what I've boiled all this information down to is that we should eat a variety of real, whole, preferably organic foods—mostly plants, and humanely raised, grass-produced meats, eggs, fish, and seafood on the side. Ideally we would consume no additives, no refined grains or sugar, and definitely no high fructose corn syrup or trans fat. In addition, it's a good idea to take a vitamin D supplement (especially in the winter), DHA (often as a fish oil supplement), and a probiotic for gut health.

If you are able to eat like this even 80 percent of the time, you've done a lot to boost your brain for optimal mental well-being. But sometimes, it's not enough.

If you are dealing with a child with behavioral or mood problems, nutrition is a key area to explore. There are so many different ways diet can be an underlying cause. The best way to determine if diet is a contributing factor is to work with a holistic dietitian and start the process by figuring out if something is missing in the diet (a deficiency) or if there is something in the diet that is causing a problem (a sensitivity)—or maybe both!

One such dietitian is Kelly Dorfman, the author of *What's Eating Your Child?* She thinks of herself as a "nutrition detective"—someone who tries to get to the bottom of any number of childhood ailments by systematically eliminating foods such as gluten or dairy, or adding nutrients such as fish oil and vitamin E.

For example, she tells the story of Tyler, who was diagnosed with "beyond ADHD" and whose doctor was suggesting treatment with Risperdal (an antipsychotic). Dorfman put Tyler on a no-sugar diet and the ADHD symptoms abated.[13] In the chapter "The Bipolar Child Who Wasn't," we meet Jessica, who had been diagnosed with bipolar disorder and was taking a cocktail of three psychiatric drugs. Turns out Jessica had gluten sensitivity, not bipolar disorder.

Even though these are anecdotes, I share them here because I want you to realize that this happens time and time again. Kids present with abnormal behavior, and pediatricians jump to a mental illness diagnosis with help of the *DSM* and the pharmaceutical companies. The whole system is stuck in the discourse that says that behavioral problems require medication. These kids are medicated to the point that it's hard to know what the original symptoms were, and then it's over. They're medicated for life, often resulting in disability down the road. However, diagnosing a child with bipolar disorder, or any mental illness, without first exploring other causes and interventions is a tragic mistake. Dorfman echoes this sentiment:

> I am disheartened when preteens are given diagnoses of bipolar disorder. The usual treatment is complicated drug trials, often accompanied by unacceptable side effects and hospitalizations. If even 25 percent of these children could be stabilized with dietary changes and simple supplements, the reduced suffering and financial savings would be immense.

One of my friends (I'll call her Anna) told me the story of her family's experience with food, chemicals, and behavior. Her daughter (I'll call her Isolde) was a very high-maintenance child from the time she was born. By the time Isolde was three or four, Anna, a special education teacher, started getting worried because she saw some bipolar tendencies in Isolde. However, she was not interested in getting a diagnosis or medication for her four-year-old. But it was exhausting to care for Isolde. Just when Anna was about to give up, she found out about the FAILSAFE diet. The diet (which stands for "free of additives, low in salicylates, amines, and flavor enhancers") is based on the elimination diet developed by the Royal Prince Alfred Hospital Allergy Unit in Sydney, Australia. It is an extremely strict diet, but Anna was willing to try anything to regain some sanity. Within forty-eight hours of starting the FAILSAFE diet, she had a different child! Through the elimination diet, they discovered that both Isolde *and* Anna were sensitive to a number of common foods, additives, and chemicals, including salicylates (present in almost all fruits), amines, artificial colors, artificial preservatives, gums, dairy, oranges and orange juice, eggs, barley, mechanically processed grains, protein alterations resulting from the ultra-pasteurization process, pesticides, many natural flavorings, rice syrup solids, and corn syrup. Thankfully, they have been able to work with acupressure to remove nearly all of their sensitivities so they can be on an almost completely "normal" diet. You definitely don't want to stay on a strict diet if you don't have to.

The book *Food and Mood* by Jude Burger describes the author's own experience with the FAILSAFE diet and how it freed her from a lifetime of depression and anxiety. She provides a number of resources for treating food sensitivities and relays anecdotes from others who have also found relief from symptoms of depression, anxiety, and ADHD by eliminating certain chemicals and substances from their diets.

Another good case for the connection between food and behavior is made in the book with the same name. In *Food and Behavior: A Natural Connection*, former probation officer Barbara Reed Stitt describes the nutrition program she used during her twenty-year career to turn delinquents and criminals into well-adjusted adults with a bright future:

> Instead of sending my subjects off immediately to a psychiatrist, I placed them on the diet I found in the Low Blood Sugar booklet. It consisted of a total ban on sugar, white flour products, chemical additives, caffeine and alcohol, and emphasized the consumption of fresh fruits and vegetables, whole grains and such lean meats as chicken, fish, and plenty of water.[14]

Barbara had realized that most, if not all, of the probationers that came to her office were junk-food junkies and addicted to sugar. Because they weren't eating any real food, their brains and central nervous systems were actually malnourished and not able to function properly. Once their brains received proper nourishment, they were able to stay out of the correctional system.

If you think improving mental health with dietary changes sounds too good to be true, consider this: would you rather give your child medication, which may or may not be approved for kids and only manages symptoms, or would you rather try feeding your child nourishing food and work with a dietitian to determine if he is reacting to something in his diet? It comes back to trying the safest and least risky options first.

Considering how important food is for our general well-being, we should take great care to eat only the most nutritious and clean foods. And we should be even more careful when it comes to feeding our children. One of the things I'll discuss in the last part of this book is how school food needs to be revamped to optimize mental health. We tell kids to "eat healthy" in health class and then send them to the cafeteria for processed junk. No wonder everybody's confused about food! The good news is that improving our diets can only make things better. Good nutrition is an important tool in the mental health optimization toolbox.

Before we move on to the next section, I do want to note that due to Rebecka's history of disordered eating, we did not try to adjust her diet in any way. In order for her to heal, it was very important for her to be empowered to make her own food decisions. All I could do was set a good example in my own eating by minimizing processed foods, but also emphasizing that there are no "bad" foods, just "special occasion" foods. Introducing a whole foods diet is easiest if done from birth, but a family can certainly ease into it by substituting whole foods for junk. The key is to make sure nobody feels deprived, because that is an open invitation to a disordered eating future.

Rest and Sleep

According to the Centers for Disease Control and Prevention, preschool-aged children need eleven to twelve hours of sleep per day. School-aged children need at least ten hours of sleep a day, and teenagers need nine to ten hours.[15] Unfortunately, most kids and teens don't get enough sleep. Indeed, according to a study conducted with fifty-six adolescents ages fourteen to nineteen in Rhode Island, the teens got on average 7.5 hours of sleep—not nearly enough.[16]

Adequate sleep is imperative for proper brain function. As you can imagine, sleep is also important for mental health.[17] It's long been known that people with depression, anxiety, and other symptoms of poor mental health have disturbed sleep. And until recently, psychiatrists and other mental health professionals viewed poor sleep purely as a symptom of the mental disorder, or possibly of the medication.[18] However, studies now show that it is more of a two-way street.[19] Poor sleep can in fact exacerbate symptoms of depression, anxiety, bipolar disorder, and ADHD, and contribute to stress.[20]

Evaluating sleep should be part of any initial mental health consultation. This is seldom the case. Rather, with the pills-as-first-resort approach, disordered sleep is often overlooked and can even be worsened by the medication.[21] A 2012 *New York Times* blog post titled "Attention Problems May Be Sleep-Related" confirms:

> Many children are given a diagnosis of A.D.H.D., researchers say, when in fact they have another problem: a sleep disorder, like sleep apnea. The confusion may account for a significant number of A.D.H.D. cases in children, and the drugs used to treat them may only be exacerbating the problem.

The article goes on to quote Merrill Wise, a pediatric neurologist and sleep medicine specialist at the Methodist Healthcare Sleep Disorders Center in Memphis: "No one is saying A.D.H.D. does not exist, but there's a strong feeling now that we need to rule out sleep issues first."[22]

If you have a child who is not getting enough sleep, the best thing to do is to establish a consistent bedtime routine. The routine should provide enough time for the mind to start winding down. Some kids may respond to a bath, while others may benefit from soothing music or a bedtime story. Regular exercise also contributes to better sleep—at any age.[23] Sleep experts recommend shutting off screens and electronic devices at least two hours before bedtime to make sure that the body's internal clock doesn't get confused. This is especially important for adolescents.[24] I am the first to acknowledge that this is easier said than done in our hyper-connected society. However, don't be afraid to take control of your family's technology usage. When Rebecka was on the road to recovery and we realized just how important sleep was for her mental health, we unplugged the wireless router at night. I have also talked to parents who collect all mobile devices before bedtime each evening to ensure their kids get a good night's sleep.

Beyond sleep, it is also important to rest from work, school, chores, and commitments on a regular basis. This means having time weekly to relax and play. I am a big proponent of observing a "day of rest" (a.k.a. "the Sabbath" in the Jewish and Christian traditions). When I was growing up and was forced to observe the Sabbath as a child, it was a bit annoying, mostly because we couldn't go shopping. However, as an adult, I have realized the significance of weekly rest for optimal wellness. The primary objective during my day of rest is to unplug. I turn off my computer and smartphone. I also avoid doing things I consider to be chores or otherwise stressful. I take advantage of the extra time to read for fun, take long walks (ideally in the woods), spend time with friends and family, and nourish my soul through music or meditation. It's important to design the day of rest to *your* needs. And please note that you need not be religious to embrace this practice.

A couple of years ago, I had the opportunity to attend an informal parlor discussion with Henry Emmons, an integrative psychiatrist with Partners in Resilience and the author of several books, including *The Chemistry of Joy: A Three-Step Program for Overcoming Depression Through Western Science and Eastern Wisdom*. We talked about a number of topics during the discussion, but the topic that stuck with me was Dr. Emmons's take on one of the reasons why so many people in our culture get depressed. It's because we never slow down and rest! With electricity, we can work 24/7 if we so choose. This was not possible just a few generations ago. We no longer live in harmony with the natural cycles of our environment. Normally, winter would be a time to slow down, because it's dark and cold. Now we plow through winter (both literally and figuratively) and don't think for a second that we should do anything differently.

Unfortunately, it's not just adults who go, go, go and never rest. Many children are so over-programmed they barely have time to catch their breath. And our schools encourage this by placing importance on homework and extra-curricular activities over unstructured play. This is the premise of the 2009 documentary *Race to Nowhere*. According to this film, children and teens around the country feel an enormous amount of pressure to succeed in school. And "succeed" means taking hard classes, getting excellent grades, and scoring well on standardized tests, not necessarily developing critical thinking skills and a love of learning. It also means participating in a large number of extra-curricular activities such as sports, music, dance, community service, and other clubs. Our schools do not promote rest.

However, there is a different way. Says Ann Robinson, a pediatrician interviewed in the film, "So much of this has to do with bringing the community together and deciding that we value student health and well-being—and that that can coincide with academic achievement and excellence. And that well-rested, well-balanced students perform better academically and in every aspect of their lives."[25] I'll talk more about the role of education in optimizing kids' mental health in chapter 20.

For now, it's up to parents and other caring adults to let our kids know that getting perfect grades and acing standardized tests isn't all there is to life. It's more important to be able to think critically about the world around you and figure out what you love to do. And take a break every now and then!

Just keep in mind that this may not always sit well with the school. Rebecka captured some of these thoughts in the essay she wrote for her National Honor Society application, and was denied membership her junior year in high school. The faculty who communicated this to our family cited "disdain for academia" and "making bad choices." They clearly misunderstood what she was trying to say. But as parents, we would rather Rebecka think critically about the education system and the definition of success than become a member of an honor society.

Being In Nature

When I was eight years old, my family moved from the heart of San Francisco to a small town with a population of 1,200 in the Swedish province of Småland. I remember to this day how excited I was that I would actually be able to walk to school without an adult. Such freedom!

Woods with tall pines and fir trees surrounded our neighborhood, and there was a creek nearby—full of tadpoles when the season was right. My siblings and I walked home from school and into nature. I even "ran away from home" a time or two, taking shelter in the cozy wooden "house" on our neighborhood playground. I loved hiding in there on rainy days with a stack of comics. The first year back in Sweden, we didn't even have a television, so there wasn't much to do other than find some friends and go outside. We built stick shelters in the woods, collected ladybugs, and identified the first flowers by name as they pushed through the snow every spring. We went bird-watching, cross-country skiing, and camping. Nature was part of life, not a once-in-a-while special outing.

Some lucky kids still have this experience, especially in more rural settings, but most kids don't. A combination of fear (of bugs, strangers,[26] injuries, damage),[27] enhanced indoor recreation (TV, video games, Internet),[28] and increased school demands (homework, AP classes, extracurricular activities), and thus a loss of unstructured playtime, has resulted in kids not having the same experience with nature that I—and others of my generation and older—had growing up.[29]

This is a huge shift in how we exist in this world. Humans have always lived, worked, and played in close proximity to nature. It is only the last few generations that have moved away from active outdoor living toward sedentary indoor dwelling—mostly due to technological advances—and it's taking its toll. Chris Rowan, a pediatric occupational therapist, describes some of the fallout in the *Huffington Post* article "The Impact of Technology on the Developing Child":

> So what is the impact of technology on the developing child? Children's developing sensory, motor, and attachment systems have biologically not evolved to accommodate this sedentary, yet frenzied and chaotic nature of today's technology. The impact of rapidly advancing technology on the developing child has seen an increase of physical, psychological and behavior disorders that the health and education systems are just beginning to detect, much less understand. Child obesity and diabetes are now national epidemics in both Canada and the U.S., causally related to technology overuse. Diagnoses of ADHD, autism, coordination disorder, developmental delays, unintelligible speech, learning difficulties, sensory processing disorder, anxiety, depression, and sleep disorders are associated with technology overuse, and are increasing at an alarming rate.[30]

In the book *Last Child in the Woods: Saving Our Children From Nature-Deficit Disorder*, journalist and author Richard Louv comprehensively covers the topic of children's disconnection from nature and what to do about it. I was especially interested (but not surprised, based on my own experience) to learn that being in nature contributes greatly to stress relief.[31] Considering that chronic stress is one of the biggest causes of illness (both physical and mental),[32] this is a big deal! Further, Louv points to research that shows that nature can be used as an effective therapy for ADHD.[33] For example, researchers at the Landscape and Human Health Laboratory at the University of Illinois at Urbana-Champaign have found that when kids diagnosed with ADHD spend time in green spaces, their ability to pay attention improves.[34]

Depending on where you live, it may be easy or somewhat difficult to find green spaces. I am fortunate to be able to look out my window and see trees and bluffs, and hear birds chirping. And there are trails and parks within walking distance. However, in more urban settings, especially low-income neighborhoods, finding safe green spaces may be quite challenging. One thing to remember is that nature is more than parks and trails. Indeed, Rebecka recently stated to my sister Priscilla that she doesn't like to be in nature.

Priscilla replied: "But you love spending time with our cat. He is nature." Rebecka has also sent joyful pictures from her study-abroad experience of her host family's bunny snuggled up in her bed. The bunny is nature. There is such a thing as "animal therapy," and it's effective.[35] Nature can also be an herb garden on a kitchen windowsill and going up on the roof to gaze at the stars.

Natural and Free "Therapies"

Just like exercising, eating whole foods, and getting enough sleep, spending time in nature is one of the natural ways of being in the world that are now considered "therapy." These are the building blocks for the foundation of a healthy life. What's ironic about this is that it is how we lived for most of human history. No wonder we are feeling shaky when we have rapidly altered every one of these foundational building blocks.

The good news is that these "therapies" are accessible to most people. And some activities combine several of them. For example, going for a walk in the woods takes care of your exercise and your need to be in nature—*and* can help you sleep! Gardening connects you to the earth, provides exercise, *and* can result in whole foods for you to eat. Camping often includes a hiking component (exercise), being in nature, *and* resting (especially if you leave your electronic devices at home).

I think a few reasons why we don't take advantage of these free, natural therapies are:

- **Pills are a first resort:** As I've emphasized throughout this book, we have a paradigm of treating most forms of illness with medication (the biomedical model). It's how doctors are trained. And it's how the pharmaceutical companies make money for their shareholders. Fortunately, there is a shift toward a more integrated approach (the biopsychosocial model) that also takes psychological and social factors into consideration.[36]

- **We aren't aware of the benefits:** Nobody makes money promoting free therapy. As Louv says, "nature is often overlooked as a healing balm for the emotional hardships in a child's life. You'll likely never see a slick commercial for nature therapy, as you do for the latest pharmaceuticals."[37]

- **We get conflicting messages:** Trying to figure out what "eating healthy" means or what kind of exercise is best for us can be a full-time job. It's best to stay away from the latest fad diet books and go back to what's natural, such as moving your body throughout the day; eating local, real food that gives you energy; sleeping when you're tired; and interacting with nature daily.

- **It takes time:** Cooking real food takes a lot more time than picking up fast food on the way home from work.

- **It requires effort:** It's easier to let the kids sit in front of the TV or computer than to get them to a natural space (especially if you have to go with them).

- **It seems too good to be true:** Can food, exercise, sleep, and nature really help my child when I've been told she will need to be medicated the rest of her life?

I hope you will take what I've written in this chapter to heart—for your own well-being and the well-being of your children. The evidence is clear: getting back to a natural state of being in this world and taking care of our physical needs improves our mental health.

It might feel overwhelming, but the rewards are great. If you feel like you can only tackle one of these "therapies" right now, start with exercise. Find ways to get exercise into your and your children's day. Just don't call it "exercise." It should be fun and natural! I have included several resources to get your kids outside and moving in the "Take Action" section in the back of this book.

14

❧

Mindful Awareness, Belonging, and Being Part of Something Bigger

There seems to be something about having ties to others that is basic to health. Of course, this is intuitively understandable. It is deeply human to have a strong need to belong, to feel a part of something larger than oneself, to be in relationship with others in meaningful and supportive ways.

—Jon Kabat-Zinn, *Full Catastrophe Living*

I first learned about the concept of mindfulness on Leo Babauta's popular blog *Zen Habits*. I read posts such as "The Mindfulness Guide for the Super Busy: How to Live Life to the Fullest"[1] and "How to Master the Art of Mindful Eating."[2] But it wasn't until I learned about dialectical behavior therapy that I realized that mindfulness could be a way to alleviate symptoms of mental distress. (Of course, people in Asia have known this for thousands of years.)

As I have noted throughout this book, our culture has a lot invested in the biomedical model of psychology. In *The Spirit and Science of Holistic Health*, authors Jon Robison and Karen Carrier explain that this model is based on a mechanistic worldview that developed over the last four hundred years, starting with the Scientific Revolution. This worldview reduces everything in nature to component parts that can be fixed by focusing on an isolated problem (for example, a serotonin deficiency).[3] This model stands in stark contrast to the biopsychosocial model, initially introduced in the 1970s by George Engel and John Romano at the University of Rochester Medical Center. The biopsychosocial model takes into consideration biological, psychological, and social factors in trying to understand human health and illness. It takes a holistic and integrative approach to medicine—considering the whole person and her environment, not just the physical body or portions of the physical body.

In this chapter I will discuss three important concepts that tie in with a holistic approach to psychology:

- Mindful awareness
- Sense of community and belonging
- Having purpose and being part of something bigger

Mindful Awareness

What are you thinking about right now? Are you reflecting on something you just read or worrying about a yet-to-be-completed task? Or are you actually fully aware of reading these words? If you're like most people, many thoughts are going through your head as you are reading. You may even find that you have read some portion of this book without really being aware of the content. Your mind was elsewhere; it was wandering. In *Full Catastrophe Living*, Jon Kabat-Zinn, who developed the widely used Mindfulness-Based Stress Reduction (MBSR) program at the University of Massachusetts Medical Center, explains that we are less happy when our minds are wandering than when our minds are focused.[4]

Modern life in the United States is a never-ending stream of going, coming, doing, worrying, planning, researching, buying, and worrying some more. Even though we have created timesaving technologies, we don't seem to find time in the day to slow down and be fully present. Yet this is the healthiest state for your brain to be in. Bringing your awareness to what you are doing at this very moment helps you brain calm down and de-stress. And that's just the beginning of all the benefits associated with a disciplined mindfulness practice. Here are a few more:

- Emotional self-regulation
- Pain relief
- Improved relationships
- Happiness
- Anxiety relief
- Compassion

- Empathy
- Ability to focus
- Enhanced immune system[5]

It's no wonder that there's been a lot of buzz about mindfulness meditation the past few years. It works!

Jon Kabat-Zinn defines mindfulness as "the awareness that arises by paying attention on purpose, in the present moment, and non-judgmentally."[6] I also like Inner Kids Foundation cofounder Susan Kaiser Greenland's description:

> Mindfulness is a mirror of what's happening in the present moment. In other words, when practicing mindfulness, you see life experience clearly, as it happens, without an emotional charge. We learn how to do this by feeling our present moment experience, as it happens, without analyzing it—at least for the time being.[7]

While the concept of mindfulness is based in the Buddhist tradition, the mindfulness practices taught in MBSR and similar programs are secular. They are simply a way to train your mind to be aware of your thoughts and be present. You can hone your mindfulness skills through consistent practice. The best way to start to practice mindfulness is to focus on your breath. This is called "mindfulness of breathing." In MBSR, there are two ways to practice mindfulness of breathing:

1. **Formal practice:** setting aside time on a regular basis to lie or sit down and focus on your breath.[8]

2. **Informal practice:** using your breath throughout the day to bring awareness to the present.[9]

Here are Susan Kaiser Greenland's instructions for beginners:

> Concentrate on the feeling of your breath as it moves through your body. If your mind wanders, that's perfectly natural; just bring it back to the physical sensation of your inhalation, you exhalation, and the pause between the two. Remember, don't think about your breathing to change it in any way, just feel your breath as it is right now and rest.[10]

MBSR practices include sitting meditation, body-scan meditation, hatha yoga, and walking meditation. You can learn the details of these practices by reading *Full Catastrophe Living* and listening to the accompanying CDs. Greenland's book *The Mindful Child* is a complete guide to teaching mindfulness to children. It focuses on making mindfulness fun and accessible by preceding it with playing, singing, dancing, and creating.[11] She explains how mindfulness practices can help children who are feeling sad and anxious, children diagnosed with ADHD, and perfectionists "soothe and calm themselves, bring awareness to their inner and outer experience, and bring a reflective quality to their actions and relationships."[12]

Based on the efficacy of mindfulness practice in relieving and preventing stress, depression, anxiety, and attention problems—and making people kinder and more compassionate—it's not surprising that there is a strong movement to bring mindfulness into our nation's classrooms. The 2013 documentary *Healthy Habits of Mind* depicts kindergarten teacher Renee Harris incorporating mindfulness into her teaching, and provides glimpses into the work of Mindful Schools, an organization devoted to integrating mindfulness into education. Harris explains why mindfulness training is necessary in her classroom:

> Reading and writing used to be taught in first grade and it's moved to kindergarten. And there is a lot of debate about whether that's appropriate, but the reality is that that's what is expected right now—whether you believe that it's right or not. And I do see kids struggle with not being able to sit down and do a task. And it is because they cannot focus long enough. If we are going to ask them to do all of these things, it's so important that we give them the tools to do it. I think it's so important for this age. Otherwise, they're floundering.[13]

During a teacher training session, Mindful Schools program director Megan Cowan emphasizes that we can't just tell kids to pay attention, we need to show them—for life: "What we're addressing when we're saying that mindfulness teaches how to pay attention is what does it take, not just to pay attention in a moment, but what does it take to sustain attention, or sustain awareness," she says.[14]

It is important to note that mindfulness in education should not be used for crowd control or to create super achievers. Rather, through mindfulness, we are giving kids the *ability* to make a choice about whether or not to pay attention—and to focus on learning and creating and simply being.

All the scientific and anecdotal evidence of the power of mindfulness—and my own experience with it—has encouraged me to partner with other parents and members of our community to bring mindfulness to our teachers and kids. Along with the physical needs I documented in the previous chapter, mindfulness appears to be a key component in setting our children up for optimized mental health. We need to break the cycle of stress, depression, anxiety, and distractions that prevents kids from experiencing life to the fullest. Teaching mindfulness practices in school can help the cause—and makes so much sense.

Sense of Community and Belonging

All humans want to belong somewhere. As young children, we want to feel like we belong in our family. We want loving adults to feed us and cuddle with us and keep us safe. When we get a little older, we want to be part of a friend group (even if it's just one other person). In adolescence, we start searching for an identity. This might lead us to start listening to a particular genre of music, play certain video games, get involved with a political party, or join (or leave) a faith community.

It is clear that people who experience a strong sense of community feel better and are more resilient. Indeed, "community" is one of the "Power 9 Principles" of the Blue Zones Project (based on the book *The Blue Zones* by Dan Buettner, mentioned in chapter 12).[15] The Blue Zones Project website notes that "all but five of the 263 centenarians interviewed in the original Blue Zones areas studies belonged to some faith-based community." It goes on to say, "it doesn't matter if you're Christian, Buddhist, Muslim, Jewish or another religion. What matters is that you attend regularly and truly feel part of a larger group."

In this case, we're talking about a religious community, but it can certainly be another kind of group. In fact, one of the top reasons kids join gangs is to have a sense of community. Many kids who join gangs don't feel like they belong in their family, at school, or anywhere else. There is a sense of security that comes from having close connections and being part of a group. You know that if something bad happens to you, someone's there to catch you.

In *Full Catastrophe Living*, Jon Kabat-Zinn points to evidence of social connections greatly influencing health, including mental health:

> People who have a very low degree of social interactions in their lives, as measured by marital status, contacts with extended family and friends, church membership, and other group involvements, are between two and four times as likely to die in the succeeding ten-year period as are people who have a very high level of social interaction, when all other factors such as

age, prior illness, income, health habits such as smoking and alcohol consumption, physical activity, race, and the like are taken into account. Social isolation and loneliness are now considered demonstrated risk factors for depression and cancer.[16]

Recent studies show that singing in a group has a variety of health benefits, including stress reduction and improved mental health. For example, a year-long study in the UK found that "60 [percent] of participants had less mental distress when retested a year after joining, with some people no longer fulfilling diagnostic criteria for clinical depression." One of the reasons may be that the singers feel they are part of something meaningful, but also that they are synchronized in their breathing.[17] One interesting reflection is that Rebecka's mental well-being started to decline when she was no longer singing in a choir. She had been singing in choirs since she was in preschool, but stopped after her first year in middle school. Now she is part of a wonderful choir again, and she is happy and content. I realize this may be pure coincidence, but who knows?

There are a number of options for kids to get involved and belong. Most importantly, kids need to feel like they belong in their family. Obviously, this may depend on a large number of factors, but we know that regular family meals are one of the best ways to keep kids engaged and out of trouble. Physician and author Mark Hyman provides some specifics in the *Huffington Post* article "How Eating at Home Can Save Your Life":

> Research shows that children who have regular meals with their parents do better in every way, from better grades, to healthier relationships, to staying out of trouble. They are 42 percent less likely to drink, 50 percent less likely to smoke and 66 percent less like [sic] to smoke marijuana. Regular family dinners protect girls from bulimia, anorexia, and diet pills.[18]

With teenagers, it can be tricky to find a time when everybody is available in the evenings. At our house, we got into a habit of eating breakfast together when we had to supervise Rebecka's meals. I cook eggs, toast some bread, and make time to sit down at the kitchen table with Rebecka. We light candles and either sit together in silence or talk about whatever is going on in our lives. I love having that time in the morning, because then it doesn't matter as much if we're not able to pull off a family dinner.

Outside the family, kids might enjoy getting involved with sports, theater, choir, politics, volunteering, or other groups or clubs through the school, library, community center, or other youth organizations. The key is to make sure it's not too much, because that's not good for the parents or the kids. You have to figure out the right mix for your family. Rebecka has enjoyed being part of the Gay-Straight Alliance and the Community Club at her school. She was also one of the managers for the girls' and boys' swim teams this past season and had a small role in the musical *Tom Sawyer*. She finds that staying busy with these kinds of activities gives her enjoyment and a sense of purpose, which in turn reduces her anxiety.

Having Purpose and Being Part of Something Bigger

Recently, I was sitting at the Eastern Iowa Airport bar, having a glass of wine with a newfound friend after finding out that our flight was at least two hours delayed. We started with the easy stuff (kids, dogs, careers), but eventually moved on to some deeper topics. We talked about our mothers, both of whom had lost their husbands within the last few years—and specifically about the importance of having purpose. "My mom makes cookies," my new friend said. "For me and my brother and sister—and the grandkids. That's her purpose. So I worry what will happen when she is no longer able to bake." I told her about 101-year-old Don Faustino, featured in *The Blue Zones*, who rides the bus into town every Sunday to visit the farmers market, the butcher, and the general store to buy food so he can make Sunday soup for his family. That's his purpose. It's what gets him out of bed in the morning.[19] Indeed, "Purpose" is the second of the nine common denominators among the people around the world who live longer, happier lives. According to the Blue Zones Project website, "knowing your sense of purpose is worth up to seven years of extra life expectancy."[20]

People who are members of a religious community often find their purpose through their religion. By believing in God or a higher spirit, we feel connected to one another and part of something bigger than ourselves. But this doesn't work for everybody. In *Radically Open: Transcending Religious Identity in an Age of Anxiety*, Robert Shedinger, a professor of religion at Luther College (and the person who encouraged us to read *Anatomy of an Epidemic*), describes his tumultuous spiritual journey to overcome debilitating anxiety by finding his true identity. Inspired by Carl Jung, Shedinger states, "anxiety results from a narrow and constricted view of our own nature, from a lack of depth and a narrowed spiritual horizon."[21] He found that only when he moved beyond religious identity and embraced the mystery of being "a child of the universe" was he able to live radically open and free from anxiety.[22] Just as humans want to have close relationships and feel like they belong in a community, many humans want to be connected spiritually and feel like they are part of a larger story. It makes their lives have meaning and purpose.

When Rebecka emerged on the other side of the lost year, we started thinking about how she could feel purpose in her life. This was something she struggled with at the time. She wasn't really involved in anything at school and often said that she didn't feel like her life had meaning. We knew that she was passionate about human rights and equality—especially related to gender and sexual preference. So we talked to her about that and explained that her purpose could be to get involved more in these issues and work toward an equitable world. Within a year, she was involved in the Gay-Straight Alliance at her school and volunteering for a political campaign. When asked what gives her life purpose now, she answers, "I just try to be somebody who makes everyone else feel like a somebody. It's so important to me that everyone feels safe and welcome wherever they are. I try my best to do this through actions in my life, whether it be simply being friendly to others, or working with organizations like the GSA."

While we were waiting for Rebecka to get a spot in the DBT group in Rochester, we worked through *The Dialectical Behavior Therapy Skills Workbook* as a family. This workbook has an excellent section called "Identify Your Higher Power . . . And Make Yourself Feel More *Powerful.*" The authors remind us that "having faith in something bigger and more powerful than yourself can often make you feel empowered, safe, and calm. . . . Believing in something divine, holy, or special can help you endure stressful situations as well as help you soothe yourself."[23] We also appreciated the following "High-Power Activity":

> Remember that your higher power can also be something other than God. Your higher power can be a person who makes you feel stronger and more confident to deal with the challenges that you face. Think of someone you admire who can be your higher power. Describe that person. What makes that person special? Then, next time you're in a difficult or distressing situation, act as if you are that person, and notice how you handle the situation differently.[24]

It might seem challenging to help kids find purpose, but it could be as simple as giving them full responsibility for a family pet or assigning them a plot of land in the family garden—*and* giving them space and time to reflect on what it means to be a child of the universe, so they can identify their place in it.

15

Beyond Talk Therapy: Family Therapy, the Maudsley Approach, and DBT

*My goal is always to help families help themselves
without drugs or stigmatizing diagnoses.*

—Marilyn Wedge, *Suffer the Children*

Before our family was thrown into the world of mental illness, I didn't know much about therapy. I knew that a therapist worked with individuals and couples—and even families. And I had gathered from pop culture that therapists helped people dig into the past to reveal traumatic experiences such as sexual or emotional abuse. I imagined this revelation would then start the process of forgiveness and healing from emotional distress. However, I was not aware that there are other types of therapy—therapies focused on what's happening in the present—that can be more effective than talk (or play) therapy, depending on the situation.

In *Saving Your Child from Depression*, Dr. Berlinger holds up cognitive-behavioral-therapy, interpersonal therapy, and family therapy as the types of psychotherapy most relevant for teens with depression. He emphasizes that parents should try "to make the closest possible match between [their] teen's particular problem and the therapeutic approach."[1]

In our experience (and during my research) three types of therapies emerged as being particularly helpful in addressing mood and behavioral problems in kids and teens. I will explore these in more detail in this chapter:

- **Family therapy** frames the child as a member of a larger system.

- **The Maudsley approach**, or family-based treatment, highlights the family as part of the solution, rather than part of the problem, when treating an adolescent struggling with anorexia nervosa.

- **Dialectical behavior therapy** is a specific form of cognitive-behavioral therapy, which includes a group therapy/skills component and is influenced by Eastern Zen philosophy.

Please note that this is not even close to being an exhaustive list of therapeutic approaches to helping kids who are feeling sad, lonely, anxious, or out of control. I could also include art therapy, music therapy, equine therapy (horse therapy), animal therapy, laughter yoga, biofeedback, Emotional Freedom Technique, Reiki, acupuncture, and healing touch. These are all therapies and techniques that can help reduce emotional distress. However, that's another book!

Family Therapy

You may recall from chapter 1 that the first doctor we saw when Rebecka started complaining of depression and losing weight did suggest family therapy.

Of course, at the time this did not appeal to us at all. Personally, I was worried about what difficult issues from the past the therapist would dig up. It just felt like this would add to the stress we were already experiencing. Logistics were also a concern. Todd was only around one weekday each week and it seemed like it would be really difficult to pull it off. In hindsight, I wish the doctor had been in a position to *prescribe* family therapy, because we sure needed it. It's just really hard to see it when you're in the middle of living your life.

Not until Rebecka had been hospitalized a few times and the outlook was grim did Dr. Z force us into that ad hoc family therapy session on the floor of the quiet room. And as I envisioned, it was painful, but also very helpful. Once Todd and I were able to get past our defensiveness, we realized that our actions and moods greatly affected Rebecka's health and happiness. (Go figure.) That one session helped us realize that Rebecka felt like she always had to perform well in school and be "the perfect daughter," or we would become even more stressed-out than we were, and be unhappy with her. Of course, we didn't feel that way. But, it's amazing how much we rely on perceptions of reality. So we did our best not to focus on schoolwork, and I started making plans to leave my job, which was a big source of stress and negatively impacted my mood. It helped.

Child-focused family therapy is all about listening to the child—who often provides great clues into family dynamics and dysfunction[2]—and observing interactions between family members. Children often act out or become depressed based on something that is happening within the family structure. What I found most intriguing when researching effective approaches to family therapy was that children at times "behave badly" or display other psychiatric symptoms to distract a parent from the parent's own suffering. As such, the child is acting as the parent's helper. Marilyn Wedge, a family therapist in Westlake Village, California, explains that if she suspects a young patient is in a helper role, she reassures the child that *she* will be the parent's helper now. Once the child is off the hook, the symptoms abate. As Wedge explains, "strategically reframing a child's problem as helpfulness rather than a psychiatric symptom, and communicating to the child that the therapist is ready to take on the role of the parent's 'helper', are powerful instruments of change."[3]

Another important aspect of children's mental health is obviously the health of the parents' relationships. This includes the relationship the parents have with each other (regardless of whether they are married or not), relationships with grandparents and other siblings, and even relationships with teachers and doctors. Children are so perceptive, and they pick up on even the slightest nuances when it comes to marital and familial health. Maintaining strong relationships is not for the faint of heart. It's hard work! But when you think of the benefits, including emotionally healthy children, it's well worth it.

If your child is struggling and the teachers and your pediatrician are suggesting medication, I urge you to consider family therapy. You may not think that anything is amiss in your family, but most of the time, we're too close to the problems to see them. While medicating a troubled child can relieve symptoms temporarily, it may do more harm than good by glossing over deeper family issues that may come back with a vengeance down the road.[4] A family therapist is a neutral party who is trained to ask the right questions and suggest behavioral and environmental changes to alleviate the child's symptoms for good.

❧

The Maudsley Approach

The Maudsley approach is a family-based approach to treating adolescents with anorexia nervosa (unhealthy weight loss due to restrictive calorie intake). Contrary to the traditional approach to treatment (hospitalizing teens in order to get them away from their dysfunctional families and help them regain weight), the Maudsley approach views parents as essential partners in treatment and empowers them to take charge of re-feeding their son or daughter. Not only does this approach make parents feel better about their role in the recovery process—it is the only treatment that has a high level of efficacy over the long term in treating anorexia.[5]

One of the goals of the Maudsley approach is to keep teens out of the hospital by providing an intensive outpatient treatment in which parents play a crucial role. The treatment has three well-defined phases:

Phase 1: Weight restoration

During this phase, the main goal is to help the adolescent reach a normal body weight based on height and age. The therapist highlights the dangers of low body weight to emphasize the seriousness of the situation, assesses the family's eating habits (often by observing a family meal), and supports the parent in helping their child regain weight. It is important during this time—and throughout the treatment—that parents remain uncritical of their child, by separating the illness from the person. (This really helped me be more compassionate toward Rebecka when she was going through the recovery process.)

Phase 2: Independent eating

In the second phase, the adolescent is gradually given independence in eating. When we were going through this phase, we started by reducing the amount of time we monitored Rebecka after meals and then eliminating after-meal monitoring completely. The next big step toward independent eating was unmonitored lunches. Eventually, we were all comfortable that Rebecka could manage eating and weight on her own.

Phase 3: Addressing general issues of adolescence

Once maintaining body weight is no longer an issue, therapy shifts to address general issues associated with adolescence, including "establishing a healthy adolescent identity," as it may have been impacted by the illness. This includes figuring out as a family the appropriate level of autonomy for the adolescent, and parental boundaries.[6] In our case, it was primarily establishing curfews (since Rebecka was now able to go out with friends) and making sure that she had an appropriate amount of independence.

As you may recall from chapter 8, the treatment approach at the Mayo Clinic in Rochester, Minnesota, where Rebecka was treated, was slightly different from the Maudsley approach. It was certainly a family-based treatment, but included an inpatient component at the beginning of the program with a singular focus on weight restoration. Considering where we were as a family at that time (exhausted and frustrated), this worked well for us. Also, since we didn't have a therapist trained in the Maudsley approach in our area, it was a good alternative.

I think the most helpful aspect of the Mayo Clinic eating disorder program for us parents was learning how to respond to the restrictive eating and purging. Until we met the director, Dr. Sim, and started the program, nobody had been able to tell us concretely how to help Rebecka reestablish normal eating patterns. Because we were afraid of making things worse, we were paralyzed. We didn't know if it was appropriate to require a certain number of calories at each meal and remove privileges when the eating disorder didn't comply. At the Mayo Clinic, Dr. Sim and the rest of the staff framed it in a way that made sense: If you don't eat, you can't expend any extra energy; hence, you have to stay in bed.

Anorexia nervosa is a serious illness that can lead to death. Thankfully, there are effective treatment approaches such as the Maudsley approach and the family-based treatment program at the Mayo Clinic. It's best to nip it in the bud, so don't sit around and watch your child wither away. Take action as soon as you have a hunch something is wrong. And know that you don't have to rely on medication to treat an eating disorder.

Dialectical Behavior Therapy

I first learned about dialectical behavior therapy (DBT) from one of the social workers at Sanders Psychiatric Hospital. At the time, they were thinking that Rebecka had symptoms of borderline personality disorder (BPD), even though it is not traditionally diagnosed in adolescents. (However, that is changing.)[7] People with BPD have attachment issues, maintain rocky relationships, engage in reckless and dangerous behavior, exhibit recurrent suicidal behavior, and often react strongly to negative events, among other symptoms.[8] Not surprisingly, a high percentage (81 percent) of people with BPD experienced major trauma as children.[9] As you can imagine, it is a difficult disorder to treat.

I never really believed Rebecka had BPD, but I was intrigued by DBT. When I looked it up online, I learned that DBT is a form of cognitive behavioral therapy designed to help people manage emotional distress and reduce the chances of destructive behavior in response to overwhelming emotions. It teaches four key skills:

1. **Distress Tolerance:** To build up resiliency and find ways to cope when upsetting things happen.

2. **Mindfulness:** To spend more time in the present moment than in a potentially painful past or worrisome future. Also to overcome negative judgments.

3. **Emotion Regulation:** To recognize emotions and be able to observe them without becoming overwhelmed.

4. **Interpersonal Effectiveness:** To be able to express beliefs and needs while maintaining healthy relationships.[10]

The skills are taught in a group setting and reinforced in individual therapy. Therapists provide a sheet for clients to fill out before arriving at individual therapy sessions to indicate which skills they used to cope with distress or difficult situations the past week. This encourages clients to practice the skills in their daily life and spend the time in therapy to reflect on what worked and what didn't work. A key aspect of DBT is that the therapist is available 24/7 by phone to help clients work through distressing situations using the skills, but clients are expected to try different coping strategies before they call. For example, somebody who usually turns to self-harm to cope with overwhelming emotions may try to use a "coping thought" to get through the emotional distress. However, if they can't get the skill to work for them, they can call the therapist to coach them through it.

What's great about this approach is that it provides a concrete plan for how to deal with emotional distress before the difficult situation happens. And it builds resilience that helps people for the rest of their lives.

Finding DBT groups and trained therapists may not be the easiest task in the world. However, if you have a child who is suicidal, prone to self-harm, and clearly has trouble managing his or her emotions, I would recommend that you do what it takes to get them into DBT. We drove seventy miles (one way) every week for several months so Rebecka could attend a group for adolescents. But if you don't have the means to make this happen, working through a DBT workbook, such as *The Dialectical Behavior Therapy Skills Workbook*, is a good alternative.

When it comes to kids, we should assume their problems *do not* stem from an inevitable, lifelong mental disorder. This should be our first and basic assumption. We should try to get to the bottom of the problem using integrative medicine approaches coupled with helpful forms of psychotherapy as described above. Only when all else fails should we resort to psychiatric medication.

I agree with Allen Frances when he says, "Even in severely disturbed kids, there are serious clinical and ethical questions, but medicine may be needed in extremely exigent circumstances."[11] When we medicate children for behavioral problems and emotional distress, we're treating symptoms and not getting to the root of the problem. Is it a disturbance in the family hierarchy? Is the child gluten intolerant? Does the child need to spend more time running around outside? By jumping straight to medication, we avoid having to adapt the environment to the needs of the child. We can continue to ignore detrimental family dynamics. We can continue to feed her wheat and processed foods. And we can continue to send him to a one-size-fits-all school where outdoor playtime is limited and the curriculum is geared toward standardized testing, rather than intellectual growth.

We tried medication and lost a year of our daughter's life. I am grateful that I now know that this is not the only option for reducing mental distress. I have shared some alternative strategies with you above, many of which can also be used to *optimize* our children's—and our own—mental health. We'll talk about that next.

Part 5

Optimizing Children's Mental Health

While trying to figure out why well-informed doctors still prescribe psychiatric medication to kids, I came across this analogy by pediatrician John Diller:

> If as a pediatrician I were presented with an epidemic of serious diarrhea occurring in my community, of course I would treat these children with hydration, oral or intravenous fluids as necessary, and add other medications to help them get through their course of illness. But if I suspected that the epidemic was caused by drinking water that had been polluted by the effluent of an upstream factory, it would be unconscionable for me to remain silent.[1]

Diller's point is that our society is messed up, and it's causing our children to be messed up. And while we figure out how to un-mess things for our kids, he's going to treat the kids who can't take it to reduce their suffering.

This certainly helped me understand the physician's primary goal—to ease suffering at all costs. But what really stuck with me was the last sentence.

We can't stay silent about the fact that we have some significant problems in our society, which are contributing to our children's suffering. Indeed, we must figure out how to change our society fundamentally. Otherwise, we'll never break the cycle of widespread mental distress.

I started thinking a lot about the following questions: What would a society designed for optimal mental health look like? How would it be different from our current society? What fundamental values and ethics would be the foundation of this society? What first steps could we take to move in this direction? In essence, I started dreaming of a mental health utopia. I leveraged my knowledge of voluntary simplicity, social business, holistic health, community rights, progressive education theories, and ecopsychology, along with my experience of growing up in Sweden (a social democracy), to come up with some guidelines for a society designed to promote mental health. This society is based on the assumptions that the majority of human beings are in favor of cooperation, meaningful work, and equality—and value human health and happiness above material possessions. As we know, human beings are complex. We have egotistical and greedy traits, but we also express generosity and desire equality. And, as Swedish feminist, author, and journalist Nina Björk reminds us, we develop the traits that are nurtured. As a society, we can choose to nurture greed and competition, or we can choose to nurture empathy and cooperation.[2] So while my mental health-optimized society might be considered a utopia, which by definition is an *imaginary* place where everything is perfect, I have to believe it could become a reality.

After describing my mental health "utopia," I will look more closely at four broad areas that need to be addressed immediately in order for our society to promote mental health:

1. **Creating a Culture of Enough:** Our endless cycle of looking for bigger, better, and more exciting is not sustainable and creates a culture of competition, over-consumption, and discontent. In order to keep up, we must work harder and longer, which increases stress that we pass to our kids.

2. **Establishing a Just Republic:** Our government does not serve the people, but rather corporations and their bottom lines. This has resulted in poverty, mental distress, wage inequality, chronic stress and disease, environmental crisis, and "race to the top" education. We must enact significant change.

3. **Compassionate Parenting:** While all parents want what's best for their children, most parents are not trained or equipped to practice compassionate parenting, which is one of the keys to optimizing children's mental health.

4. **Student-Centered Education:** Traditional education is focused on standards, tests, and competition. We're missing the boat by not allowing our students' intellectual, social, and emotional needs—coupled with the needs of a just society—to be the foundation for our curriculum and teaching approach.

16

A Society Designed to Optimize Mental Health

If we dream about the sun shining equally on all people, it requires that we go beyond viewing upward mobility as a goal of the good society. It requires that we see the benefit of well-being for all people. It requires a utopia.

—Nina Björk, *Happily Ever After*

Here in the United States, our society has moved as far away as it possibly can from being optimized for mental health. I believe this is in part the result of rampant consumerism, a profit-at-all-costs economic system, our warped definition of success, and the tragedy of the commons. I further believe that we didn't consciously set out to de-optimize our society for mental health. We didn't think of the consequences of viewing humans as disposable "human resources," of separating kids from their parents at six weeks of age, of giving limitless political power to corporations, of making everything a competition starting with our first report card in kindergarten, of giving dangerous medications to unruly children, of viewing natural resources as private property, and of separating ourselves from nature and our food supply.

Okay, some people imagined the consequences, but the bulk of us didn't listen.

We were too busy "going with the flow"—going to school, learning that having as much money and power as possible equals success, getting jobs, starting families, working hard, getting promotions, buying bigger houses, dreaming about the weekend, and watching TV. (Trust me, I've been there!) And here we are. Many of us are depressed, anxious, and stressed (forty million adults suffer symptoms of anxiety disorders[1]). A whopping 117 million of us have chronic diseases that are strictly related to our stressed-out, sedentary, processed lifestyle.[2] Many adults spend forty-plus hours each week doing work that clashes with our values—and that is plain boring and uninspiring. And some of us are starting to dream about a different society and a different world. Because the one we have isn't working for 99 percent of us—and if we think globally and more long-term, not any of us.

I would like to take a stab at outlining this different society and, to a lesser extent, this different world. An architect starts with a blueprint, a tailor starts with a pattern, and a software developer starts with an algorithm. If we are to build something great—a society optimized for human well-being—we need a model. I don't have all the details figured out (in the software world, waiting until everything is figured out is called "analysis paralysis"), but I believe that if enough people subscribe to this model, we will find a way to make it happen. I realize that this topic could fill a book on its own, so I won't address every single aspect of life and society (for example, I will rudely gloss over transportation, entertainment, and defense). Rather, I will focus on the big-ticket items that affect our ability to raise healthy, compassionate children.

A Government for the People

It's important for people to feel like they have a say in how things should be— that their voices are being heard. A society designed for optimal mental health would allow for a significant amount of local and regional government. It would encourage political involvement, and everybody would understand the political process and stay abreast of current events.

Elections would be publicly funded and each party or candidate would get a certain amount of money to spend on their campaign based on some set of criteria. This could be based on party membership numbers, previous performance, or other metrics. Funds from individuals and businesses would not be allowed, nor could candidates use their own money for the campaign. This way, our elected officials could focus on making smart legislative decisions based on the needs of the people, as opposed to spending a large chunk of their time campaigning and doing everything in their power to retain financial support for the next election. And ideally, we would have a multiparty system to encourage voter participation and create a more diverse political landscape.

Social Business and Worker Cooperatives

In this society, the traditional corporation with its singular focus on economic growth, expanded market share, and the bottom line is an antiquated thing of the past. Rather, many people work independently, providing services to people in their community, ranging from holistic health services to landscaping to accounting. Bottom-line-focused corporations are replaced by social businesses and worker cooperatives.

As defined by Muhammad Yunus, an economist and social entrepreneur who was awarded the Nobel Peace Prize in 2006, a social business is "a non-loss, non-dividend company dedicated entirely to achieve a social goal."[3] That is to say, this type of business operates as any other business, but profits don't go to investors; rather, they are reinvested in the business. Investors eventually get their money back, but without interest. Who would want to make this type of investment, you might ask? According to Yunus, philanthropists, who typically give to charity, would be the people to hit up for this type of venture.[4] (At least in our current society. In our new society, I imagine there would be interest-free loans to help people start social businesses).

So what are some examples of "social goals?" Well, it's really anything that is needed to provide humans with basic needs and enhance the human experience:

- Food production
- Clothing and shoe manufacturing
- Food service for schools and hospitals
- Health services
- Child care
- Home design and building
- Cleaning supplies manufacturing
- Bicycle manufacturing
- Furniture manufacturing
- Renewable energy

In this model, everybody working for a given social business earns a living wage and contributes to making the world a better place. Consumers benefit, because since huge profits are not the ultimate goal, prices can be reasonably low. And the environment is better off, because, by definition, a social business will care for the earth and follow these basic principles of responsibility:

1. The business should not put anybody's life in danger.
2. The business should make the planet safer than if the business didn't exist.
3. The business should obey the laws put in place to promote safety and environmental sustainability.[5]

Another widespread business model in our new society is the worker cooperative. In this model, all the workers at a factory or design firm or taxi business are owners and make business decisions together. It is a truly democratic model. There are many types of worker cooperatives in the United States already. Here are just a few examples:

- **Hometown Taxi** (a.k.a. "the friendliest cab service in the Midwest") in my hometown, Decorah, Iowa, operates as a worker cooperative with seven partners.[6]

- **Alvarado Street Bakery**, a worker-owned bakery in Petaluma, California, produces organic whole grain breads and bagels.[7]

- **Design Action Collective**, a worker-owned design firm in Oakland, California, provides new-media services to the social justice movement.[8]

There is even a "US Federation of Worker Cooperatives" organization, which has signed on to the basic standards for worker cooperatives as outlined in the World Declaration on Cooperative Worker Ownership. On their website, they indicate that there are "over 350 democratic workplaces in the United States, employing over 5,000 people and generating over $500 million in annual revenues."[9]

The most important aspect of business in our society is that it is humane. All workers are valued and compensated with a living wage and plenty of time off. Hours are flexible to allow parents to work part-time or from home as needed to care for children. And all workers have a sense of purpose, because they know that the work they are doing is for a good cause. They are putting clothes on people's backs, feeding them, or making them laugh. No job is more important than another. One person's success is everybody's success.

How Business and Ownership Will Change

Let's take a look at how my "favorite" industry, the pharmaceutical industry, might look in our society. First of all, a medical breakthrough is not something an individual should be able to patent or claim as his or her own. If there is ever a cure for AIDS, everybody who suffers from AIDS should have access to this medication. As such, I can see medical research as collaboration between government, academia, and pharmaceutical companies. Research is focused on finding cures to the most devastating illnesses at the time. Right now, examples would be cancer, AIDS, Parkinson's, and Alzheimer's. Research is *not* focused on inventing more of the same, which is what is currently happening in Big Pharma.[10] Once there is a breakthrough, the "recipe" is provided to social businesses, whose employees manufacture the medication and distribute it to pharmacies and hospitals. As in many European countries, our new and improved society has universal healthcare, so anybody who needs the medication gets it. And just like that, the industry saves over $27 billion by not having to advertise,[11] and around $250 million from not having to lobby.[12] I'm thinking this could bring the cost of medication down a bit—that and not having to pay dividends to investors and multi-million dollar salaries to CEOs.

In our society (as it was before European settlers arrived in North America), there are certain things that are not available for ownership. For example, water, fossil fuels, and the air. Rather, the airwaves are governed by the people and cannot be utilized for profit. They are used to communicate, collaborate, and promote the arts. No, we won't take away the TV (my family would not approve), but perhaps we can make it a useful tool rather than a democracy-killer.[13] But we probably won't watch as much, because for one, we know that it isn't good for our children,[14] and we won't have as much need to escape a drab reality. I personally love a good movie, so I'm not saying that we'll avoid digital entertainment, but I doubt that this society would be in favor of television shows and films including violence for the sake of violence or making fun at the expense of others.

One last note before we move on: for years, I've been intrigued by Germany's impressive recycling system. Everybody is involved, from manufacturers, to the government, to citizens. Since 1996, German manufacturers have been required to avoid waste, recycle what little waste they have, and properly dispose of waste that can't be recycled—in a manner that is safe for the environment.[15] In our society, businesses will be required to adhere to the highest standards regarding waste management and pollution. Businesses that have a negative impact on the earth will simply not be allowed to exist. Further, businesses will create durable products, rather than design for obsolescence (that is, planning for the product to break or go out of style quickly to increase demand), which will decrease waste. Humans have lived in harmony with the earth for many thousands of years until the twentieth century, so there is really no reason why we cannot get back to such a state.

A Sharing Economy

In addition to social businesses and worker cooperatives, another important aspect of our society's economy is the *sharing economy*. In a sharing economy (also known as collaborative consumption), participants share products and services—or rent them to each other. On a small scale, it could be something like sharing equipment with your neighbors. For example, our family shares a lawnmower with the family next door. Neighborhoods might organize to have an equipment checkout system. This way, everybody doesn't have to own one of everything.*

Bartering and trading are common and highly encouraged. All of us have special skills that others need. Some of us know how to cut hair. Others know how to fix computers. And others have a green thumb and can work magic in the garden. In our society, we have a system of service exchange that allows us to help each other while using our skills. And no skill is valued more highly than another. A trade is always an hour for an hour.

The sharing economy is already alive and well in the United States through websites such as Couchsurfing, Lyft, TaskRabbit, and Craigslist. If you live in a large-enough city, you can participate in ride-shares, rent out your spare bedroom to tourists, and rent somebody else's time to run errands for you.

Aside from the obvious financial and environmental benefits, one of the best things about the sharing economy is that it builds trust. We have been taught not to trust strangers. However, in the sharing economy, thousands of people are discovering every day that strangers make excellent hosts and taxi drivers. It's an economy worth nurturing and expanding.

---

* The website Nextdoor is one way to organize neighborhood sharing.

Intentional Communities

One of the worst things that ever happened to the United States was the suburb—the sprawled-out, car-dependent, residential "community" that caused a mass exodus from city centers, leaving behind dilapidated buildings and food deserts. I remember walking through the middle- to upper-class suburb where we lived before we moved to Iowa, looking at the big houses with their tall fences, and almost crying because it felt so isolated, so impersonal. I imagined the people living in those houses being trapped behind their big façades, feeling small and alone. I had a vision of barbed wire to keep each family in its home, and strangers out. It made me long for a different kind of community—a community that was designed to minimize our carbon footprint and to foster relationships.

In this visionary society, some people live in the country and farm as a social business (always organic, using permaculture principles) or perhaps as self-sustaining homesteaders. However, others live in urban areas and intentional communities modeled after the Danish cohousing concept. As described in the film *Happy*, in Danish cohousing communities, "multiple families live on a plot of land, or even in a single building, where certain chores and benefits are shared by everyone." In the film, a single mother with three children says that after her divorce, she was isolated, and that "if I had to move in a flat alone, I would go down. I would be depressed. I would isolate." One of the children explains, "It's like a big family. . . . It's very nice, because I have many friends." Another child continues, "It's nice to have grownups who are always looking out for us." The families also eat together almost every evening. Everybody (fourteen and up) takes turns cooking, so it's less of a burden on the individual parents, since they only have to cook once or twice a month.[16]

Cohousing communities can vary in how they are designed and managed, but most have six common characteristics:

1. Members participate in the design of the community.
2. The neighborhood is designed to foster a sense of community.
3. Members share common facilities such as laundry, community gathering space, and guest rooms. Some also have common gardens and equipment.
4. Members manage the properties and surrounding areas.
5. Decisions are made democratically.
6. There is no shared community economy (the community is not a source of income for its members).[17]

By design, cohousing communities are sustainable and encourage social interaction. We know that people who have strong relationships live longer, happier lives. Cohousing communities are the perfect place to build these relationships. And if something bad happens to you, your community is there to support you.

In our new society, communities are designed in such a manner that all community members have easy access to schools, a post office, grocery stores, farmers markets, natural spaces, a library, shops, restaurants, and coffee shops. By easy access, I mean it's safe to walk or bike to these places. Main streets are for pedestrians and bikes only, and cars have to stay on the outskirts of town in parking lots designated for out-of-towners. With such a design, people are nudged to walk more, and it makes for a cleaner, more pleasant environment. (This is how many European towns are designed, so this idea is definitely not utopian.)

A Humane Life Cycle

I've heard people say, "there should be a test you have to pass before you're allowed to be a parent." While I consider comments such as this one elitist and arrogant, it does highlight an important point: Being a parent is by far the most intellectually challenging and emotionally exhausting job on the face of this earth. Yet often, the only thing we have to go on is how our parents raised us. And if that wasn't such a great experience, we basically try to do the opposite. But mostly, we have no clue how to raise a happy, healthy child. Humorist Jenny Isenman agrees:

> As a fairly normal adult with the means to raise a child, I admittedly had no clue what I was doing with my first child . . . I remember leaving the hospital thinking, *He's mine? I own him? You guys trust me to walk out that door and raise a child because I made the obligatory poop and demonstrated my ability to put him in a car seat?*[18]

Although we can't force expectant parents to take classes on child-rearing (and we certainly can't prevent unsuitable parents from procreating—extinction, anyone?), a society designed to optimize mental health would have a comprehensive prenatal support system for expectant mothers and their partners and families. This would include things like parenting classes focused on raising optimistic children, nutritional counseling, childbirth preparation, and natural options for delivery. Pregnancy and childbirth would be more of a social, family-oriented experience than a medical experience (most pregnant women are not sick!).

And when the little one is born, mom is encouraged to breast-feed (if she is able), because breast milk is by far the best food for infants. It provides essential nutrients, protects the child from illness, and protects mom from certain cancers, obesity, and postpartum depression. Beyond the health benefits, it saves money and is better for the environment (no waste). In this society, breast-feeding is socially accepted. Moms don't get weird stares when they nurse in public, because it's a natural way to feed a baby.

To encourage breast-feeding and allow parents to bond with their baby, both moms and dads are allowed to take parental leave when a baby is born or adopted. It's so important for parents to spend lots of time touching and holding the baby, responding quickly to her needs, and for the child to feel secure and loved. A low-stress pregnancy and a secure infancy set the stage for optimal mental health.

As the child is weaned from the breast, her diet is replaced by organic whole foods prepared in such a way that the baby can eat them. There is no such thing as "baby food" (sorry, Gerber). Babies eat mashed-up versions of whatever the rest of the family is eating. This will ensure that she develops sophisticated taste buds and doesn't become a picky eater. Kids are never forced to eat everything on their plate. Rather, parents and caregivers allow them to listen to their built-in hunger and satiety cues. And we have a culture of eating meals together—breakfast, lunch, afternoon tea, and supper—rather than snacking throughout the day.

Parents have a number of options for childcare. They may choose to organize their work in such a way that the child can be raised at home. They may also consider joining a childcare cooperative, where parents take turns caring for the children. Some parents might choose a more traditional childcare setting where well-compensated, compassionate caretakers practice positive childrearing, all toys and other equipment from furniture to art supplies are made from natural materials, organic whole-food meals are prepared on-site, children spends lots of time outdoors in unstructured playtime (discovering, building, climbing, running, resting), and, best of all, everybody can afford to enroll their kids. Obviously, this means that the government must subsidize a portion of the cost, but I really can't think of a better use of government money than giving all kids a fair shot at a healthy and happy life.

At home, parents are not their children's servants (any fellow servants out there?). But they are not slave drivers either. Rather, all family members chip in to keep the household running smoothly: cooking, cleaning, washing dishes, doing laundry, walking the dog, feeding the dog, grocery shopping, paying bills, gardening, etc. When kids learn practical skills and are allowed responsibility, their self-esteem improves. And parents are less exhausted. (*And* the dog gets fed.) Mealtimes are sacred, because everybody knows that regular family meals help parents engage with their children and keep teens out of trouble.

When a child reaches adolescence, our mental-health-optimized society ushers him into adulthood through a meaningful and supportive rite of passage. The nature of the coming-of-age ceremony will depend on the family's religious and cultural background, but there is something for everyone. Surrounding the rite of passage is a support network that envelops the adolescent as he makes the difficult transition from childhood to adulthood.

In our current sink-or-swim culture, this is the time when many kids get lost. They suffer in silence, not knowing if their emotions and erratic behaviors are normal or pathological. They start drinking, smoking marijuana, and engaging in self-harming activities such as cutting. By the time the adults in their lives figure out that they are hurting, these kids are so entrenched in depression that medication seems like the only option.

In our "utopia," adolescents have mentors to guide them through the years between puberty and leaving home. These mentors may include a favorite uncle or aunt, neighbors, clergy, teachers, craftspeople, and coaches. Imagine a world where every teen had a team of caring adults watching over her journey into adulthood. What a difference it would make!

Grandparents living with young families can also make a huge difference. Rather than shipping the elderly off to retirement homes, the norm is to invite parents and grandparents come live with their families or in close proximity. This is good for the well-being of both the elderly *and* the families. The older generation gets a boost from feeling safe and needed (having a sense of purpose). And the younger generation benefits from the wisdom, support (grandparents are good at *a lot* of things), and love of the older generation. And when retirement and nursing homes are a necessity, they are combined with daycare centers and schools so cross-generational interactions, learning, and bonding can still take place.

Death is considered a normal part of life, and as often as possible, people are allowed to die in the comfort of their own homes, without aggressive medical intervention, if that is the wish of the dying person and her family. We take our time to say goodbye to loved ones. We cry out loud. We hold each other.

We remember happy moments and smile. We are present with our grief and are allowed to feel sad—for a long time, if needed. Our loved ones are laid to rest in an ecologically responsible manner, which means a natural burial, void of chemicals and non-compostable materials—or cremated, based on their wishes or the wishes of the families, if there was no will.

A Brief Note on Education

I will address education in more detail in chapter 20, but it is just too important not to include at least a few paragraphs about it in this chapter as well.

The most important thing about public education in our new society is that it offers consistent quality learning for *all* children, based on their needs and interests. This is not achieved through suffocating standards and rigorous testing, but rather through empowering highly educated teachers to assist children with the learning process in a child-centered learning environment. As well-known author Alfie Kohn points out, students should not be viewed as "empty glasses into which information can be poured."[19] Rather, the teacher's role is to spark curiosity, facilitate learning, and model critical thinking. And school is not just about "book learning." Rather, education is designed for the whole child—and emotional and social learning are considered just as important as reading, writing, and arithmetic.

I envision a school where academic learning is interspersed with hands-on, practical learning, such as sewing, woodworking, gardening, baking, and fixing bikes. Children and adults cook real food together, eat together, and clean up together. Lunchtime is considered an important learning opportunity, rather than a chore that should be rushed. Music and the arts are valued and encouraged. In addition, students spend significant time outside exploring woods, prairies, and creeks. By getting to know the natural world, children are more likely to grow up to be ecologically responsible adults. Being in nature is also good for mental health and can alleviate attention and other behavior problems we associate with the diagnoses of ADHD and oppositional defiant disorder.

Excellent education comes with a price tag. But again, I can't think of a better use of tax dollars than preparing children for a happy, healthy, and purposeful life.

⚜

Health-Promoting Care

Even in a society optimized for wellness, people will get sick (or at least I'm assuming that's the case, but who knows?). Mostly, we spend time promoting health and preventing illness. This starts when children are born, by making sure they are cared for and properly nourished, and continues at school, with healthy food, self-care education, and promoting a fitness-for-life mentality. Workplaces encourage behaviors that promote wellness, such as walking and biking to work, flexible work hours, frequent stretch breaks, nursing rooms, space for meditation and yoga, and purposeful work.

When people get seriously ill, they receive health-promoting, integrated care. This means they have a team of professionals, from nurses, to physicians, to mental health counselors, to yoga teachers, to mindfulness-based stress reduction practitioners, to acupuncturists. The members of this team all have one thing in common: the patient's best interest. They are not driven by profits or worrying about whether or not a specific procedure will be covered by the patient's health insurance, because health care is free or close to free for everyone. After all, medical care is a *human right* according to the United Nations's Universal Declaration of Human Rights, Article 25.[20]

I don't know about you, but I'd give a lot to live in a society designed to optimize mental health. And I'd give even more to provide my daughter and her hypothetical children and grandchildren with the opportunity to live in such a society.

17

✿

Creating a Culture of Enough

*The world has enough for everyone's need, but
not enough for everyone's greed.*

—Mahatma Gandhi

When I started working in Corporate America in 2002, I didn't have any
world-changing plans. My main priorities were to earn a decent living, take
care of my family, stay healthy and fit, and enjoy life. I never dreamed of fast
cars or a mansion, but I longed for the day when we could afford a slightly
larger house and have enough money to visit my family in Sweden every year.

I was a good worker. I completed tasks quickly and took initiative. After
less than a year, I received my first promotion and pay raise. As my role at
the company became increasingly demanding, I started working longer hours.
While I had started at forty-five hours per week (company policy), I soon found
myself working fifty to sixty hours each week, taking work home with me every
weekend. I became obsessed with my work, which led to additional promotions, but wasn't good for my family or my overall well-being. I was like the
antagonists in Hollywood workaholic conversion stories such as *Elf* and *Up
in the Air.*

When I was promoted to product manager, Todd and I decided we had
enough money to buy a bigger house. I fell in love with a 2,800-square-foot
home with a view of downtown Nashville. It was way more space than we
needed, but we had the money, so why not? After filling our house with IKEA
furniture (I am Swedish, after all), we hosted a housewarming party for friends

and colleagues. Everybody loved our house, and I loved being able to have so many friends over at one time. While resting on a couch after the party, a straggling guest (a free-spirited colleague from New Zealand) said something that will stick with me always: "Congratulations! You have achieved the American Dream. You have this great big house and no time to spend in it." It hit me in my core. Wow—yes, that had happened. I had become trapped in the corporate hamster wheel, running faster and faster and faster.

While I didn't do anything about my hamster wheel situation immediately, my colleague had planted a seed in my brain—an idea that perhaps something was wrong with the picture that was my life.

Not long thereafter, I stumbled across the simple-living blog *Zen Habits,* by Leo Babauta. This blog changed my life forever. Literally. Leo (and guest bloggers) wrote about how to slow down,[1] how to declutter your life,[2] minimalism,[3] and other fascinating topics. Reading this blog quickly became the favorite part of my day, and it led me to explore a whole new world of voluntary simplicity literature such as *Simple Prosperity* by David Wann, *Radical Simplicity* by Jim Merkel, and *Your Money or Your Life* by Vicky Robin and Joe Dominguez. The following opening paragraph from *Radical Simplicity* gave me the perspective I needed to realize that life wasn't just about me and my family having enough—it was about *everybody* having enough:

> Imagine you are at a potluck buffet and see that you are the first in line. How do you know how much to take? Imagine that this potluck spread includes not just food and water, but also the materials needed for shelter, clothing, healthcare and education. It all looks and smells so good and you are hungry. What will you heap on your plate? How much is enough to leave for your neighbors behind you in the line?

Until this point, I had never considered that shopping for fun might negatively impact the earth and other human beings (think sweatshops). I happily threw away plastic grocery bags, not realizing that it would take hundreds if not thousands of years for them to break down. I had never stopped to think about how much of the world's resources I was using up while others used barely any. Yes, of course I thought (occasionally) about the fact that people around the world were starving, but only when I heard about it on TV, and then only fleetingly. It seemed like something beyond my reach to address. Anyway, I was busy building software to help big box retailers increase their profits, so when would I have time to save the planet or work toward ending world hunger?

But once I got clued in to the tenets of sustainable living, I started making personal changes. Some were small changes, like bringing cloth bags to the grocery store and getting rid of unnecessary clutter. Other changes were bigger, like creating a philanthropy plan for the year and attempting to buy mostly organic and local food. But the biggest change of all, my 2009 New Year's resolution, was to stop buying clothes unless I really, really needed them. I wasn't a compulsive shopper or anything, but the idea of buying based on *need* rather than *want* was revolutionary to me. When I recapped this experience on my blog at the end of the year, I wrote that the only clothing items I bought were a pair of athletic shorts, two workout shirts, and a pair of SmartWool socks.[4] So that was a success, but more importantly, I realized that I enjoyed *not* buying clothes unless absolutely necessary. I enjoyed it so much, in fact, that I decided to apply this idea to all my buying—inspired by Judith Levine, author of *Not Buying It: My Year Without Shopping*—and haven't looked back.

The moral of this story is that people can change—even software executives caught up in the cycle of working harder, making more money, and buying bigger and better stuff. I think many of us come to a point in our lives when we realize that the material world is not what matters. We start to recognize how messed up it is to buy so much stuff that we need to buy bigger houses or rent additional storage space to be able to keep it. We also discover that having a lot of stuff sucks up our energy and resources. Every new thing we bring into our home takes up space, it malfunctions, it goes into the dumpster—and beyond that, we don't want to know what happens to it. And we realize that we have enough. We are content with what we have, because we know that by owning less, we save money, save time, and, most importantly, help save the planet. So why are most of us still consuming at a rate that is detrimental to the health of the planet?

A Culture of Consumerism

We live in a culture of consumerism. It started with the Industrial Revolution, which enabled manufacturers to mass-produce products at affordable cost and transformed the household from a site of production to a site of consumption. What used to be produced in the household was increasingly getting "outsourced" to factories. As these products became available to the average person, we started consuming more—because we could. And since corporations must experience constant economic growth, the leadership of these companies hired marketers ("Mad Men") to create demand for new models of products. We started buying new products even if the old products still worked just fine. Fashion is perhaps the most obvious example of this (bell-bottoms, anyone?), but also interior design ("Eeww! That '70s wallpaper will have to go!"), automobiles ("Why would I drive last year's model when the new one has rain-sensing wipers?"), and, of course, electronics ("Yes, I will upgrade my fully functioning phone to get Touch ID."). This was one side of the "planned obsolescence" coin of industrial design, the other being the design of poor-quality products intended to break after a certain period of time. ("They just don't make things the way they used to.")

Here's the thing, though: mass consumerism didn't *really* take off until after World War II. In fact, during the war, it was fashionable to be frugal. Posters during this time proclaimed: "Use It Up – Wear It Out – Make It Do!" and "All Fuel Is Scarce – Plan For Winter Now!" People were encouraged to grow their own food and eat just enough—and save the leftovers. We were doing so well! Then the war ended, and we celebrated by consuming more than any culture at any time in history had ever consumed—and we haven't stopped.

It got even worse after 9/11 and the financial crisis that followed. A free market (capitalism) depends on spending. Consumers must spend, so factories can keep cranking out stuff, so that our neighbors can keep their jobs. That's why President George W. Bush and his brother Jeb Bush made statements such as "we need to respond quickly so people regain confidence and consider it their patriotic duty to go shopping, go to a restaurant, take a cruise, travel with their family. Frankly, the terrorists win if Americans don't go back to normalcy."[5] All of a sudden, being frugal wasn't just weird; it was unpatriotic—un-American.

I remember arriving at a company board meeting in Atlanta, Georgia, during the 2007–2009 recession, noting to a board member that I had to stop by the mall to buy a belt (I had forgotten to pack the one black belt I owned). He congratulated me on doing my patriotic shopping duty—and he wasn't being sarcastic. This consumerism-as-civic-duty mentality has slipped into Europe and other developed nations as well. Nina Björk laments the fact that it is acceptable to dream about designer sunglasses, a remodeled kitchen, and luxury vacations, but it is *not* acceptable to dream about a different, more sustainable economic system.[6]

⚜

An Unsustainable Economic Model

Mass consumerism and continued economic growth are not sustainable.[7] Think about it. With ongoing accelerated production and consumption, we use more and more of the earth's resources. And the earth isn't getting any larger. We are depleting fossil fuel, lumber, and topsoil at an alarming rate. We are polluting the water and the air. Just this week, the average atmospheric carbon dioxide values reached an all-time high of 401.33 parts per million—the highest they've been in human history.[8] We create an enormous amount of waste (4.3 pounds per day per person)[9] and, according to the World Wide Fund for Nature, we are losing at least ten thousand species each year (some we don't even know about).[10] So the prognosis is not good for the planet, and if we're not careful, we might end up being one of the species to disappear. Further, our consumerism in the West doesn't leave enough resources for the rest of the world's population. What I learned from Jim Merkel is that if we divided up the Earth's bioproductive land among all the people in the world, we would get 4.7 acres each (and of course, we'd need to share some of that with the animals).[11] However, that was 11 years ago, and the world's population was 6 billion. Now we have 7.2 billion people, so that number is closer to 3.9 acres. The average American has an ecological footprint of 24 acres.[12] That's more than six times our allotment, if we are to consider ourselves part of a global community. Indeed, our planet is currently 20 percent overpopulated based on consumption versus resources.[13]

Not sustainable.

There Is A Better Way

We have all been tricked into thinking that we need more than we really do. It's called marketing. It happens to me when I get the latest Athleta catalog in the mail. Suddenly, I feel like I *really* need a new pair of yoga pants and maybe a cute yoga hoodie, even though I already have a perfectly fine pair of yoga pants and several hoodies (albeit not designed specifically for post-yoga wear). Simultaneously, I start feeling bad about my body and wishing that I looked like the athletic models on the colorful pages. Then I take a deep breath and walk over to the coat closet and toss the damned catalog in the blue bin we use for paper recycling.

Advertisers spent approximately $140 billion in 2013 to make sure that we remain discontent—unhappy with everything in our lives: our bodies, our hair, our clothes, our kitchen appliances, our cars, even our significant others.[14] But we don't have to be victims of the advertising of wants. We can learn to recognize when we're being influenced by ads, whether on TV, in a newspaper, or on Twitter. But most importantly, we need to find contentment. We need to realize that we have everything we need. We need to create a culture of enough.

The good news is that there is already a voluntary simplicity and minimalism movement in our country. Bloggers such as Leo Babauta (*Zen Habits*), Joshua Fields Millburn and Ryan Nicodemus (*The Minimalists*), Joshua Becker (*Becoming Minimlist*), and Tammy Strobel (*Rowdy Kittens*) reach millions of readers with the message that living a meaningful life is so much more important than collecting money and stuff. The folks at the Tumbleweed Tiny House Company have started a downsizing revolution with their tiny house plans and workshops. And The Center for a New American Dream "helps Americans to reduce and shift their consumption to improve quality of life, protect the environment, and promote social justice."[15] By consuming only what we need and selecting locally produced, responsibly manufactured, recyclable, high-quality products, we can become part of this movement and show the world that less is truly more.

Consuming only what we need and sharing the world's resources in a sustainable manner is the foundation upon which a society optimized for mental health is built. Beyond preventing the unhappiness and psychological problems that may stem from materialistic values,[16] when we adopt the value of enough, we are freed from the stress of working long hours to buy bigger and better possessions. As a result, we don't pass that stress on to our kids. We can spend time every day taking care of ourselves—and not feel guilty about it. It gives us the freedom to pursue our passions and find meaningful occupation. Further, it allows us to prioritize the health of our children and all the things that go along with that, such as bonding with our babies, preserving natural spaces, providing opportunities for exploration and creativity, and finding ways to adapt environments to children's needs versus the other way around (and I'm not talking about Go-GURT and fast-food playgrounds).

Taking Action and Spreading the Word

If we are to create a culture of enough, we must take these two steps:

1. Adopt the value of enough in our own lives.
2. Share the benefits of simple living with our friends, family, and coworkers (without judging or coming across as a know-it-all).

Adopting the Value of Enough

As you can tell, I get immense enjoyment from reading about voluntary simplicity and sustainability. I love reading about people who move off the grid, grow all their own food (or source it locally), become "No Impact Man," reduce their carbon footprint to a single digit, and move into tiny houses built on trailers. These people are admirable and show us how simple and sustainable life could be—and used to be.

But I also recognize that for most people living in our current mass-producing, over-consuming, debt-ridden, competition-focused world, making such drastic changes is not possible or practical, at least not in the short term. So I challenge you to do what you can right now—today. Here are some ideas:

- Make a decision to buy only what you need—or really, really love.
- Eat mostly real food (not processed/packaged food-like substances).
- Bike, walk, or ride the bus or train instead of driving a car.
- Patronize brands and businesses that are truly trying to make the world a better place.
- Find ways to trade services, and trade, share, reuse, and repair goods.
- Realize that you don't have to be involved in everything. In fact, you'll be more effective (and less stressed) if you do less.

As I mentioned above, it comes down to contentment. This you must arrive at on your own. However, I can highly recommend *The Little Book of Contentment* by Leo Babauta to point you in the right direction. And I am confident that once you start implementing some of these "enoughness" ideas, you will realize that you're actually happier without all the stuff, and its accompanying hassle and overcommitments. You might find that you have extra money available in your checking account every month and that you have to take the trash out less frequently. You will experience a new level of gratitude for the necessities you do have and find time to do nice things for others. And if you implement the biking and walking idea, you may even lose some weight.

(Not that you need to…) It will be awesome! So awesome, in fact, that you'll want to spread the word to everybody you know.

Sharing the Benefits of Simple Living

When I wear my marketing consulting hat, I often say, "word of mouth is alive and well." What I mean by that is while it's important to have an up-to-date, useful website, most people are not going to buy your product, hire you, or sign up for your program because you have a shiny new website or they saw an ad on Google. Rather, they will explore your products or services because they *talked* to somebody who had a great experience with your product or working with you. We trust information we get from friends and family—and even strangers writing reviews on websites—*way* more than we trust information we get from businesses and organizations through advertising.

Word of mouth applies to ideas and societal change as well—perhaps even more so. We could advertise the benefits of simple living on TV, radio, and on the Internet, but that would not convince many, if any, people to take action. A better option is to live a life of contentment, to show and tell others how amazing it is, and to encourage friends and family to embrace the value of enough in their own lives. I have led workshops on the topic of creating space in your life through simple living, and I can tell you that people are ready for this message. They are ready to simplify, eliminate mindless shopping, and reduce both physical and mental clutter. They are ready to think about buying food that doesn't come packaged in future trash and to find other ways to reduce their carbon footprints.

You might consider creating a book club on the topic of voluntary simplicity and read and discuss some of the books I mentioned above.* And if you're chomping at the bit to do some community educating around simple living and the resulting happier, healthier life, read Cecile Andrews's classic *The Circle of Simplicity: Return to the Good Life* for ideas on how to start a "Simplicity Circle" or what she now calls a "Community Happiness Circle." The point being that voluntary simplicity is not "a life of 'self deprivation.'" Rather, "it is a turning away from activities that have failed to deliver satisfaction—activities such as shopping and scrambling up the career ladder—in order to embrace activities that bring true joy and meaning—creativity, community, and the celebration of daily life."[17] Andrews's latest book, *Living Room Revolution: A Handbook for Conversation, Community and the Common Good,* is another great resource.

---

*Additional suggestions are available in the "For Further Exploration" section at the back of the book.

It "provides a practical toolkit of concrete strategies to facilitate personal and social change by bringing people together in community and conversation." Andrews emphasizes that social change has to start at the local level: "local starts with small groups, meeting in places like people's living rooms, cafes, meeting rooms and auditoriums."[18]

We also can't escape the fact that the Internet can be a channel for enacting change. As much as I prefer *not* to spend my precious free time in front of a screen, I appreciate the power of connections and an online community. If spending some time online will result in positive social change, perhaps it's worth it. Change.org, where anyone can create a petition and encourage friends, family, and strangers to support their cause, is a great example. Recent victories include the Boy Scouts voting to allow openly gay young men to earn their Eagle awards,[19] United Airlines replacing Styrofoam cups on flights,[20] and Pepsi and Coca-Cola removing an ingredient called BVO, a flame retardant that has been banned in Europe and Japan.[21] Other social movements online include Occupy Wall Street, with over 170,000 followers on Twitter and over 600,000 likes on Facebook, and ThinkProgress, with over 314,000 Twitter followers and over a million likes on Facebook.

However, all this progressive activity on the Internet is primarily preaching to the choir and has counter-movements with just as big a following. I think the real key is for all of us who believe that health and happiness is more important than money and stuff to live it, share it, and plant seeds among our family, friends, and coworkers. It could be something as simple as posting an AdBusters link about "Buy Nothing Day" on Facebook, or pinning an infographic about reducing, reusing, and recycling on Pinterest.[22] But most of all, we must emphasize the *benefits* of a simpler lifestyle, like the Center for a New American Dream did with their "More Fun, Less Stuff" campaign.[23]

With time, simplicity will not be voluntary, because we won't have a choice. But let's not wait until we're plumb out of resources—let's start embracing a culture of enough *now* and let those around us know how sweet it is.

18

❧

Establishing a Just Republic

*In the United States we have an unfortunate tradition of separating
our work and our politics. Or, more specifically, of treating our work
practice as if it were essentially non-political. This is, of course, an
illusion. All work is political. All mental health assessments and
interventions are political. The job of progressive health care activists
is, first, to recognize the political nature of everything we do, and
secondly, to seek out and practice those forms of politics that will ensure
the best possible health care system for all people everywhere.*

—Dawn Belkin Martinez, "Mental Health Care After Capitalism," *Radical Psychology*

In early May 2013, I attended a weekend-long workshop called "Becoming We
the People," led by Paul Cienfuegos, a regional leader in the Community Rights
movement and a partner with Community Environmental Legal Defense
Fund, and community song leader Laurence Cole.

The weekend kicked off with a potluck on Friday evening in the basement
of the local United Church of Christ church. Most people in attendance were
those I usually associate with the "crunchy crowd"—people who have been
practicing simple living for years, live off the grid, grow their own food, and
homeschool their kids. The group also included social justice activists, musi-
cians, college students, and people generally interested in making the world a
better place. After dinner and a few songs, we dove into the core of the workshop—learning about the history of corporate rule and our rights as citizens. It
opened my eyes as no other workshop has opened my eyes before.

I learned that not too long ago, the United States had very strict corporate laws. Indeed, after the American Revolution, incorporation was a time-bound *privilege* that was granted to very specific projects intended to benefit the public, for example building a bridge or a railroad. This privilege was granted through a charter, which could be revoked if the corporate leaders violated any laws. Corporate leaders had to reapply to renew their charter, which would only be granted if the corporate mission was still deemed to benefit the public. And, most importantly, corporations could not spend money to influence politics.[1]

That all sounded great to me, so I wondered how we got from there to where we are now—a country governed by the corporate elite. Of course, Paul had the answers. He told us about significant legislative developments that led us to where we are today, including the Dartmouth Decision of 1819, which established constitutional protections for corporations for the first time in US history; the Supreme Court decision in 1886 that led to corporations having the same rights as persons in the 14th Amendment to the Constitution, which was really designed to protect freed slaves;[2] and, of course, the 2010 Supreme Court case *Citizens United v. Federal Election Commission*, which allowed corporations to use *unlimited*, undisclosed funds to influence our elections and legislation under the guise of free speech.

It was a lot to process. We were all frustrated, but also determined to learn more about what we could do to improve the situation. Most importantly, it reminded me why pharmaceutical companies are allowed to keep doing what they're doing. Between lobbying (the pharmaceuticals and health-products lobby spends the most money of any lobby on Capitol Hill every year—$226 million in 2013 alone),[3] election contributions, and revolving doors (former federal employees taking jobs with special interest groups and consulting with big business),[4] Big Pharma has our elected government officials wrapped around its little finger. This "undue influence over government" is the very definition of *big* business.[5] Corporations should not be able to influence our elected officials' decisions.*

I could go into lots of detail about all the ways our current form of corporate-ruled government is *not* in the best interest of all people, but I will stick with this grim summary by Jeff Clements, author of *Corporations Are Not People*, of the results of the last thirty years of campaigning for corporate

---

* When I talk about corporations in this section, I am referring to corporations that have so much money and power that, when left unchecked, they can sway our government to make decisions that are in favor of corporate shareholders, but not necessarily in all people's best interest.

rights and power:

> Massive job outsourcing abroad; destruction of our manufacturing
> capacity; wage stagnation for the vast majority of Americans and
> unprecedented enrichment of the very few; uncontrolled military
> spending and endless wars to secure energy supplies from a
> region from which we should have cut our dependence long ago;
> out-of-control healthcare spending at the same time that millions
> of people cannot get health care at all; bloated and unsustainable
> budgets and debt at every level of government; national and
> global environmental crisis; loss of wilderness and open land, and
> the takeover of public hunting and fishing grounds; chain store
> sprawl and gutting of local economies and communities; obesity,
> asthma, and public health epidemics; and a growing sense that the
> connection between Americans and our government has been lost.[6]

"The agenda of the largest corporations," Clements reminds us, "will never
be the agenda of the American family and the American community."[7] Rather,
many corporate leaders will go to extreme lengths to protect the bottom
line—including sucking the planet dry of its resources and leaving a trail of
layoffs, poverty, and mental distress in their path. They have a responsibility to
the shareholders to achieve constant growth, and if they don't, they get fired.[8]
What's ironic is that this greedy attitude is not socially acceptable in any other
part of society. As the short film *The Story of Citizens United v. FEC* points
out, you wouldn't leave your child with someone who says "all I care about is
money."[9] Yet for some reason we continue to give corporate leaders leeway to
behave however they want, even though it clashes with our value system. This
is a significant moral dilemma.

Politics Affect Everything

But enough about the problems. We're here to talk about solutions—how
to optimize children's mental health through policy changes.

"Wait, what?" you may be thinking. "What do policy changes have to do
with mental health?"

Everything.

Politics affect *everything* in our lives. And when I say politics, I don't mean
Republican versus Democrat or gun rights versus gun control or pro-life versus pro-choice. Let's move beyond that and think about politics in a larger
sense—how it affects everything from our children's education to access to
holistic health care to parents' ability to put food on the table, factors that all

play a role in children's mental health outcomes. It is impossible to avoid the topic of politics and have an honest discussion about mental health. Indeed, any book that attempts to address mental health but ignores the politics of it is a fairy tale. So stay with me!

Between lobbying and campaign-bashing, we have forgotten that politics is supposed to be about serving the common good—or to "promote the general welfare," to quote the Preamble to the US Constitution. What would constitute "common good" as it relates to children's mental health? Guaranteeing parental leave for all new parents. Ensuring that no child has to go hungry or worry about where they're going to sleep tonight. Pulling families out of poverty and creating safe neighborhoods. Providing student-centered, holistic education to all children. Creating and preserving natural spaces so all children can experience unstructured play. Restructuring the mental health system to take profits out of the equation. (The list goes on...)

As we continue our discussion, keep in mind this connection between policy and our ability to optimize children's mental health. Mental health is a social concern as much as it is an individual concern. And currently, policy is dictated by a handful of wealthy, mostly white, mostly male owners of giant corporations pursuing their individual interests—more money and power. Unless we change this structure, our politicians cannot serve the common good.

So how do we go about upgrading our country from an unjust oligarchy (where power rests with a small number of privileged people) to a just republic (where power rests with the people via fairly elected citizen representatives)?[10] In the remainder of this chapter, I will describe four important changes people are *already working on* and describe how we as individuals can help make these changes happen:

- **Get corporate money out of politics,** because as long as big business can keep buying our elected officials and swaying legislative decisions, the corporate elite will continue to control our country—and we saw the awful results above, including public health epidemics, gutting local communities, environmental crisis, loss of wilderness, and disenchantment, which all impact mental health.

- **Hold corporations accountable,** because it is our right and duty.[11] Yes, it is our duty as citizens to ensure that corporations serve the public and not the other way around. Corporations should exist for good, not for greed.

- **Discontinue corporate welfare subsidies,** because this is money that could be used to optimize children's mental health through parental leave, high-quality school food, protection of natural areas, and more resources in education to accommodate all children's various learning styles.

- **Raise minimum wage to a living wage,** because it's the right thing to do, and it will improve parents' ability to raise mentally healthy kids by removing the stress of financial hardship—which is considered a traumatic experience—from childhood.[12]

Get Corporate Money Out Of Politics

Until that workshop with Paul in the spring of 2013, I had no idea that corporations have the same constitutional rights as citizens. Honestly, it sounded like a bad joke. Why in the world would corporations be protected in the same way people are protected by our constitution? Of course, it all comes down to money. Big corporations don't want to have to deal with regulations, and they want to be able to influence government decisions and spending in their favor. We have an unsustainable economic system that requires constant economic growth.[13] In order for corporations to make that happen, they need to have the government on their side.

Thanks to the precedent set in 1886, Citizens United was able to argue that corporations should have freedom of speech like anybody else. And freedom of speech was interpreted to include spending money on propaganda or any other mechanisms to sway people to vote one way or another. This led to the 2010 midterm elections being the most expensive elections in history with a total spend of $4 billion.[14] What's the point of trying to stay informed when you can't trust what you hear on TV and radio? And what's the point of voting when you know that most candidates are bought by big business? (I'm assuming that's what some of the 58 percent no-shows at the 2010 general election wondered, anyway.)[15]

Based on this, one of the first steps to get corporate money out of politics must be to reverse *Citizens United* and declare that corporations are not persons.[16] Several groups, including "Free Speech for People" (co-founded by Jeff Clements) and "Move to Amend" (a coalition of organizations and individuals) have proposed versions of a 28th Amendment to the Constitution to address these very topics. You can read these amendments online and determine if you would like to add your name to the list of supporters and maybe even get involved with this cause. These organizations' websites also include lists of state resolutions in support of amending the constitution and a number of related proposed amendments introduced by various members of Congress, such as Senators Patrick Leahy (Democrat of Vermont) and Tom Udall (Democrat of New Mexico).[17]

Is it difficult to get enough votes to institute a new amendment? You bet.* But we've done it before—twenty-seven times, in fact. And we can do it again. The very best way to make it happen is to become an involved citizen, understand the platforms of the political candidates in your city and state, vote for candidates who are more likely to support such an amendment, and encourage others to do the same. It's going to take a lot of us!

In addition to reversing *Citizens United* and corporate personhood, we need to create laws that regulate election funding and prevent excessive lobbying—or what Clements accurately calls "corporate bribery and corruption of government"[18]—and other shady practices, such as the "revolving door" problem noted above. The website OpenSecrets.org has a wealth of information about money's influence on US elections and public policy, including the amount of money spent on lobbying (over $3 billion each year), revolving door examples, and contributions by Political Action Committees or PACs ($1.4 billion in 2103). Imagine if all this money were used for the greater good! In my opinion, the fairest campaign-funding model would be to give each candidate a certain amount of money and airwaves (ad spots) using tax dollars. It would give all candidates a fair shot.

A more popular idea currently being pursued is the small-donor public financing model. A version of this model is outlined in the Fair Elections Now Act (H.R. 269), reintroduced in the House of Representatives by Congressman John Yarmuth (Democrat of Kentucky), along with fifty-two original co-sponsors, on January 15, 2013. According to the organization Public Campaign's website, "the bill would allow federal candidates to choose to run for office without relying on large contributions, big money bundlers, or donations from lobbyists, and would be freed from the constant fundraising in order to focus on what people in their communities want."[19] What a concept! So what can we as individuals do to help move this along? First, educate yourself on the issue. The websites mentioned above include lots of great information. You should

---

* On September 11, 2014, all forty-two Senate Republicans voted against advancing Senator Udall's constitutional amendment on campaign spending, effectively blocking this important amendment (the senate requires sixty votes to advance amendments).

also find out if public campaign financing is in place—or is being suggested—at the local level where you live. Second, stay up to date on developments related to bills supporting public financing so you can make your voice heard when it matters. Third, tell your friends. People need to know there is a better—and fairer—way.

Hold Corporations Accountable

Once we have Big Money out of politics, it will be easier to hold corporations accountable through legislation, but we don't have to wait until then to take action. In *Corporations Are Not People*, Jeff Clements suggests two principles to guide corporate law reform:

1. "Incorporation is a privilege," which means that we should hold corporations to high standards, make sure they serve the public interest, and not let them get away with harming the planet or its inhabitants.[20]

2. "Incorporation is a national or international matter," which means that when a corporation reaches a certain size, it should be regulated at the national or international level, not by a single state, such as Delaware.[21]

Clements further explains that most states (even Delaware) still have laws that allow for revocation of corporate charters, which can be put into effect if the leaders of the corporation don't play nice. Clements's organization Free Speech for People has actually requested a charter revocation in conjunction with Appalachian Voices regarding Massey Energy Company, "based on its criminal and immoral conduct as a corporation."[22] But Clements also encourages new legislation "to modernize the corporation to serve our present needs."[23]

One such exciting modernization that's happening right now is a new type of corporation called a "Benefit Corporation" (not to be confused with B Corporation, which is a certification, kind of like Fair Trade or Certified Organic). This is a legal status, which is available in twenty-seven states as of this writing. Fourteen additional states are working on it. These laws give business leaders and investors "new freedom to make decisions that are in the best interests of society as well as their bottom line."[24] According to the Benefit Corporation website, benefit corporations

> 1) have a corporate purpose to create a material positive
> impact on society and the environment; 2) are required to

consider the impact of their decisions not only on shareholders
but also on workers, community, and the environment;
and 3) are required to make available to the public an
annual benefit report that assesses their overall social and
environmental performance against a third party standard.[25]

This is the closest thing we have to the social business model I outlined in chapter 16, and it's a big deal! I have a dream that there will come a day when benefit corporations are the norm, because consumers demand it. The best way to make change happen is to "B the change," per the B Corporation slogan. If you are a business owner, find out if Benefit Corporation is a legal status in your state. As a consumer, support these businesses and other businesses whose owners strive to make the world a better place, avoid big business, and be mindful about where you spend your hard-earned money as you work toward making just corporate laws happen.

Discontinue Corporate Welfare Subsidies

If you are still with me after reading the above subtitle, I applaud you. (And I wouldn't blame you if your eyes just glazed over.) Government subsidy is a big, complicated, and not very sexy topic. So I will try to keep it short and sweet and get to the point. First let's clear up a few things. Government subsidies (for example, grants, interest-free loans, tax breaks, and insurance) are not inherently bad. When used appropriately, they can help small farms survive a disastrous year, support the arts, and encourage entrepreneurs to create businesses that generate renewable energy. When we talk about "corporate welfare" subsidies, we're talking about money (tax dollars) given directly or indirectly to profitable corporations, many which are not necessarily making the world a better place (think Monsanto, Bank of America, and Chevron).

Recent online news and blog headlines hint at some of the problems with corporate welfare and why we should be considering other options:

- "Government Spends More on Corporate Welfare Subsidies than Social Welfare Programs"[26]
- "Should We Subsidize Multinationals or Repair Our Infrastructure?"[27]
- "Fossil Fuels Receive $500 Billion A Year In Government Subsidies Worldwide"[28]
- "General Electric Avoids Taxes By Keeping $108 Billion Overseas"[29]
- "Average American Families Pays $6K a Year in Big Business Subsidies"[30]

Governments at all levels (federal, state, county, city) are spending money on the wrong things, and we, as taxpayers, are paying for it, while most multinationals pay little to no taxes.

According to *The New York Times'* "United States of Subsidies" interactive database, cities, counties, and states dole out $80.4 billion in business subsidies each year. One might expect these incentives to go to eco-focused startups, organic farmers, social enterprises, and renewable energy—that is, initiatives that have promise of making a positive societal and environmental impact. And some do. However, when I click on my home state, Iowa (a small piece of the pie), I see incentives to, among others, John Deere ($76.4 million), DuPont ($57.5 million), and Monsanto ($23.2 million). Last time I checked, these companies were doing quite well.[31] Perhaps the incentives are keeping these businesses in Iowa, providing high-quality jobs for Iowans. However, herein lies the problem, right? Corporations are so driven by the bottom line that they will follow the money, even if it means handing the local workforce a pink slip.* What if there were no money to be followed? What if this money were spent on education, preventive health care, and conservation of natural spaces instead?

Americans are getting pretty fed up with corporate welfare. Indeed, just last year, the Agricultural Act of 2014 was signed into law. Among lots of other things, this bipartisan Farm Bill repeals direct payments to farmers (a.k.a. "welfare for farmers"). This is a great step in the right direction, because before this reform was put into place, a number of wealthy landowners—including actors, professional athletes, and other millionaires—received payments from the government, even though they didn't farm![32] But we have a long way to go. We need to address the tax breaks and loopholes that allow big business to pay single-digit taxes, or in some cases no taxes. We need to stop subsidizing fossil fuels (petroleum, coal, and natural gas), which are non-renewable and whose gases contribute to global warming. And we need to continue to make sure that subsidies serve their purpose, that is, the common good—not welfare for corporations. The federal government has lost $2.4 trillion in revenue since 2001 due to tax cuts introduced during the Bush era.[33] We could do a lot of mental health optimizing with that kind of money.

---

* I don't think that still happens, but it's a good visual.

'Raise Minimum 'Wage to a Living 'Wage (and Other Options)

During my high school years in Sweden, I worked at a quaint, seasonal restaurant by a lake close to my home. It was hard work, but most guests were friendly, and I enjoyed my co-workers. But most importantly, it was good money. I made sixty Swedish crowns an hour, or approximately $9. This was *twenty-three years ago*. I was seventeen years old, and I made today's equivalent of $15—or more than double the minimum wage in the United States ($7.25 as of this writing) for adults. And guess what? People showed up to eat, paid a reasonable amount of money for high-quality, home-cooked food, and the restaurant thrived.

The low minimum wage in the United States is the epitome of corporate injustice and greed. A wage of $7.25 an hour equals an annual salary of $15,080. Only with a family of one does this put you above the poverty line,[34] which is too low to begin with. It is no wonder that 49 million people in our country are considered food insecure (not having access to enough affordable and nutritious food).[35] The impact on kids is devastating. We have known for quite some time that kids are more likely to be anxious and depressed when they are food insecure.[36] While programs such as the Supplemental Nutrition Assistance Program (SNAP) and the Special Supplemental Nutrition Program for Women, Infants, and Children (WIC) are important for families who are unemployed or otherwise unable to put food on the table (our family certainly benefited from WIC when Rebecka was born—with Todd in grad school and me making $12,000 per year working at a private school), they are not the solution. We need to raise the minimum wage so working parents can feed their families, provide a healthy living environment, and make sure their children are prepared—academically, socially, and emotionally—to enter adulthood.

When you really dig into it, a low minimum wage is really just another form of very indirect corporate welfare. Several recent reports indicate that the employees of big corporations such as Walmart and McDonald's cost taxpayers billions of dollars in public assistance each year.[37] If Walmart and McDonald's and similar corporations were forced to pay higher wages, we could use this money for other purposes, because their employees wouldn't need the assistance. Seems like a win-win situation to me. What's exciting is that fast-food workers and their allies are fighting aggressively for a higher wage. Just a few days ago, two thousand fast-food workers gathered at McDonald's headquarters in Oak Brook, IL to make their voices heard. They were asking for two things: a fifteen-dollar-an-hour wage and permission to form a union (without negative repercussions). The Oak Brook police arrested approximately 150 people for trespassing.[38] The demonstrators received lots of national media attention and support on social media. This is just one example, but it shows that people are fighting for what's right. And that gives me hope.

I know some of you wonder what will happen to the economy if we raise the minimum wage, even just to the level proposed by President Obama, which is nine dollars an hour. Will people lose their jobs? Will it really help poor people? And will it double the price of my Big Mac? It's complicated, and I don't have space to go into the details in this book. So, I highly recommend that you read the *New York Times* article "The Business of the Minimum Wage" by Christina Romer, an economics professor at the University of California, Berkeley, and former chairwoman of President Obama's Council of Economic Advisers. Her conclusion is that "the costs in terms of employment and inefficiency are likely small." But she also questions whether raising the minimum wage is the best solution, providing other options such as a more generous earned-income tax credit and universal pre-kindergarten education.[39] I say we should explore *all* the options and put together a poverty-reduction package that is likely to pull the highest number of people, especially children, out of poverty. I do think the gross wage is an important number from a justice and equality standpoint. Who feels good knowing that the CEO of their company makes 587 times their salary (a search for Walmart on the website Executive Paywatch turned up the following statistic: "In 2013, [Walmart CEO] Michael T. Duke received $20,693,545 in total compensation. By comparison, the average worker made $35,239 in 2013. Michael T. Duke made 587 times the average worker's pay.")?[40]

In the words of former labor secretary Robert Reich, "inequality is bad for everyone."[41] Let's work together for a just republic by getting involved in politics, learning about the issues, raising our voices for justice, and supporting those actively working for change. This will create the political conditions required to optimize mental health for all.

19

✧

Compassionate Parenting

We all want to raise healthy, happy children, and we all want to be good parents. Every child desires nothing more than to be loved and accepted. In the end, the work of parenting involves learning to love well.

—Scott M. Shannon, MD, *Parenting the Whole Child*

I never really read parenting books when I was in the thick of parenting Rebecka. Between taking care of my much-younger sister Miriam growing up and working at a childcare center for a year, I figured I had plenty of childrearing experience. Indeed, I did get a few things right: I wasn't depressed or very stressed during my pregnancy. I had a natural childbirth. I breast-fed. I stayed home with Rebecka as long as financially feasible. I responded to her basic needs during those first months of her life. I sang lullabies. I encouraged her to follow her dreams. And I told her that I loved her—often.

But I got a few things wrong too: I used rewards and consequences to manage behavior. I fed her Lunchables (gasp!). I talked a lot about my weight and kept "bad" food out of the house. I was insensitive at times. I was a workaholic and complained excessively about my job. And worst of all, I didn't listen to her when she was telling us in so many ways that our family was hurting—until after the shit hit the fan.

When Rebecka started complaining of stomachaches, depression, and weight loss, and engaged in self-harming behaviors, I never stopped to think that these symptoms could be reflective of a problem within our family. Well, that's not exactly true. We *did* bring up to every doctor we met that our family was separated half of the time, with Todd teaching at Luther College and coming home on the weekends, but nobody seemed to think this was significant information. Of course, we had also learned through mainstream media and pop culture that mental illness was a brain disorder—something you were born with. Something inevitable. So we didn't push the environmental factors too much.

Now I know better. Based on our own healing process as a family and lots of research, I have learned that parent-child relationships and other family dynamics play a *huge* role in a child's ability to be emotionally healthy. If we do it right, we optimize our child's mental health, but if we don't truly see our children and don't take our cues from them, we can do some real damage. When I say "doing it right," I refer to *compassionate parenting*. At the core of compassionate parenting is the belief that we should treat our children with respect and as equal human beings. We as parents are not above them just because they happen to be smaller than we are, or because our own parents exerted their power over us. Rather, it is our privilege and responsibility to nurture them, love them, listen to them, learn from them, keep them safe, and guide them through childhood and adolescence. And if we operate from this belief, we raise children with high self-efficacy and resilience, which greatly affects their future mental health.

Today, most informed mental health professionals and researchers agree that we are born with genes that make us more or less susceptible to depression, anxiety, and other mental distress. But, as psychology professor Elliot Valenstein explains, "predisposition is not a cause. How and whether a predisposition is expressed depends on many nonbiological factors, especially on life experiences and on input from the environment in many different ways."[1] This is why compassionate parenting and other factors I discuss in this book can determine if the "mental illness switch" gets turned on.[2] In other words, nurture has the upper hand over nature. Of course, this is a very sensitive topic, and I think this is one of the reasons we cling to the "broken brain" explanation for mental illness. We don't want to place blame on the parents (and we shouldn't!). However, excluding environmental factors and family dynamics from the mental health equation leads to bad diagnoses and unnecessary—and potentially harmful—prescriptions for antidepressants, stimulants, and antipsychotics.

I eagerly accept the responsibility that comes with being a parent and actually find it comforting that the art of parenting is an acquired skill.[3] This means we as parents can *learn* how best to interact with our children and provide a nurturing environment to optimize their mental health. It also means that as a society, we can offer concrete support to parents in their quest to raise happy, healthy children. In this chapter, I will share some of the key philosophies and concepts about mental-health-optimizing parenting that I gleaned from pediatric mental health professionals with over one hundred years of combined experience working with suffering kids and their families.

The Importance of a Good Start (Pregnancy and Early Attachment)

One of the most surprising findings from my research for this book is that mental health optimization starts during pregnancy. I knew good nutrition during pregnancy has a big impact on a child's development, but I didn't know the mother's *mood* makes a difference. Clinical psychologist Bob Murray and therapist Alicia Fortinberry explain in their excellent book *Raising an Optimistic Child* that a depressed, stressed-out mother can pass harmful stress hormones to her fetus, "causing the child to be born depressed or anxious or with a disposition to become so."[4] On the flip side, moms who are relatively stress-free, excited to be expecting, and have a good support network "will send the fetus positive and health-giving neurochemical messages."[5] The message here, which is one of the recurring themes in compassionate parenting, is that parents must take care of their own mental health if they are to raise mentally healthy kids. And this process starts at conception.

When a child is born, the best thing a mother can do for him is to breast-feed, if physically possible. (It's estimated that 1 to 5 percent of Western women have an insufficient milk supply.)[6] Not only is breast milk the best option from a nutritional standpoint, but the sheer act of breast-feeding has a positive impact on the child's mental health.* Among other things, it releases the anti-stress hormone oxytocin, calms the infant, and significantly contributes to the child's attachment to the mother, who is often the primary caregiver.[7] And that secure attachment is crucial to early mental health optimization. A secure attachment is formed between a child and her primary caregivers when she is confident that her needs will be met.[8] That means that somebody will feed her when she's hungry, change her when she's wet, comfort her when she's startled, and be constantly available to attend to her needs. Jon Kabat-Zinn

---

* If you are not able to breast-feed your child, don't beat yourself up about it! Your happiness is a key factor in determining the mental health of your child.

succinctly summarizes the importance of early attachment for future mental health: "Secure attachment leads to a robust sense of well-being in the child as he or she gets older."[9]

Do you want to know something that helps parents bond with their infants? Having enough time to spend with them! This is one of the reasons parental leave is so important. I was honestly shocked when I found out that many mothers in the United States have to go back to work after only six short weeks of bonding with their child. And most fathers don't get any leave at all! In addition to separating parents from children at too young an age, going back to work too soon is associated with increased maternal depression and overall family stress.[10] These are exactly the things we want to avoid in order to optimize our children's mental health. Despite all this evidence that paid parental leave is really good for families, the United States is one of only four countries in the world to offer *zero* days of paid leave, save a few progressive states and territories—Puerto Rico being the most generous, with eight weeks of maternity leave at 100 percent pay. So again, we see that our mental health is adversely impacted by our political-economic system, which is about profit at all cost. Paid parental leave is a cause worth fighting for.

One group fighting for this and a number of other family-related causes is MomsRising.org. If you're interested in getting involved with this issue, I highly recommend you visit their website to learn more about maternity and paternity leave in the United States.

Children's Behaviors Teach Us How To Be Better Parents

If you are a parent, you know that children are excellent communicators from the time they are born. Babies scream as they enter our bright, cold, and unfamiliar world, saying, "please put me back into my mommy's tummy!" Of course, we can't do that, but we can quickly place the newborn on his mother's breast and make sure that he is safe and warm. Not only are children quite competent at communicating their needs, but they are also great at giving us feedback that allows us to become better parents. This is what I learned from Jesper Juul, a family therapist from Denmark, while reading his book, *The Competent Child*. Juul explains that one of the main reasons we have so much conflict in the parent-child relationship is that traditional child-rearing theories have been based on the assumption "that children are potentially uncooperative, asocial, or egocentric. Therefore, the task of adults has been to teach children how to cooperate, adapt themselves, and take others into consideration."[11]

Juul argues that children are cooperative by nature. In fact, they will go to such lengths to cooperate with their parents that they compromise their own integrity—nine times out of ten.[12] To explain what he means by cooperation, Juul gives a beautiful example of a mother who is going back to work after six months of maternity leave. Her infant daughter Lily cries and is unhappy whenever mom drops her off at daycare, but not when dad drops her off. Juul explains why:

> Children like Lily cry with mom because, quite simply, the mother (for good reasons) is not emotionally ready to be separated from her child. She is anxious, sad, nervous, and unhappy—and has been since giving birth . . .
>
> Even though the mother is no longer conscious of these feelings, Lily senses them—and copies them. The child, in other words, is cooperating by competently communicating a message that can be translated as "Dear Mother: Something is wrong between us—something is unclear. I am just letting you know that I know this, and assume that you will take the responsibility for solving the problem, so that we both can feel better."[13]

What a wonderfully different way to look at behaviors traditionally considered uncooperative and asocial. This ties back to what we learned in chapter 15 in the Family Therapy section. Children with behavior problems and mental distress are not the problem. Rather, they are reflecting that something is amiss in the family system or in their environment. Holistic child psychiatrist and author of *Parenting the Whole Child* Scott M. Shannon agrees:

> Children teach us every day. Over the course of my 30-plus years of practice, I have found that the greatest source of learning and truth about how to heal our children comes not from a diagnostic manual or from a pharmacy but from our children themselves. Our kids, given the chance, can tell us (even in nonverbal ways) what's bothering them. It's our job to listen to them attentively and openly, to resist labeling them, and to remove any barriers impeding their mental and emotional health.[14]

So one of the best things we can do to become better parents is to pay attention to our children and pick up the signals they are sending us related to how we treat them and how they feel about being part of our family. We can then help them express these signals using clear and direct language (more on that below) and address potential problems in the family system.[15] Our children love us and want to connect with us, so they imitate us every chance they have. Hence, if we want to raise mentally healthy kids and decent human beings, we must look ourselves in the mirror and see ourselves—the good, the bad, and the ugly. Want to raise respectful children? Be respectful. Want to raise compassionate children? Be compassionate. Want to raise joyful children? Be joyful.

Respect and Value Your Child As She Is

It is in our nature to praise our children. We want them to know that we think they did a good job. We also believe this will encourage future excellence in sports, music, and academics. We've all done it: rewarded a successful soccer game with a trip to the local pizzeria; handed flowers to our children after a dance recital or theater performance; given incentives for good grades and other desirable behavior. Unfortunately, praising your child for what she *does*, rather than who she *is*, is not helpful to building your child's self-esteem. And good self-esteem is one of the best predictors of future mental and emotional well-being.

Juul writes that "our self-esteem is nurtured by two experiences: when one of the most important people in our lives 'sees' and acknowledges us as we are, and when we sense that we are of value to other people as we are."[16] Isn't this what we expect from our significant others? Unconditional love?

Of course, we do love our children unconditionally—we're just not very good at expressing this, because all of the performance-based praise and our own self-absorption get in the way. So let's talk about a few ways we can make sure we see and acknowledge our children *as they are* and make them feel like they are a valuable part of the family.

The first thing we can do is to replace our praise for what our children *do* with a continual celebration of our children as they *are*—in all their ordinariness, as Shefali Tsabary,* clinical psychologist and author, would say.[17] This is difficult, because it goes against how most of us were raised and the type of feedback we cling to for our own floundering self-esteem. A simple example is to express to your child that you were really paying attention and "seeing" her, rather than doling out a generic "Great job!" at the end of a sports game or music performance. In my case (since Rebecka is in choir), it would be "I really liked the third piece your choir sang, and it looked like you had fun singing it!" versus "Great job on that concert. The choir sounded beautiful!" (See the difference?)

---

* Shefali Tsabary goes by Dr. Shefali, so this is how I refer to her in the rest of the book.

Secondly, we can make a conscious effort to let children be who they are without imposing our hopes and dreams on them. As Dr. Shefali so elegantly puts it: "When you parent, it's crucial you realize you aren't raising a 'mini me,' but a spirit throbbing with its own signature."[18] Conflict arises and self-esteem plummets when we don't respect our children's need for autonomy and being their own person separate from us. This starts when our two-year-old begins to assert his independence and continues all the way through high school and college. The child is not looking for conflict. Rather, he is looking to find his self-identity, another key component of mental health.[19] We can support this important developmental process by seeing our children as distinct persons with their own hopes and dreams, separate from us. If our two-year-old wants to wear the yellow dress, we let her wear the yellow dress. If our ten-year-old would rather take an art class than play football, we let him take the art class. And if our eighteen-year-old wants to go to a college other than the college we had hoped for, we let her enroll at her preferred college (assuming it is within financial reach).

Thirdly, we can show our children that they are valuable members of the family—just as they are. We can do this by asking children for their help when we truly need it. According to Juul, it's better to ask children for help with chores as needed than to assign chores because it's "good" for kids to have chores. In the first scenario, children feel valuable to their parents. In the second, they feel more like objects in a parenting experiment.[20] We can also open ourselves up to receive gifts from our children. This includes receiving their love, flowers plucked in the backyard, and breakfast in bed. However, the greatest gift we receive from our competent children is their keen perception and assistance in helping us see ourselves as we really are.[21] And reversely, in Dr. Shefali's words, "the ability to see—really see—our children separate from who we are is our greatest gift to them."[22]

Clear Family Communication Is Key

In *Your Competent Child*, Juul introduces the idea of "personal responsibility." He defines personal responsibility as "the responsibility we have for our own lives—our physical, psychological, mental, and spiritual health and development."[23] Juul believes that "the overwhelming majority of conflicts between children and adults—and among adults themselves—develop in a destructive way precisely because the parties are unable (or unwilling) to take responsibility for themselves."[24]

Maintaining personal responsibility in the context of interaction with others requires that we can express how we're feeling, what we need, and set limits. Juul proposes that parents and children learn to express themselves verbally and emotionally using a "personal language."[25] The following phrases are at the heart of a personal language:

> I want to. I don't want to.
> I like. I don't like.
> I will. I will not.

For example, rather than yelling at your kids because they're being too loud, you can say "I want to have some quiet for a while. Please go outside and play." Likewise, a child might say, "I don't want to take a nap. I'm not tired."

In order to encourage the development of personal responsibility and personal language—and as a result, optimal health—it is vital that parents don't take over their children's personal responsibility. For example, in our culture, it has become the responsibility of parents to ensure that kids do their homework. When parents take over this responsibility, it is a missed opportunity for the child to develop personal responsibility, and it often leads to conflict.[26] Continuing with the homework example, Juul describes wonderfully what can happen when parents go against the grain and allow their children to assume responsibility for their homework—and for their own personal wellness:

> One glorious day, the parents will feel free to express their genuine interest in their child's schoolwork in a way that does not cause their child to turn off. And on another glorious day, the miracle actually takes place: you ask your twelve-year-old son if he has a lot of homework to do for the following day, and he answers, "Yes, piles! But I've decided to go down to the harbor and do some fishing instead. It's just the day for fishing!"[27]

According to Juul, parents are fully responsible for the quality of family interactions, and we often make mistakes. When we do, it's important that we take responsibility for our mistakes and do not blame our child. You might say, "I'm sorry I yelled at you when we were leaving the house. I overslept, so we were running late, and it was stressing me out. It wasn't your fault. It was my fault, and I'd like to apologize."[28]

One way we can improve interactions with our children is to validate their emotions. As soon as a young child is able to recognize emotions (around eighteen months), she needs to know that it is acceptable to express these emotions.[29] For parents, this means that we empathize and validate her feelings. For example, if a child cries because a play date was canceled, a compassionate parent might say, "I can tell you were really looking forward to playing with your friend. I understand that you are really sad that it didn't work out." This simple acknowledgement of her feelings contributes to the child's ability to bounce back and feel better.

I first learned about validating children's emotions when Rebecka was a young teen (better late than never, right?). These two sentences in the book *Helping Teens Who Cut: Understanding and Ending Self-Injury* radically changed my interactions with Rebecka, in the best sense: "Validation means communicating that you understand the other person's experience. This doesn't mean that you have to *share* the opinion."[30] It was so simple. All I had to do was acknowledge that I heard her. That I understood that she was upset. I didn't have to agree with the reason she was upset. And it worked! Whenever I remember to validate Rebecka's emotions, our interactions are greatly improved, because she knows that I'm hearing her and acknowledging her feelings.

Finally, if you are interested in learning additional compassionate communication strategies, I recommend that you look into Nonviolent Communication (NVC). From the website:

> NVC begins by assuming that we are all compassionate by nature and that violent strategies—whether verbal or physical— are learned behaviors taught and supported by the prevailing culture. NVC also assumes that we all share the same, basic human needs, and that each of our actions are a strategy to meet one or more of these needs. People who practice NVC have found greater authenticity in their communication, increased understanding, deepening connection and conflict resolution.[31]

Practice Conscious Parenting

We learned about the positive impact of mindfulness on mental health in chapter 14, where we explored alternative treatment options for mental distress. What's exciting is that mindfulness can also be incorporated into parenting and thus prevent mental distress from happening in the first place. This is the topic of Dr. Shefali's best-selling book *The Conscious Parent*, which I will draw heavily from in this section.

The essence of conscious parenting is being present with your child in everyday life. It's not a set of techniques, but rather a philosophy—a way to live and be with your children. And as we've already learned, when we pay attention to our children, we learn from them and grow as parents and human beings. Put another way, "consciousness informs us moment-by-moment how best to go about the task of parenting."[32] Dr. Shefali explains:

> A conscious parent doesn't look outside the parenting relationship for answers, but is confident the answers can be found for both parent and child within the parent-child dynamic. For this reason, conscious parenting is learned through the actual experience of relating to our children, not through reading books that offer quick fixes or taking classes that specialize in techniques.[33]

So how do we become present with our children? *By learning from them.* Children are born knowing how to be present. They notice bugs on the ground and birds soaring up above. They don't fret about the past or worry about the future. Rather, they relish the present moment. Dr. Shefali writes about how children teach us to be present:

> While a parent is called upon to provide their child with emotional guidance, stability, acceptance, and safety, the child is invited into the parent's life to teach something only a child can: how to engage life with the presence, authenticity, and joyful spontaneity that adults have lost as a result of their own unconscious upbringing.[34]

When we practice conscious parenting, we are able to let go of overly high expectations of our children. While it can be difficult to do, it's one of the best things we can do for our kids. As Scott Shannon reminds us, "too many children are crumbling inside under the burden of high parental expectation and feel 'worthless' or 'bad' if they can't always perform as expected."[35] When we remove the pressures of becoming a top athlete, a straight-A student, or class president, we allow our children to remain in their inherent state of being joyfully present. And avoiding overscheduling makes it possible to take Dr. Shefali's advice and allow room for stillness in our child's schedule. "It's helpful to encourage our children to sit in stillness, so that they learn to exist in a state of quiet without the need to converse."[36]

If the whole family is starting a mindfulness practice, you can set aside ten minutes every day to sit quietly with your children. You might start with just one minute of sitting quietly and focusing on the breath entering the body and leaving the body. You can also buy books such as *Sitting Still Like a Frog* by Eline Snel or Thich Nhat Hahn's *Planting Seeds* for some ideas for teaching formal mindfulness practices to your children. By establishing a mindfulness practice, not only are you assisting in the optimization of your children's mental health—you are also setting them up for living life in the present, which is the only way to really live.

Beyond Personal Action

In this chapter, I have shared some basic concepts associated with compassionate parenting. I hope you are sufficiently intrigued by these concepts to want to explore them further. Take a look at the "For Further Exploration" section at the back of the book for further reading.

If all parents (and grandparents, uncles, aunts, and other caring adults) who read this book implement compassionate parenting, we're doing well. If you also share this philosophy with your friends and family, that's even better! However, it will still only be a very small percentage of the population. We need to think of ways to spread the messages that (1) parenting and childhood experiences have a great impact future mental health, and (2) compassionate parenting is the best way to optimize our children's mental health.

Several of the mental health professionals I have referred to and quoted in this chapter are doing their part:

- Dr. Shefali recently did a show with Oprah, and *The Conscious Parent* is number thirty-one on Amazon.com as of this writing.
- Dr. Scott Shannon runs the Wholeness Center, an integrative medicine center in Fort Collins, Colorado, with holistic health services for all ages.
- Jesper Juul is the founder of Family Lab International, which offers parenting workshops, seminars, and other resources with a goal of "making good families better."

However, it's not enough. We need a system to reach *all* families. Indeed, when I interviewed a couple of seasoned teachers who work in a low-income school in Las Vegas for this book, they said that the first thing they would do if they had extra time and money would be to offer parenting classes. They said children watch too much TV, play too many video games, and do not get outside to play. Many children come from divorced homes and are constantly confused about where they are supposed to be on a given day. And a good many of their students are already medicated for behavioral problems. These parents clearly are not getting the support they need to implement compassionate parenting.

The Our Emotional Health website, the online home of psychologist Robin Grille, includes a *Children's Wellbeing Manifesto*, which is a list of ways we should support parents. The very first item in this manifesto suggests that we should establish community "hubs" or centers for parent support in every municipality. Parents-to-be should be introduced to the centers during pregnancy, to get to know the local community of parents and learn about available services.[37] I love this idea! Since we know that the first six years of a child's life are the most important in establishing personality and the ability to be optimistic and resilient,[38] we should make absolutely sure to support parents during these early years. It will require a reprioritization of how we spend our money, but that's the case with pretty much every action I've suggested in this book so far. But what could be more important than raising mentally healthy and resilient kids?

Student-Centered Education

How we educate kids should follow from what defines them as kids.

—Alfie Kohn, *Feel-Bad Education*

Before we get started with this chapter, I'd like to make it known that I come from a family of educators. My mother was a teacher, as were her four sisters. My dad was a pastor, but went back to school when he was fifty years old so he could teach at a Swedish folk high school (kind of like a community college, but more vocation-oriented, and often with older students). I also started my working life as a teacher at a Swedish junior high school (*högstadium*) for one semester, and then at a preschool and a private school in Atlanta, Georgia for three years. Oh, and did I mention that I'm married to a teacher?

The point is, I understand teaching is challenging, emotionally exhausting, and can be amazingly rewarding. I admire teachers who save the best versions of themselves for their students and serve as life-changing mentors to kids. There are lots of tremendous teachers who want to do things differently, but they're locked into a system that doesn't allow for as much creativity, active learning, and exploration as they'd like. So this chapter is not about our teachers doing a poor job. It is about what education could look like if we properly funded it, emphasized collaboration, deemphasized testing, provided resilience training, and gave kids time to be kids, while also allowing them to have input into the direction of their schooling.

A Note About How School Is Not Working for Many Kids

Before we dive into the various ways we can improve the education system to optimize our children's mental health, I want to point to a few ways that current US public education is *not* so good for our children's mental health—or learning.

1. **A Reward-and-Punishment-Based System:** We learned in the previous chapter that rewards and punishments are not conducive to raising children with high self-esteem and healthy brains. When we focus so much on grades, detentions, and standardized testing, kids lose the joy of learning. They also learn that they only have value if they excel. This is detrimental to self-esteem and consequently, mental health.

2. **Teaching to the Test:** If you know a teacher or pay attention to the news, you've probably heard about this problem. Our obsession with standardized tests has gotten out of control. Mandates from above dictate that teachers focus on preparing students for standardized testing. Not only does this limit the time spent on teaching other important skills, such as social and emotional skills, but it can also cause a lot of stress for the students.

3. **Teacher-Centered Education:** In most schools, the teacher (or the government in conjunction with corporate philanthropy and assessment companies) creates the curriculum, and the students do not have a say in what they will or will not learn—or *how* they will learn. Combined with pressures to "teach to the test," this method relies heavily on lectures, textbooks, and memorization. We know this is not the best way to get kids excited about learning.[1]

4. **One-Size-Fits-All Model:** Between Bush's No Child Left Behind and Obama's Race to the Top program, the message to the schools is clear: make your curriculum and schools work for *all* children. The problem is, every child is different. Some kids do better in more intimate settings, but school districts lean toward bigger and consolidated to save money. Some kids are auditory learners, while others learn best by doing. However, our schools cater to visual learners. We expect kids to adapt to the environment rather than the other way around. This inflexibility may be one of the leading causes for the surge in ADHD diagnoses and resulting medication. (Close to 10 percent of US children ages three to seventeen have

received an ADHD diagnosis.)[2]

5. **Competition Over Cooperation:** Everything about the US school system is tied up in competition. From class ranking to competitive athletics to spelling bees, our schools are full of winners and losers. Children who were friends become enemies when they realize they are competing for the same prize. Students have to think twice about helping others, should it become a competitive disadvantage. Yet there is no evidence that competition is healthy. Indeed, competition can have a negative impact on self-esteem and cause anxiety—for both winners and losers.[3]

6. **Over-Scheduling and Extreme Pressure:** The documentary *Race to Nowhere* details how over-scheduling and the pressure to succeed are taking a toll on our children. Hours of homework, activity-packed schedules, and Advanced Placement tests all reduce our children's lives to success at all costs. When every minute of the day is booked, children don't have time to be kids, spend time with their family and friends, or just be. School stresses kids out, doesn't allow for enough sleep, and is causing children to get diagnosed with a variety of mental illnesses, including depression and anxiety.[4]

7. **Junk Food and Reduced Recess/PE:** Although school food has gotten slightly better the last couple of years thanks to new government standards, school food is still not nutritionally optimal for kids. Much of the food is made from subsidized commodities, and cafeteria workers have been reduced from cooks to food re-heaters. In addition, many schools still have sugary beverage and junk food vending, because it's a source of income. Add to that the fact that many schools are reducing or eliminating recess and PE. We know from chapter 13 that nutrition and physical exercise greatly impact mental health, so why are schools not at the forefront of providing the best possible food and fitness opportunities for our children?

With all these problems, why do we even bother? Why don't we homeschool, unschool, or place our children in progressive schools such as Montessori or Waldorf and be done with it? Well, some people do (approximately 3 percent of children in the United States are homeschooled). The thing is, I believe in public education. My husband and I were adamant that Rebecka attend public school—even when we had the means to place her in a private school—because we wanted her to be exposed to diversity of race, socioeconomics, ideology, and so on. But beyond a desire for diverse experiences for my daughter, the reason I will always support high-quality public education is because there are so many children who don't have an alternative. I want public education to be top-notch for them—because the more disadvantaged a child's background, the more important the quality of his or her school experience. So let's see what we can do to turn our public schools into student-centered, mental-health optimizing institutions!

Adopt a Philosophy of Unconditional Teaching

In chapter 19, we discussed the importance of parents clearly expressing their unconditional love for their children to ensure future mental health. Alfie Kohn, one of the most outspoken critics of the US education system and the author of a dozen books on education, parenting, and human behavior, has written an entire book dedicated to this topic, called *Unconditional Parenting*. Drawing on this concept and relating it to education, he also coined the term "unconditional teaching." Kohn's views on this topic are summarized in a 2005 *Educational Leadership* article aptly titled "Unconditional Teaching."[5] In this section, I will draw from this article to summarize some of the scientific evidence in favor of unconditional teaching, examples of conditional acceptance, and what teachers can do to practice unconditional teaching.

Over the last twenty years or so, psychologists and researchers have discovered that "the best predictor to mental health may not be one's level of self-esteem but the extent to which it fluctuates." In other words, constantly low self-esteem isn't as bad as self-esteem that depends on some set of factors—for example, praise from parents, teachers, or bosses for a job well done. On the flip side, "kids who have an underlying sense of their own value are more likely to see failure as a temporary set-back, a problem to be solved. They're also less likely to be anxious or depressed." And what causes children to have an underlying sense of their own value? "The extent to which they have been accepted unconditionally by others," Kohn writes. It's important that children experience unconditional acceptance both at home and at school.

We know this to be true, yet our public education system is set up to promote favoritism and acceptance based on performance and behavior. Teachers are evaluated based on their students' performance on standardized tests. So it's only natural that teachers would be more accepting of academically successful kids. And as Kohn points out, "if some children matter more to us than others, then all children are valued only conditionally." In addition, most schools and classrooms employ a punishment-and-reward system, which identifies some kids as bad via visits to the principal's office, detention, and suspension. Kohn provides two examples of conditional acceptance that may contribute to kids feeling that the teacher only cares about them if they perform or behave in a specific way:

1. **Acceptance Based on Performance:** There is a difference between "valuing excellence" and "leading students to believe that they matter only to the extent they meet our standards." Kids actually perform best when they know that they are accepted no matter what. "It's the experience of being accepted without conditions that helps people develop a healthy confidence in themselves, a belief that it's safe to take risks and try new things."

2. **Acceptance Based on Obedience:** When we single bad kids out or reward good behavior, we send the message that we only accept children when they behave a certain way. Kohn writes, "The real alternative to making children suffer for their offenses (or dangling goodies in front of them for doing what they're told) is to work *with* them to solve problems." While it might seem impossible to manage difficult kids without a "behavior management system," the compassionate way to handle these kids is to think about *why* they are acting this way (remember how we can learn about parenting from our kids—the same thing goes for teaching). Kohn suggests that perhaps these kids aren't testing limits, but rather testing if we will accept them unconditionally.

Kohn makes the following suggestions for how to teach unconditionally:

- Let kids know that you are glad to see them and that you care about them.
- Show your students respect by asking them what *they* think about a given situation.
- Don't be afraid to be yourself in the classroom.
- Bring treats for no good reason and eat lunch with your students.
- Remember details about the kids' lives and ask them about them.
- Look for goodness in every child.

While it may be challenging to pull this off in large, impersonal schools, the good news about unconditional teaching is that it is free! It is simply a matter of rethinking our teaching philosophy and deciding that our kids' mental health is more important than test scores and perfect behavior.

Establish a Culture of Cooperation

Having spent time in both US and Swedish schools (both as a student and as a teacher), the biggest difference I've seen is the level of competition that is present in US schools compared to Swedish schools. When I was a young student in San Francisco, I would come home at the end of each semester with certificates for good behavior, being the teacher's best helper, and being a good friend (do we really need certificates for friendship?). I received report cards starting in kindergarten (always straight As) and wound up with a number of ribbons from speech meets, art fairs, and a semester-long reading competition. When I moved back to the homeland at age eight, I realized that Sweden, on the other hand, didn't do awards. The only option for winning *anything* was at track and field meets.* Well, I suppose I *did* receive an award for my senior paper, which discussed the allegorical qualities of C.S. Lewis's *Chronicles of Narnia*. But that was it! Since I had gotten used to lots of competing and winning, I didn't like the Swedish system much. However, as an adult, I recognize the benefit of the Swedish approach: it didn't pit students against each other, but rather fostered a culture of cooperation.

Competition is at the core of our education system and our society as a whole. It stems from our economic and political system, which is completely based on competition, or the "free market." It seems that we think we must incorporate competition into our schools to prepare our children for what is to come: the cutthroat, sink-or-swim corporate environment. I marvel at the fact that US schools have managed to turn *everything* into a competition: sports, music, art, speech, debate, attendance, grades (class rank), volunteerism, and character (think National Honor Society). Is this really necessary? My go-to education guru, Alfie Kohn, says no. In *No Contest: The Case Against Competition*, he debunks a number of myths about competition, including the myths that competition is an inevitable part of human nature and that it makes people more productive.[6] According to Kohn, "natural selection does not require competition; on the contrary, it discourages it."[7] Indeed, cooperation is more important for our survival than competition. And beyond not being helpful, competition can in fact be harmful, including having a negative impact on self-esteem and causing anxiety.[8]

Establishing a culture of cooperation is a long-term commitment. We need to evaluate our own contributions to a competitive culture and determine

---

* I was the kid at the back of the pack hoping to make it around the whole track witout passing out. I did bring home a shot put medal once, though—it was a big deal.

what changes we can make on a personal level. Beyond this, we must question the status quo. This will not be an easy task. I've been to a number of high school graduation parties and the main attraction at these events are the awards, medals, trophies, and other recognitions of the graduate spread across long tables and hung on walls and displays. Competition is deeply engrained in our culture.

Some radical ideas for reducing competition include:

- Remove class rank and valedictorian recognition.* Some schools have already done this, or are pursuing it, because students place too much emphasis on their rank.
- Deemphasize importance of athletics results and rankings.
- Emphasize the benefits of teamwork, fitness, and friends for life.
- Sing for the joy of singing. Paint for the pleasure of painting. Read poems and short stories for the bliss of reading. Debate topics for the thrill of debating. Volunteer for the satisfaction of helping others. Don't make these creative, intellectual, and compassionate activities into a competition and suck all the joy out of them!

To promote collaboration:

- Design projects where success is defined by how well children work *together* to solve problems or discuss controversial topics.
- Encourage students to help each other learn instead of focusing on individual success via tests (which encourages cheating).
- Let kids make mistakes without fear of repercussions, because making mistakes is part of creativity, learning, and forming original ideas.
- Welcome healthy conflict and guide students through the process of conflict resolution.

So what will happen to collaborative children when they get to the "real world"? Will they be able to survive the fierce competitiveness of corporate America? My hope is that the upcoming generation will bring collaboration and kindness and balance to the workplace and change the culture forever. I see in young people today a resolve *not* to go down the path of workaholism and material success at any cost. They give me hope.

---

* This would also require colleges and universities to rethink how they evaluate students for higher education readiness. Perhaps students could submit portfolios showing writing samples, problem solving, etc.

Embrace Student-Centered Learning

Our current education system was originally designed to produce workers for factories and other businesses that grew out of the industrial revolution. At the time, the most important skills were the ability read, write, and do basic arithmetic. The most important values were "punctuality, regularity, attention, and silence."[9] Guess what? The world has changed since then, but the way we educate our kids has not. That's a problem.

Student-centered learning is an approach to learning that is based on the interests and self-direction of the students. In this approach, the teacher is a facilitator or a coach (or in the most extreme cases, absent, as in the "School in the Cloud" experiment).[10] Rather than punctuality and regularity, student-centered learning fosters problem solving, collaboration, and interpersonal skills—qualities today's business leaders look for in their employees. While many proponents of student-centered learning (especially technology leaders) are driven by the need to create a workforce that can allow companies to compete in a global economy,[11] the reason I include it here is twofold:

1. It is a superior method for children to learn and doesn't kill creativity.[12]
2. It allows children to focus on what interests them, which in turn increases focus and reduces the need to label and medicate "inattentive" children.

Superior Learning Method

We all know from experience that we remember very little of the information we crammed into our heads in school, even in college. I personally do not remember much at all. What I do remember, though, is how to research (*find* information) and how to communicate my ideas effectively. Yet we continue to fill our children with information that they regurgitate on exams and later discard. Not only is this method of learning not effective, it kills the joy of learning and lessens kids' abilities to think for themselves, experiment, make mistakes, and form their own opinions of the world.[13]

You may have read the story about elementary school teacher Sergio Juárez Correa, who teaches at an impoverished school in Matamoros, Mexico, just south of the US border. He and his students made headlines in late 2013 when one of his students received the highest math score in the country and several other students ranked in the 99.99th percentile in math. What was Sergio's secret? He had discovered student-centered learning and implemented it in his classroom. Instead of giving students formulas and handing them the answer, he let the kids figure it out using simple prompts. The very bright students, who were normally bored in the classroom, thrived in this environment and pulled students we would consider average or below average along with them. They all learned together by working out problems in small groups. Other examples of student-centered learning success include Montessori schools, Finland's public school system, and educational technologist Sugata Mitra's "minimally invasive education" in rural India.[14]

Children Focus When They're Interested

The reason student-centered learning is especially important for optimizing mental health is that children are more likely to pay attention when they're interested and engaged. Clinical psychologist and activist Bruce E. Levine confirms:

> Studies show that most ADHD-diagnosed children will pay
> attention to activities that they enjoy or that they have chosen.
> In other words, when ADHD-labeled kids are having a good
> time and in control, the 'disease' routinely goes away.[15]

With close to 10 percent of US children having received an ADHD diagnosis, it makes sense that we would be looking for ways to help kids focus at school.

In his famous TED talk, "How Schools Kill Creativity," arts-education expert Sir Ken Robinson relates an inspiring interview with a world-class choreographer, Gillian Lynne:

> Gillian and I had lunch one day and I said, "Gillian, how'd you get
> to be a dancer?" And she said it was interesting; when she was
> at school, she was really hopeless. And the school, in the '30s,
> wrote to her parents and said, "We think Gillian has a learning
> disorder." She couldn't concentrate; she was fidgeting. I think now
> they'd say she had ADHD. Wouldn't you? But this was the 1930s,
> and ADHD hadn't been invented at this point. It wasn't an available
> condition. (Laughter.) People weren't aware they could have that.
>
> Anyway, she went to see this specialist. So, this oak-paneled
> room, and she was there with her mother, and she was led
> and sat on this chair at the end, and she sat on her hands for
> twenty minutes while this man talked to her mother about all
> the problems Gillian was having at school. And at the end of it—
> because she was disturbing people; her homework was always
> late; and so on, little kid of eight—in the end, the doctor went
> and sat next to Gillian and said, "Gillian, I've listened to all these
> things that your mother's told me, and I need to speak to her

> privately." He said, "Wait here. We'll be back; we won't be very long," and they went and left her. But as they went out [of] the room, he turned on the radio that was sitting on his desk. And when they got out [of] the room, he said to her mother, "Just stand and watch her." And the minute they left the room, she said, she was on her feet, moving to the music. And they watched for a few minutes and he turned to her mother and said, "Mrs. Lynne, Gillian isn't sick; she's a dancer. Take her to a dance school."

Gillian went on to have a successful career at the Royal Ballet in London and later worked with Andrew Lloyd Webber to choreograph *Cats* and *Phantom of the Opera*. Robinson wraps up the story with the scary truth: "Somebody else might have put her on medication and told her to calm down."[16]

It's for kids like Gillian—and Andy Warhol and Beethoven and Sir Isaac Newton and many other world-changing people dead and alive—that I am devoting significant time to the writing of this book. I can't bear to think that we are crushing and medicating away the spirit and creativity of extraordinary and talented kids because they do not conform to our obedience-focused, "information pouring," one-size-fits-all approach to education.

Teachers, I urge you to explore the student-centered learning philosophy and decide if this is an approach you can get behind. I know you already want to focus on the individual, but our factory-style educational system makes it difficult to do so. According to some organizations, such as Jobs for the Future, student-centered learning will be required to meet the expectations of the Common Core.[17] Use that as your excuse to transform your classroom into one centered on the interests of your students. And remember that all children are different and approach learning in different ways. Hopefully, we can get you the support you need to meet the needs of every child.

Incorporate Social and Emotional Learning

After Rebecka went through the dialectical behavior therapy group skills training—and I witnessed how these skills enabled her to tackle difficult situation with ease—I started thinking, Why don't we teach these skills to all kids in school? We all face difficult situations, so everybody could benefit from this.

As you may recall, DBT includes mindfulness, distress tolerance, emotional regulation, and interpersonal skills—skills that are all part of what we call resilience, or "the ability to thrive even in the face of great stress."[18] The Adverse Childhood Experiences in Iowa report, which shows that childhood trauma has a strong link to negative physical and mental outcomes, suggests that resilience is the best way for children and families to "cope in positive ways with everyday challenges."[19] This message is clear and consistent throughout the all the literature that I have studied on the topic of mental health. Resilience is one of the foundations of strong mental health.

While I thought I had come up with a revolutionary idea to teach resilience in schools, I quickly realized that others had conceived of the same bright idea. The most widely discussed form of this is what is called Social and Emotional Learning (SEL). The Collaborative for Academic, Social, and Emotional Learning (CASEL), the nation's leading organization advancing the development of academic, social and emotional competence for all students, defines SEL as follows:

> SEL involves the processes through which children and adults acquire and effectively apply the knowledge, attitudes and skills necessary to understand and manage emotions, set and achieve positive goals, feel and show empathy for others, establish and maintain positive relationships, and make responsible decisions.[20]

Obviously the best way to get SEL into public school curricula is to create a policy that requires SEL and has clear measurements. A handful of states, such as Pennsylvania and Tennessee, already have standards for SEL.[21] I hope other states will follow suit. Another "way in" for SEL is through bullying prevention programs. Research shows that SEL is successful in creating an environment that inherently prevents bullying. CASEL provides a guide called "Social and Emotional Learning and Bullying Prevention," available on its website, if you want to learn more.

Another approach to teaching resilience is mindfulness in education. We've discussed mindfulness a number of times already, because it is such an essential ingredient of resilience and emotional health. Since mindfulness is now going mainstream, and because mental distress is an identified problem, school communities are primed to be receptive to bringing secular mindfulness practices into the classroom. There are a number of organizations working to bring mindfulness (including yoga) to schools, such as Mindful Schools, MindUp, The Garrison Institute, and Inner Kids.* Not only is mindfulness good for kids; it can be a lifesaver for teachers, if they develop a personal practice.[22]

---

* For a more comprehensive list, see the "Take Action" section at the back of the book.

A Grassroots Approach

In February 2014, I was sitting at a local café, chatting with a friend about my book project and getting her insights on nonviolent communication and eco-psychology. I mentioned that I had talked to several parents and community members about trying to do something related to optimizing mental health in our school district. However, I didn't feel like I had time to start something new, since I was already heavily involved with another wellness initiatives in our county—and writing this book! We talked a while longer, and then she said, "I think you should do it." I though about it for two seconds and said, "Okay, let's do it!" I agreed to pull some people together for an information session and see where it went.

Around eight people showed up to the first meeting in my basement. We talked about mindfulness in schools, shared knowledge about various programs and resources, and ate chocolate. The meeting lasted a couple of hours and people left that night feeling excited and hopeful. I stayed up late compiling all the ideas we had come up with and looking up research in support of mindfulness in schools.

Since that first meeting, the group has already accomplished a lot. So far, we've:

- Facilitated a two and a half hour "mini-course" at the middle school on mindfulness and yoga
- Presented to the school district's Wellness Committee (including the health teachers and our amazingly supportive school superintendent) and worked with this group to incorporate a goal related to emotional wellness in the action plan for the upcoming school year
- Raised awareness about the benefits of—and the real need for—social and emotional learning with the entire school district during an educational session for teachers
- Worked with the district's wellness coordinator to facilitate her mindfulness training and selection of a mindfulness-based SEL curriculum that she is teaching in the younger grades this school year

I tell you this to show that you can accomplish a lot with a small number of passionate people (and some chocolate). The key is to have somebody from the school involved from the start (one of our core members works at the middle school) and work through existing channels, if possible (in our case, the school district's Wellness Committee).

Social and emotional learning in schools makes so much sense. Not only does it help kids be mentally healthy, but it also increases academic learning. It is imperative that schools incorporate SEL. Child psychiatrist Scott Shannon agrees:

> I believe a social emotional education curriculum should be part of every child's education, beginning with elementary school. This approach would enhance the emotional growth of all kids long before being identified as being at risk. I know some people argue that this kind of education is the purview of parents. I agree that responsibility for teaching core values should fall to parents, but the development of healthy emotional and social skills is one that crosses all areas of life and should be part of our public educational process.[23]

We're all in this together. Let's make social and emotional learning happen for our kids.

End the Race

As documented in the film *Race to Nowhere*, some kids are literally getting sick from the pressure to perform at school, stress over too much homework, and over-scheduling. Indeed, some children are committing suicide because the pressure is too great to bear. And the drive to get into the right college, have a prestigious career, and make lots of money is pushing some teens over the edge.

The film highlights that the pressure stems from different family situations. There is the pressure from high-achieving families for kids to perform as well as their parents did. On the other hand, there is also pressure on low-income kids to perform, because their parents want their children to have a better life than they have. It also discusses the issue of kids who take a look at the crazy system and decide it's not for them. These are the kids we lose at some point during high school, because we are not able to meet their learning needs and goals.

Let's discuss a few ways we can lessen the pressure on our kids, while not losing any learning in the process.

Homework

In some cases, the pressure and stress comes from having more homework than is appropriate for the given grade level. While we rarely experienced this at our house (Rebecka is a big fan of getting much of her work done *at* school), children and parents in *Race to Nowhere* lament over hours upon hours spent on homework every evening. Kids are staying up late at night, sacrificing their precious sleep to make sure that they get everything done. In addition, family time is reduced, and squabbles about homework lead to tension at home. (Why is it the parents' job to monitor homework anyway?)[24]

As progressive education experts remind us, it's important to take a look at the effectiveness of homework. Do kids really need homework to learn? According to Denise Pope, co-founder of Challenge Success at Stanford University, it depends: "There's almost no correlation between academic achievement in elementary school and homework. When you get to middle school there's a slight correlation, but anything that you're doing after an hour, pretty much that correlation fades. And in high school, there is a link, but really, we see a fallout after two hours."[25]

This sounds reasonable to me. However, one interesting twist on homework, which had never crossed my mind, is that it contributes to the gap between the rich and the poor. Etta Kralovec, Associate Professor at the University of Arizona and author of *The End of Homework*, explains:

> Some kids go home to well-educated parents, access to all kinds of resources. Other kids go home to parents who may work at night, no Internet access—to parents who may speak a second language, so they can't help them with the homework. So the inequalities that exist in our society are actually magnified by the practice of homework.[26]

Alfie Kohn, who also wrote *The Homework Myth*, makes the bold claim that "homework may be the greatest single extinguisher of children's curiosity."[27] In a short YouTube video, "Healthy Homework Guidelines: A New Vision for Homework," produced by the *Race to Nowhere* team, Kohn outlines three simple guidelines to ensure that homework is meaningful:

1. Homework should advance a spirit of learning. (Teachers should have to make a good case for homework.)
2. Homework should be student-directed. (For example, kids reading books of their own choosing.)
3. Homework should promote a balanced schedule. (Give kids time to be kids!)

The *Race to Nowhere* website has a section devoted to helping parents and other concerned community members advocate for healthy homework guidelines in their schools.[28]

Overscheduling

Another symptom of the race to get into the best colleges that we hear a lot about is the immense over-scheduling of some kids. And the reason we hear about it is that it's a real problem. This goes back to the point about letting kids be kids. Children need time to be bored, to sit under a tree and wait for an apple to fall on their head, to run around in unstructured play, and to learn practical skills from their parents.

The biggest problem is the prevalent myth that kids have to be involved in everything: sports, music, clubs, and, of course, community service. This simply isn't true. College admissions officers are a lot more interested in seeing a student really engaged in one or two things. Being a leader and making a difference. And those are the kinds of adults we want to produce anyway, right? Adults who are passionate about one or two things and pour their hearts and souls into them? Success comes from focus on quality over quantity.[29]

There is a simple solution to this problem. Sit down and talk to your child about her activities outside of school, and find out what she really loves and what she could do without. If she feels comfortable enough to tell you the truth, she may surprise you with her answers. Cut out the activities that she doesn't love and move on.

Redefining Success

Toward the end of *Race to Nowhere*, one of the featured teachers, Darrick Smith, summarizes the crux of the matter:

> You can put as much money as you want into schools, but if you don't change the ideology of what makes a good educational system, what type of individual are we trying to create? If you don't prioritize, you know, classes, agendas that do character development, that give kids free time, unscheduled time, if you don't prioritize making cities safe enough so that parents can let their kids have unscheduled time to roam around in the first place—taking the responsibility for raising kids out of advertisers' and corporate hands, giving parents more time off work. It's a social issue.[30]

We must redefine success for the "type of individual" we are trying to create. It's not about perfect grades. It's not about what college you go to. It's not about the kind of job you get or how much money you make. It's about loving what you do, making the world a better place, and being healthy and happy.

In early 2010, I wrote a short blog post called "The Definition of Success." It was inspired by a monologue from the 2009 remake of the movie *Fame*. The monologue started by defining what success is not. "It's not *fame* or *money* or *power*." Rather,

> success is waking up in the morning, so excited about what you have to do to literally fly out the door. It's getting to work with people you love. Success is connecting with the world and making people feel. It's finding a way to bind together people who have nothing in common but a dream. It's falling asleep at night knowing you did the best job you could. Success is joy and freedom and friendship. And success is love.[31]

In the blog post, I wrote that when we left the movie theater, I said to Todd, "I'm not successful." At the time, I was a vice president making a six-digit salary. Todd, who is a professor and was making about a third of my income, responded, "I was thinking the exact opposite."

This is the definition of success I want for my daughter—and for all the children of the world: being so excited about what you have to do that you literally fly out the door.

Serve Real Food and Encourage Play

I would be remiss not to spend a little bit of time addressing nutrition, recess, and fitness in a chapter about student-focused education. School nutrition is actually what got me started in school wellness several years ago. As I mentioned in chapter 2, Rebecka started eating school food in seventh grade. When I eventually looked at the menu to see what they were serving—after discovering that Rebecka had been subsisting on "a la carte" items such as Pop-Tarts, cookies, and chips—I was dismayed. They were feeding our kids junk food! Needless to say, I started researching if this was a problem in other parts of the country, and realized that yes, yes it was—and is. Mostly, subpar school food is an issue of cost, training, and access to fresh food—that is, classic American shortsightedness.

When we moved to Decorah, I decided to join the Wellness Committee. I wanted to work for better food in our schools, but also for adequate recess and effective physical education. Fortunately, Decorah is in much better shape than most school districts because we've had the opportunity to be a W.K. Kellogg Foundation Food and Fitness Initiative community the past five years. As such, I've had the opportunity to work with, and learn from, a number of passionate wellness leaders, parents, and community members.

In this section, I want to talk about two ways schools can help optimize kids' mental health by meeting their most basic physical needs: serving real food and letting kids move their bodies.

Serve Real Food in a Relaxed Setting

Close your eyes and imagine yourself in a middle school cafeteria. Smell the deep-fried chicken nuggets and French fries. Hear the overwhelming cacophony of loud chatter, scraping chairs, and clanking lunch trays. See the pounds of food being wasted because kids had to rush through their meal in order to get to their next activity. Is this where you would want to eat lunch five days a week? How do you think you would feel?

It doesn't have to be like this.

First, schools need to make an effort to serve real, homemade food. This means relying less on processed commodities and more on farm-to-school programs and school gardens. It also involves building functional kitchens staffed with trained cooks to plan nourishing menus that meet the federal guidelines—and cook appetizing, kid-friendly food.

Second, schools should consider involving children in food production, preparation, serving, and cleanup. Few kids are getting cooking skills at home, so why not teach them at school? Planting a garden, harvesting the bounty, preparing meals, setting the table, and washing the dishes are all valuable life skills—and kids love doing them!

Third, schools must create space—both temporal and physical—for relaxed eating. Many states do not have a policy regarding the minimum amount of time students should be allotted for lunch, but the states that do require twenty to thirty minutes of time, once kids have received their food. Children should have plenty of time to chew and taste their food. This helps with weight management and digestion. So does being able to eat in a calm, quiet environment. Ideally, schools would have multiple smaller dining rooms with kid-sized furniture made of natural materials, smaller tables, and family-style dining.*

Schools have the opportunity to provide two of our kids' three meals a day. We should take advantage of this! As Alice Waters, founder of the Edible Schoolyard Project, says: "Right there, in the middle of every school day, lies time and energy already devoted to the feeding of children. We have the power to turn that daily school lunch from an afterthought into a joyous education, a

---

* This is not utopia, my friends. Several European countries have figured this out.

way of caring for our health, our environment, and our community."[32]

Let Kids Play and Move Their Bodies

In *The Story of a Soul, The Autobiography of St. Therese of Lisieux*, Saint Therese writes about her habit of telling stories to her friends during "recreation" (or recess). The stories were so good that even some of the older girls would gather around her to listen. "But," she writes, "soon our mistress, very rightly, brought my career as an orator to an end, saying she wanted us to exercise our bodies and not our brains."[33]

The Story of a Soul was published over one hundred years ago in 1898. Saint Therese's mistress understood the value of exercising the body long before there were scientific studies and brain research to back it up. How much wisdom we have lost over the past hundred years, which we are now rediscovering.

Not only is recess important because it allows kids to move their bodies and get a break from the stress of academics, but children also learn important skills when they play. In 2012, the American Academy of Pediatrics released a new policy statement on recess, "The Crucial Role of Recess in Schools." In the summary, the authors state:

> Recess serves as a necessary break from the rigors of concentrated, academic challenges in the classroom. But equally important is the fact that safe and well-supervised recess offers cognitive, social, emotional, and physical benefits that may not be fully appreciated when a decision is made to diminish it. Recess is unique from, and a complement to, physical education—not a substitute for it. The American Academy of Pediatrics believes that recess is a crucial and necessary component of a child's development and, as such, it should not be withheld for punitive or academic reasons.[34]

And, of course, unstructured play in a natural environment is *so* important for kids with attention and hyperactivity problems[35]—and kinesthetic learners.

I would also like to suggest that we revamp our outdated version of physical education, which is very much geared toward athletic kids. Those of us not fortunate enough to come from the correct gene pool fake illnesses to get out of the most painful class periods (dodgeball, anyone?). Rebecka has told me that PE makes her feel belittled, because she feels like she is so bad at anything that involves balls or speed. She will do whatever it takes to get out of it. That's not what we want for our kids.

Rather, how about renaming PE to "Fitness for Life" or "Self Care"—because that's what's important. We want children to find fitness activities that they can carry with them to adulthood and enjoy for life, not simply endure. Perhaps schools could offer different tracks for kids to choose from:

1. Team sports, for kids who enjoy balls and don't mind getting knocked to the ground every now and then.
2. Individual fitness, for kids who like to run, swim, bike, and do their own thing in their own time.
3. Martial arts, for kids who crave the discipline and structure of the sport.
4. Dance, for kids who prefer to move their bodies to music.

Beyond this, all kids should be exposed to appropriate and accessible weight bearing and stretching activities such as kettlebells, calisthenics, Pilates, yoga, and tai chi, so they can find something that works for them.

Now that's what I call student-centered physical education.

Prioritizing Education—and Our Children's Happiness

While some of the changes I've suggested in this chapter can be implemented without any added cost, others will require additional funds. We need to make teaching a celebrity-status career and pay teachers accordingly. As school districts think about building new schools, their board members should consider sustainably constructed neighborhood schools with fewer kids and teachers, so that children who are not able to thrive in large, factory-style schools can have a chance to learn and be happy. This will also simplify transportation, because kids will be able to bike and walk to school.

While we may lose efficiency, we will gain humanity.

We must ensure that schools have lots of natural spaces for kids to play, discover, and connect with nature. Schools should use natural materials for furniture and equipment as much as possible. Our kids' food should be as good as it comes: organic, local, fresh, and delicious. This will require coordinators of local food procurement, construction of functional kitchens, and training of cooks.

When we prioritize education in the manner I have described above, we prioritize our children's health and happiness. This requires vision and long-term thinking. If we spend more energy and resources upfront to ensure that every child is cared for unconditionally, is nourished in mind and body, is able to learn in a manner that is most conducive to her needs and interests, and is allowed to proceed through school at her own pace, without societal pressure to "succeed" in the traditional sense, we will realize the benefits. We will have a society filled with compassionate, mentally healthy adults possessing a solid sense of self, doing work they love, and being content in the knowledge that they have enough.

If we focus on happiness, success will follow.[36]

21

❧

Putting Vision Into Action

Whether they realize it or not, mental health professionals
who narrowly treat their clients in a way that encourages
compliance with the status quo are acting politically.

—Bruce E. Levine, *Get Up, Stand Up*

As our family emerged on the other side of Rebecka's lost year and realized the role that psychotropic medication, and a one-sided approach to psychiatry, had played in our suffering, one obvious—and very American—reaction was to sue the offending companies.

At the top of our list was Eli Lilly, the manufacturer of Prozac and Zyprexa. Rebecka took these two medications for an extended period of time, and they caused a number of harmful symptoms including suicidal ideation, psychosis, and extreme weight gain. We believe that had we allowed the medication madness to continue, the Rebecka we once knew would have been lost to us forever.

While our family normally doesn't endorse our litigious culture, I kept drawing parallels between Big Tobacco and Big Pharma. Thanks to a number of successful lawsuits against Big Tobacco, everybody is now aware of the health implications of smoking and secondhand smoke. And many states have enacted strict laws prohibiting smoking in public areas, including pubs!

The big difference, of course, is that while tobacco is all-around bad for our health, many pharmaceuticals, possibly including psychotropic drugs, save lives.

Lawsuits Against Big Pharma: Not the Solution

Regardless, at the urging of a couple of friends, I started looking around on the Internet to see if others had tried to sue the pharmaceutical companies and on what grounds.

Sure enough, a handful of Google searches quickly produced a number of articles related to thousands of lawsuits against Eli Lilly and other Big Pharma players. For example, in the 1990s, Eli Lilly reportedly paid in excess of $50 million to settle more than thirty cases related to violence and suicide as side effects of Prozac. (Prozac—and all other SSRIs—now has a so-called "black box" warning on its label to alert consumers to the suicide risk in children and young adults.) These days, people are suing Eli Lilly for birth defects linked to taking Prozac during pregnancy.[1]

Of even greater significance, in 2007, Eli Lilly paid $500 million to settle 18,000 lawsuits from consumers who had developed diabetes or other diseases after taking Zyprexa.[2] Two years later, the same company paid $1.24 *billion* to settle civil suits related to illegal marketing of Zyprexa for treating dementia in non-psychotic patients, a non-approved use of this drug.[3]

Did all these lawsuits hurt Eli Lilly? Not really. Lilly's revenue was over $23 billion in 2013. (They were hurt more by their patents expiring.) Did it change how we prescribe and take drugs in this country? Nope.

While it's good that people whose lives have been ruined by these drugs receive compensation, I've come to the conclusion that lawsuits don't result in the type of systems change that is needed to reduce the incidence of mental illness—and pharmacology-induced suffering—in this country. Young kids and teens are still being diagnosed in droves, the drugs are still out there, physicians are still prescribing them, and the narrative of the broken brain theory is still deeply ingrained in our collective consciousness.

I don't want to sue the pharmaceutical companies. I'd rather participate in creating a society that is designed to optimize children's mental health, to reduce the need for psychotropic medication. Rather than focus on what's wrong, I want to focus how things could be better—and do something about it. I'm starting small in my own community by encouraging the school district to consider social and emotional learning and contemplative practices. I'm excited about the possibility of preventing future mental illness by implementing the changes I've outlined above, and creating happier and healthier kids and adults in the process.

First Things First:
Integrated Care for Kids Who Are Suffering

Of course, first we need to provide holistic treatment for kids and teens who are suffering today—right now. We must ensure that all children and their families have access to integrated care, which considers all the different factors that may contribute to mental distress, from low self-esteem to family dysfunction to lack of sleep.

And instead of using medication as a *first* resort, physicians must be equipped and empowered to provide alternative treatment options and get to the bottom of kids' problems, rather than pathologizing, labeling, and attempting to mask symptoms with potent drugs. As Marilyn Wedge points out in the article, "Why French Kids Don't Have ADHD," French child psychiatrists

> view ADHD as a medical condition that has psycho-social and situational causes. Instead of treating children's focusing and behavioral problems with drugs, French doctors prefer to look for the underlying issue that is causing the child distress—not in the child's brain but in the child's social context. They then choose to treat the underlying social context problem with psychotherapy or family counseling.[4]

We need to adopt this same view here in the United States. Medication should be used only as a *last* resort after careful consideration—and a full explanation of the potential side effects—when the benefits are deemed to outweigh the risks. This is not to say that finally resorting to medication is a failure on the part of the patient, caregivers, or the treatment team, but rather an indication of severe mental illness and a situation where other treatment options are not effective or attainable.

In order to make this shift happen, we need additional reliable research studies to investigate the benefits of "natural cures" such as spending time in nature, engaging in unstructured play, eating real food, practicing mindfulness, exercising, and child-centered educational environments. And we need to distill this information down for busy doctors, nurses, mental health practitioners, parents, and teachers, and work on spreading this data with the same urgency as drug reps push psychotropic medications.

While this may shake the very foundation of everything psychiatrists know to be true, I believe most psychiatrists have their patients' best interest in mind, and they will find ways to reinvent their practices to be integrative and holistic, as have psychiatrists such as Drs. Henry Emmons, Scott Shannon, and Kelly Brogan. Psychiatry cannot continue to depend solely on prescribing and managing medication for its sustenance. Rather, psychiatrists should be responsible for the coordination of care—taking the whole person into consideration, and designing individual treatment plans—for suffering children and teens. Professionals on the team could include the child's regular doctor, the school nurse, specialists, a dietitian, a health coach, a physical therapist, a naturopath, a family therapist, and a yoga instructor. Parents and caregivers would also be part of the team. This is the essence of holistic, integrated care—and the key to treating people experiencing debilitating mental distress.[5]

Long-Term Solution: Optimizing 'Kids' Mental Health

While we establish a network of integrated mental health care for the children and teens who need help now, we need to work in parallel to move our society in a direction that eliminates the undue influence of the pharmaceutical industry on the mental health discourse and optimizes our kids' mental health. This is the only way to end the mental illness epidemic in our country and prevent it from getting worse.

I have provided a number of options for taking action throughout the past four chapters, but I want to summarize the key steps we must take if we truly want to put the health and happiness of our children first.

1. **Become an Informed Citizen:** Read and understand the United States Constitution. Find out who your representatives are at all levels of government, and learn about their platforms. Stay abreast of the issues that matter to you, so you can contact your representatives when critical decisions are on the table. And stand up for voting equality and encourage others to participate in our democratic process. It is our right and duty.

2. **Awaken Your Inner Activist:** We cannot let corporations continue to pacify us with brainless entertainment and allow psychiatry to medicate us into acceptance of the status quo. In Bruce E. Levine's words, we "must focus on how we can be made whole again, so as to regain strength to fight for ourselves and our communities."[6] It's time we stood up for that which matters most—our children's future health and happiness. Pick *one* cause and focus completely on this single cause (for example, education reform, paid parental leave, higher minimum wage, etc.). When we give our undivided attention to one issue, we are more likely to make change happen.

3. **Evaluate Your Lifestyle:** Is your lifestyle causing undue stress in your life and the lives of your family members? If you're like most people, the answer is yes. And stress is one of the largest contributors to physical *and* mental illness. Kids soak up stress like little sponges and then turn around and act out or exhibit other "antisocial" behaviors. Find ways to manage your stress. Evaluate how you spend your money, and determine if you can spend less to work less. Write down your list of commitments in order of importance and see what you can cross off from the bottom of the list. Get off that hamster wheel—it's not leading anywhere.

4. **Practice Compassionate Parenting:** Embrace the possibility that our children are competent—that they come to us with an innate desire to cooperate with us. By being present with our children and truly listening to them, we can become better parents. Show your children that you love and accept them for who they are—not for what they do. This will provide them with much-needed self-esteem. Maintain a balanced and flexible schedule—even though this goes against our current culture. Refuse to schedule every minute of your children's lives. They will thank you later. And above all—be kind.

And Finally…

If you picked up this book because your family is living a psychiatry story, know that there is hope. You do not have to accept your child's devastating diagnosis. It's just a label, and a subjective label at that. I hope you feel equipped with knowledge and strategies to help your child overcome his or her struggles. While it will take a while to upgrade our society to one that promotes mental health, you can take steps within your family, school, and community to improve the conditions for your child.

It is my greatest wish that by now you share my vision that collectively, we can break the cycle of mental illness and raise a generation of mentally healthy, compassionate children. Naturally, we cannot fully shield our children from pain and suffering—these experiences are part of life. However, future generations will be prepared in a radically improved way to handle life's ups and downs and feel empowered to continue to make positive social changes. This is the power of resilience, self-worth, and having enough—enough food, movement, sleep, sunshine, nature, love, friends, creativity, spirituality, and knowledge to live meaningful, high-quality lives.

I've proposed some big societal changes within these pages. Changes so big that they would usher us out of our current mechanistic, patriarchal, biomedical stage of humanity and into what evolutionary theologian L. Robert Keck refers to as Epoch III, our spiritual adulthood.[7] The good news is that we are already on our way—bumpy as the road may be. People in this country are working on every single issue I've described in this book, from getting Big Money out of politics to teaching compassionate parenting to changing the face of education. However, our vision will not materialize unless we all act *personally* and *collectively* to reshape society in the best interest of all people—and especially our children.

It's time.

A Postscript by Rebecka

The present is a million times brighter than my dark past was. Since my recovery, I have gotten to experience more and live life to the fullest. I have let go of my past and only acknowledge it when I need to stop and put things into perspective, if I am having a bad day. Without my illness, I am able to focus on the things I truly love and am passionate about, versus just brooding and feeling sorry for myself.

Having such a difficult experience at such an early age forced me to grow up a lot sooner than most other children. I was forced to face things most people won't ever have to experience. Through bouts of hospitalization, I had to learn to rely on myself and cooperate with others, even when I did not want to. And through recovery, I had to learn to listen to and love myself—something most people struggle with their whole lives. Without my experience, I might never have learned to appreciate myself and the wonderful people around me. It was a terrible experience, but it was a growth experience and something that changed who I am forever, for the better.

Next year, I will begin a new chapter of my life in college. That being said, I am currently suffering through a most intense case of senioritis, but still loving every moment I have to spend time with my friends, as we prepare to go our separate ways in just a few short months. My hope is to continue writing throughout college by pursuing an English major. I cannot be certain what the far future holds, but I can hope that whatever it is includes me living in a large city, working at my own pace, and setting my own hours. I am also hopeful that it includes the worlds of fashion and art, as those are two of my passions and coping skills, and I know I can turn to them whenever life gets a little rough.

There is so much I am thankful for beyond measure. Even though I whine and moan like most teenagers do, I know I have an amazing life that most people would love to have. My parents are extremely proud of how far I have come since thirteen and to this day support me through whatever decisions I make. They are not only my parents, but also my friends, and I know the hardest part of growing up will be to leave them. I am grateful for my friends who keep me grounded and are always there for me to talk to, and to tell me if I am being dumb.

One friend in particular deserves special thanks. My friend Maddie stood by me through the absolute darkest periods of my illness. She was friends with me when no one else wanted to be—when I was the weird, crazy girl. She never once gave up on our friendship and supported me through all of my hospitalizations. Even though we live in different states now, we still keep in contact weekly, if not daily. Without her, the dark times would have been much darker, and my bright present would perhaps not be as bright.

Lastly, I am most of all thankful for the normality of my life. I love being a normal teenager and would not have it any other way. With the help of my family, friends, and amazing dog, I am able to live a healthy, teenage life. The future looks bright indeed.

Acknowledgements

More people than I ever imagined have helped this book come to life. I am forever grateful.

Rebecka, thank you for helping me share your story through the written word. You are an inspiring and courageous young woman—and the funniest person I know. I can't wait to see how you will go about changing the world in your own, special way.

Todd, beyond being my steadfast partner through thick and thin, I will always appreciate your encouraging feedback on the manuscript, your faith in me when mine plummets, and your continuous wisdom and support. I love you!

Sophie, you're the best dog anyone could ask for. Thanks for making our family whole.

Mamma, Priscilla, Fredrik, David Å., Emily, Tobias, Miriam, Johan, Rene, Mike, David G., Caroline, nieces, and nephews, nothing beats a loving family. You are dear to me.

Bob and Emi, thank you for recommending books that brought us hope and changed the course of our lives toward healing.

Dan and Joyce, our *really long* chat on the phone helped me fully appreciate what it means to be a teacher today and the importance of good parenting.

Kate, I appreciate your invaluable insight into the mind of the bookseller. Thank you for giving us Dragonfly Books and being an enthusiastic champion of local authors.

Amalia, Andrea, Caroline, Craig, Deb, Ellen M., Ellen R., Karen, Laura, Shelby, and Todd, thank you for providing early feedback on the "shitty first draft" (as Anne Lamott would say). I appreciate your gentle, yet thoughtful and honest feedback. You made this book better.

Professor Kaethe Schwehn offered valuable feedback on the "story" parts of the book. Katherine Sharpe, author of *Coming of Age on Zoloft*, perfected the manuscript with her top-notch copyediting. My sister Priscilla Åhlén Sundqvist created the stunning cover art. Designers Terry Rydberg, Erik Berg, and Samuel Sander pulled out all the stops to make *Her Lost Year* look and feel beautiful. And Aaron Lurth captured our images. I am thankful beyond words for these creative and talented professionals.

The publication of this book was made possible through monetary contributions from over one hundred families and individuals. Rebecka and I thank you for believing in us and helping us share our story of recovery and hope. Special appreciation goes out to April, the Carroll Family, the Green Family, and Kimberly for your generous pledges. Wow, just wow!

I wrote and edited large portions of this book at my favorite coffee house, Java John's. They have the best chai latte in town and above-and-beyond customer service. If you're ever in Decorah, be sure to stop by. Tell them Tabita sent you.

Finally, to all of you who opened up and shared (and continue to share) your stories with me, thank you. You are not alone.

Notes

Chapter 3 • Side Effects from Hell

1. "Parkinsonism: Causes and coping strategies," Mayo Clinic, last modified August 23, 2011, http://www.mayoclinic.com/health/parkinsonism/AN01178.

2. "Seroquel," last modified June 13, 2014, http://www.drugs.com/seroquel.html.

Chapter 4 • Is It Contagious?

1. Valerie L. Forman-Hoffman and Cassie L. Cunningham, "Geographical clustering of eating disordered behaviors in U.S. high school students," *International Journal of Eating Disorders* 41 (2008): 209–214, doi: 10.1002/eat.20491.

2. Norman T. Berlinger, *Rescuing Your Teenager from Depression* (New York: HarperCollins, 2009), Kindle edition, location 1660.

Chapter 5 • Nobody Will Listen

1. Robert Whitaker, *Anatomy of an Epidemic: Magic Bullets, Psychiatric Drugs, and the Astonishing Rise of Mental Illness in America* (New York: Random House, 2010), 235.

2. Ibid., 245.

3. William V. Bobo et al., "Antipsychotics and the Risk of Type 2 Diabetes Mellitus in Children and Youth," *JAMA Psychiatry* 70 (2013): 1067-1075.

4. Whitaker, *Anatomy*, 207-208.

5. James Colquhoun and Laurentine Ten Bosch, *Food Matters*, Netflix streaming video, directed by Carlo Ledesma and James Colquhoun (2008; McHenry, IL: Permacology Productions, 2008).

6. Ethan Watters, *Crazy Like Us: The Globalization of the American Psyche* (New York: Free Press, 2011), Kindle edition, 238.

7. Glen I. Spielmans and Irving Kirsch, "Drug Approval and Drug Effectiveness," *Annual Review of Clinical Psychology* 10 (2014): 760.

8. Berlinger, *Rescuing Your Teenager*, location 1911.

Chapter 7 · The Turning Point

1. Alexander L. Chapman, "Dialectical Behavior Therapy: Current Indications and Unique Elements," *Psychiatry (Edgemont)* 3(9) (2006): 62–68.

Chapter 8 · Lifesaving Help

1. James Lock, *Help Your Teenager Beat an Eating Disorder* (New York: Guilford Press, 2004), Kindle edition, 121.

Chapter 9 · Breaking Free Factors

1. Marilyn Wedge, *Suffer the Children: The Case Against Labeling and Medicating and an Effective Alternative* (New York: W. W. Norton & Company, 2011), 41.

2. Berlinger, *Rescuing Your Teenager*, location 1188.

3. Pouneh G. Fazeli, et al., "Psychotropic Medication Use in Anorexia Nervosa between 1997 and 2009," *International Journal of Eating Disorders* 45 (2012): 970-75.

4. Lock, *Help Your Teenager*, 120-121.

5. Whitaker, *Anatomy*, 210.

Chapter 10 · From Psychotherapy to Psychotropics

1. Gardiner Harris, "Talk Doesn't Pay, So Psychiatry Turns Instead to Drug Therapy," *New York Times*, March 5, 2011, accessed September 27, 2014, http://www.nytimes.com/2011/03/06/health/policy/06doctors.html.

2. "A Short History of Thorazine," accessed September 27, 2014, http://katherinegscott.wordpress.com/2011/02/03/a-short-history-of-thorazine/.

3. Whitaker, *Anatomy*, 6-8.

4. Debbie M. Price, "For 175 Years: Treating Mentally Ill With Dignity," *New York Times*, April 17, 1988, accessed September 27, 2014, http://www.nytimes.com/1988/04/17/us /for-175-years-treating-mentally-ill-with-dignity.html.

5. Jim Haggerty, "History of Psychotherapy," *Psych Central*, reviewed January 30, 2013, http://psychcentral.com/lib/history-of-psychotherapy/000115.

6. Allen Frances, *Saving Normal: An Insider's Revolt Against Out-of-Control Psychiatric Diagnosis, DSM-5, Big Pharma, and the Medicalization of Ordinary Life* (New York: HarperCollins, 2013), 108.

7. Whitaker, *Anatomy*, 47.

8. J. Swazey, *Chlorpromazine in Psychiatry* (Cambridge, MA: MIT Press, 1974), 105.

9. Whitaker, *Anatomy*, 48-51.

10. Ibid., 51-52.

11. Ibid., 78.

12. Mayo Clinic, *Teens + Antidepressant Medication: Stay on your meds!* (Rochester, MN: Mayo Foundation for Medical Education and Research, 2009), 5.

13. "Zoloft Commercial," YouTube video, posted by "lemsipGY," May 19, 2007,

https://www.youtube.com/watch?v=6vfSFXKlnO0.

14. Jonathan Rottenberg, "The Serotonin Theory of Depression Is Collapsing," *Psychology Today*, July 23, 2010, accessed September 27, 2014, http://www.psychologytoday.com /blog/charting-the-depths/201007/the-serotonin-theory-depression-is-collapsing.

15. "What Is Depression?" National Institute of Mental Health, accessed September 27, 2014, http://www.nimh.nih.gov/health/publications/depression/index.shtml.

16. Qiuping Gu, Charles F. Dillon, and Vicki L. Burt, "Prescription Drug Use Continues to Increase: U.S. Prescription Drug Data for 2007–2008," NCHS Data Brief, no. 42, (Hyattsville, MD: National Center for Health Statistics, 2010), 5.

17. IMS HEALTH, *2010 Top Therapeutic Classes by Spending*, IMS National Sales Perspectives", last modified April 7, 2011.

18. Ibid.

19. "What causes depression?" Harvard Health Publications, accessed August 12, 2014, http://www.health.harvard.edu/newsweek/what-causes-depression.htm.

20. Whitaker, *Anatomy*, 318.

21. Ibid., 221.

22. Ibid., 237.

23. "What is attention deficit hyperactivity disorder?" The National Institute of Mental Health, revised 2012, http://www.nimh.nih.gov/health/publications /attention-deficit-hyperactivity-disorder/index.shtml.

24. "The Basics of ADHD," WebMD, reviewed on May 10, 2014, http://www.webmd.com/add-adhd/childhood-adhd/adhd-basics.

25. "Attention-deficit/hyperactivity disorder (ADHD) in children," Mayo Clinic Staff, Mayo Clinic, March 5, 2013, http://www.mayoclinic.org/diseases-conditions/adhd/basics /causes/con-20023647.

26. Judith Warner, *We've Got Issues: Children and Parents in the Age of Medication* (New York: Penguin Group, 2010), 241.

27. "A Study for Assessing Treatment of Patients Ages 10-17 With Bipolar Depression," ClinicalTrials.gov, accessed September 27, 2104, http://clinicaltrials.gov/ct2/show/results/NCT00844857.

28. Warner, *We've Got Issues*, 222.

29. Gu, Dillon, and Burt, "Prescription Drug Use Continues to Increase," 2.

30. Whitaker, *Anatomy*, 164-169.

31. Ibid., 5.

32. Warner, *We've Got Issues*, 221.

33. Watters, *Crazy Like Us*, 238.

Chapter 11 • Under the Influence of Big Pharma

1. Pew Prescription Project with Community Catalyst, *Pharmaceutical Industry Marketing*, (Boston: PRESCRIPTIONPROJECT.ORG, 2009).

2. ZYPREXA label, (Indianapolis: Eli Lilly and Company, 2009), accessed September 27, 2014, http://www.accessdata.fda.gov/drugsatfda_docs/label/2013 /020592s063,021086s041lbl.pdf.

3. Ibid.

4. Whitaker, *Anatomy*, 229.

5. Ibid., 230-1.

6. Warner, *'We've Got Issues*, 242.

7. Ibid., 129.

8. Liz Kowalczyk, "60 doctors took speaker fees from drug giant," *The Boston Globe*, September 29, 2009, accessed September 27, 2014, http://www.boston.com/news /health/articles/2009/09/29/60_doctors_took_speaker_fees_from_drug_giant/.

9. Shantanu Agrawal et al., "The Sunshine Act — Effects on Physicians," *The New England Journal of Medicine*, 368 (2013): 2054-2057, accessed September 27, 2014, doi: 10.1056/NEJMp1303523.

10. "Physician Payment Registry," Eli Lilly and Company, accessed September 27, 2014, http://www.lillyphysicianpaymentregistry.com/Payments-to-Physicians/Current-Registry; "Physician Payments," Janssen Pharmaceuticals, Inc., accessed September 27, 2014, http://www.hcctransparency.com/report/janssenpharmaceuticalsinc /134/hcp/yearly; "Physician engagement," AstraZeneca United States, accessed September 27, 2014, http://www.astrazeneca-us.com/responsibility /corporate-transparency/physician-engagement.

11. Warner, *'We've Got Issues*, 242.

12. Watters, *Crazy Like Us*, 189.

13. Ibid., 190-192.

14. Ibid., 225.

15. Frances, *Saving Normal*, 28.

16. "Antidepressant Medications for Children and Adolescents: Information for Parents and Caregivers," National Institute of Mental Health, accessed September 27, 2014, http://www.nimh.nih.gov/health/topics/child-and-adolescent-mental-health/ antidepressant-medications-for-children-and-adolescents-information-for-parents-and-caregivers.shtml.

17. Alex Chadwick, interview with Sydney Spiesel, National Public Radio, podcast audio, October 22, 2008, http://www.npr.org/templates/story/story.php?storyId=95985619.

18. Whitaker, *Anatomy*, 218.

19. Ibid., 325.

20. Berlinger, *Rescuing Your Teenager*, location 1721.

21. Ibid., 245.

22. Ibid., 246.

23. Frances, *Saving Normal*, 95.

24. "Major Foundation and Corporate Support," National Alliance on Mental Illness (NAMI), accessed September 27, 2014, http://www.nami.org/Template.cfm?Section= Major_Foundation_and_Corporate_Support.

25. Whitaker, *Anatomy*, 276-77.

26. American Psychiatric Association, Detail on Industry Revenue, accessed September 21, 2013, http://www.psychiatry.org/about-apa--psychiatry/annual-reports.

27. "Research Fellowships," American Psychiatric Association, accessed September 21, 2013, http://www.psychiatry.org/researchers/research-training-and-funding /research-fellowships.

28. "About NIMH," National Institute of Mental Health, accessed October 4, 2014, http://www.nimh.nih.gov/about/index.shtml.

29. "What Is Depression?"

30. "Introduction: Mental Health Medications," National Institute of Mental Health, revised 2008, http://www.nimh.nih.gov/health/publications /mental-health-medications/index.shtml.

31. Whitaker, *Anatomy*, 245.

32. Daneial J. Carlat, "Robert Whitaker's Anatomy of an Epidemic: The Carlat Take," *The Carlat Psychiatry Blog*, January 21, 2011, accessed October 4, 2014, http://carlatpsychiatry.blogspot.com/2011/01/robert-whitakers-anatomy-of-epidemic.html.

Chapter 12 · Expanding the Definition of Mental Illness

1. "DSM: History of the Manual," American Psychiatric Association, accessed October 4, 2014, http://www.psychiatry.org/practice/dsm/dsm-history-of-the-manual.

2. Edgar Z. Friedenberg, "Sick, Sick, Sick?" *New York Times*, August 22, 1965, accessed November 2, 2013, http://www.nytimes.com/books/00/12/17specials /foucault-madness.html.

3. Michel Foucault, *History of Madness* (New York: Routledge, 2006), xvi.

4. Neel Burton, "Understanding Mental Disorders," *Psychology Today*, May 27, 2012, accessed November 2, 2013, http://www.psychologytoday.com/ blog/hide-and-seek/201205/understanding-mental-disorders.

5. Ibid.

6. Friedenberg, "Sick, Sick, Sick."

7. Burton, "Understanding Mental Disorders."

8. Nancy Joseph (Editor), "Mental Illness as a Social Construct," *A&S Perspectives*, July 2010 issue, accessed August 23, 2014, http://www.artsci.washington.edu/newsletter /July10/BorchJacobsen.asp.

9. Barbara A. Mather, "The Social Construction and Reframing of Attention-Deficit/ Hyperactivity Disorder," *Ethical Human Psychology and Psychiatry* 14 (2012): 15-24.

10. Watters, *Crazy Like Us*, 13.

11. Ibid., 59.

12. Frances, *Saving Normal*, 16.

13. Margarita Tartakovsky, "How the DSM Developed: What You Might Not Know," *Psych Central*, reviewed July 3, 2011, http://psychcentral.com/blog/archives/2011/07/02 /how-the-dsm-developed-what-you-might-not-know/.

14. Frances, *Saving Normal*, 67.

15. Ibid., 69.

16. Ibid., 73.

17. Ibid., 73.

18. Ibid., 78-81.

19. Ibid., 81-83.

20. Ibid., 83-84.

21. Ibid., 84-85.

22. Ibid., 87-89.

23. Ibid., 90-95.

24. Ibid., 97-99.

25. Ibid., 103.

26. Ibid., 95.

27. Ibid., 104.

28. Anahad O'Connor, "Younger Students More Likely to Get A.D.H.D. Drugs," *New York Times*, November 20, 2012, accessed October 4, 2014, http://well.blogs.nytimes.com /2012/11/20/younger-students-more-likely-to-get-a-d-h-d-drugs/.

29. Whitaker, *Anatomy*, 33-34.

30. Ibid., 3.

Part 4

1. Ibid., 344-347.

2. Kelly Dorfman, *What's Eating Your Child?* (New York: Workman Publishing, 2001), 200-202.

3. Watters, *Crazy Like Us*, 57.

4. Henning Tiemeier et al., "Vitamin B12, Folate, and Homocysteine in Depression: The Rotterdam Study," *The American Journal of Psychiatry* 159 (2002): 2099-2101, accessed February 1, 2014, doi: 10.1176/appi.ajp.159.12.2099.; Alec Coppen and Christina Bolander-Gouaille, "Treatment of depression: time to consider folic acid and vitamin B12," *Journal of Psychopharmacology* 19 (2005): 59-65, accessed February 1, 2014, doi: 10.1177/0269881105048899.

5. Richard Louv, *Last Child in the Woods: Saving Our Children From Nature-Deficit Disorder* (Chapel Hill, NC: Algonquin Books, 2008), Kindle Edition, 32.

Chapter 13 • Taking Care of Physical needs

1. David C. Nieman et al., "Exercise and the Common Cold," *ACSM Current Comment*, accessed September 2, 2014, http://www.acsm.org/docs/current-comments /exerciseandcommoncold.pdf.

2. "ACSM Issues New Recommendations on Quantity and Quality of Exercise," American College of Sports Medicine, accessed October 4, 2014, http://www.acsm.org/about-acsm/media-room/news-releases/2011/08/01 /acsm-issues-new-recommendations-on-quantity-and-quality-of-exercise.

3. Neville Owen et al., "Too Much Sitting: The Population-Health Science of Sedentary Behavior," *Exercise and Sport Sciences Reviews* 38 (2010): 105-113, accessed February 1, 2014, doi: 10.1097/JES.0b013e3181e373a2.

4. Dan Beuttner, *The Blue Zones: Lessons for Living Longer from the People Who've Lived the Longest* (Washington, D.C.: National Geographic Books, 2008), 46.

5. John J. Ratey, *Spark: The Revolutionary New Science of Exercise and the Brain* (New York: Little, Brown and Company, 2008), Kindle Edition, location 23.

6. Ibid., location 28.

7. Ibid., location 77.

8. M. Bonhauser et al., "Improving physical fitness and emotional well-being in adolescents of low socioeconomic status in Chile: results of a school-based controlled trial," *Health Promotion International* 20 (2005): 113-22, accessed October 4, 2014, http://www.ncbi.nlm.nih.gov/pubmed/15788528.

9. Whitaker, *Anatomy*, 347.

10. Maria Carling, "Kroppen kan läka själen," *Svenska Dagbladet*, February 28, 2012, last modified October 16, 2014, http://www.svd.se/nyheter/idagsidan/kropp-och-halsa/kroppen-kan-laka-sjalen_6884649.svd.

11. Ratey, *Spark*, location 1938.

12. "How much physical activity to children need?" Centers for Disease Control and Prevention, last modified November 9, 2011, http://www.cdc.gov/physicalactivity/everyone/guidelines/children.html.

13. Dorfman, *What's Eating*, 172 – 183.

14. Barbara Reed Stitt, *Food and Behavior: A Natural Connection* (Manitowoc, WI: Natural Press, 2004), 28.

15. "How Much Sleep Do I Need?" Centers for Disease Control and Prevention, last modified July 1, 2013, http://www.cdc.gov/sleep/about_sleep/how_much_sleep.htm.

16. Kathryn M. Orzech et al., "Sleep patterns are associated with common illness in adolescents," *Journal of Sleep Research* 23 (2014): 133–142, accessed October 11, 2014, doi: 10.1111/jsr.12096.

17. David Perlmutter, *Grain Brain: The Surprising Truth about Wheat, Carbs, and Sugar—Your Brain's Silent Killers* (New York: Little, Brown and Company, 2013), 207-208.; "Teens Who Get Little Sleep, Are Glued To Digital Devices And Don't Exercise Could Face Psychiatric Risks," *Huffington Post*, February 3, 2014, last modified February 3, 2014, http://www.huffingtonpost.com/2014/02/03/digital-devices-sleep-teens-mental-health-exercise-psychiatric-risks_n_4718162.html.

18. "Treating sleep disorders may help psychological problems, reports the Harvard Mental Health Letter," Harvard Health Publications, July 1, 2009, accessed February 11, 2014, http://www.health.harvard.edu/press_releases/treating-sleep-disorders-may-help-psychological-problems.

19. Alice M. Gregory and Avi Sadeh, "Sleep, emotional and behavioral difficulties in children and adolescents," *Sleep Medicine Reviews* 16 (2012), 129-36, accessed October 11, 2014, doi: 10.1016/j.smrv.2011.03.007.

20. "Sleep and mental health."

21. Jeanie Wolfson, *It's Not Mental: Finding Innovative Support and Medical Treatment for a Child Diagnosed with a Severe Mental Illness* (Cerebella Publishing, 2010), 338.

22. Kate Murphy, "Attention Problems May Be Sleep-Related," *New York Times*, April 16, 2012, accessed February 11, 2014, http://well.blogs.nytimes.com/2012/04/16/attention-problems-may-be-sleep-related/.

23. Jon Kabat-Zinn, *Full Catastrophe Living: Using the Wisdom of Your Body and Mind to Face Stress, Pain, and Illness* (New York: Bantam Books, 2013), Kindle edition, location 8028.

24. Deborah Rice, "Experts say exposure to artificial light from tablets is causing sleep disorders," *ABC*, June 30, 2013, accessed February 11, 2014, http://www.abc.net.au/news/2013-07-01/artificial-light-leading-to-increase-in-sleep-disorders/4790448.

25. *Race to Nowhere*, DVD, directed by Vicki Abeles, and Jessica Congdon (2010; LaFayette: Reel Link Films, 2011).

26. Louv, *Last Child*, 126.

27. Gary Paul Nabhan and Stephen Trimble, *The Geography of Childhood: Why Children Need Wild Places* (Boston: Beacon Press, 1994), 9.

28. Cris Rowan, "The Impact of Technology on the Developing Child," *Huffington Post*, May 29, 2013, last modified July 29, 2013, http://www.huffingtonpost.com/cris-rowan /technology-children-negative-impact_b_3343245.html.

29. Sandra L. Hofferth, "Changes in American children's time – 1997 to 2003." *Electron Int J Time Use Res.* 6 (2009): 26–47, accessed February 18, 2014, http://www.ncbi.nlm.nih.gov/pmc/articles/PMC2939468/.

30. "The Impact of Technology on the Developing Child."

31. Louv, *Last Child*, 50.

32. Razali Salleh Mohd, "Life Event, Stress and Illness," *Malaysian Journal of Medical Sciences* 15 (2008): 9-18, accessed February 10, 2014, http://www.ncbi.nlm.nih.gov /pmc/articles/PMC3341916/.

33. Louv, *Last Child*, 100.

34. "Green Play Settings Reduce ADHD Symptoms," University of Illinois at Urbana-Champaign Landscape and Human Health Laboratory, accessed February 20, 2014, http://lhhl.illinois.edu/adhd.htm.

35. Nabhan, *Geography of Childhood*, 98.

36. Suzanne Bennett Johnson, "Medicine's Paradigm Shift: The Case for Integrated Care," American Psychological Association, accessed February 22, 2014, https://www.apa.org/about/governance/president/paradigm-shift-integrated-care.pdf.

37. Louv, *Last Child*, 49.

Chapter 14
Mindful Awareness, Belonging, and Being Part of Something Bigger

1. Leo Babauta, "The Mindfulness Guide for the Super Busy: How to Live Life to the Fullest," *Zen Habits*, accessed October 11, 2014, http://zenhabits.net /the-mindfulness-guide-for-the-super-busy-how-to-live-life-to-the-fullest/.

2. Leo Babauta, "How to Master the Art of Mindful Eating," *Zen Habits*, accessed October 11, 2014, http://zenhabits.net/mindful-eating/.

3. Jon Robison and Karen Carrier, *The Spirit and Science of Holistic Health* (Bloomington, IN: AuthorHouse, 2004), 37-38.

4. Kabat-Zinn, *Full Catastrophe*, location 363.

5. Daphne M. Davis and Jeffrey A. Hayes, "What Are the Benefits of Mindfulness? A Practice Review of Psychotherapy-Related Research," *Psychotherapy* 48 (2011): 198-208, accessed February 22, 2014, doi: 0.1037/a0022062.

6. Kabat-Zinn, *Full Catastrophe*, location 395.

7. Susan Kaiser Greenland, *The Mindful Child: How to Help Your Kid Manage Stress and Become Happier, Kinder, and More Compassionate* (New York: Atria Books, 2010), 5-6.

8. Kabat-Zinn, *Full Catastrophe*, location 1662.

9. Ibid., location 1668.

10. Greenland, *Mindful Child*, 14.

11. Ibid., 105.

12. Ibid. 10-12.

13. *Healthy Habits of Mind*, streamed online, directed by Mette Bahnsen (2013; Århus: Persona Film, 2013), http://www.mindfulschools.org/resources /healthy-habits-of-mind/.

14. Ibid.

15. "Power 9," Blue Zones Project® by HEALTHWAYS, accessed February 25, 2014, https://iowa.bluezonesproject.com/power9.

16. Kabat-Zinn, *Full Catastrophe*, location 4776.

17. Hayley Dixon, "Choir singing 'boosts your mental health'," *The Telegraph*, December 4, 2013, accessed February 27, 2014, http://www.telegraph.co.uk/health/healthnews /10496056/Choir-singing-boosts-your-mental-health.html.

18. Mark Hyman, "How Eating at Home Can Save Your Life," *Huffington Post*, January 9, 2011, last modified May 25, 2011, http://www.huffingtonpost.com/dr-mark-hyman /family-dinner-how_b_806114.html.

19. Buettner, *Blue Zones*, 180-184.

20. "Power 9."

21. Robert Shedinger, *Radically Open: Transcending Religious Identity in an Age of Anxiety* (Eugene, OR: Cascade Books, 2012), 46.

22. Ibid. 128.

23. Matthew McKay, Jeffery C. Wood, and Jeffrey Brantley, *The Dialectical Behavior Therapy Skills Workbook: Practical DBT Exercises for Learning Mindfulness, Interpersonal Effectiveness, Emotion Regulation & Distress Tolerance* (Oakland, CA: New Harbinger Publications, 2007), 39.

24. Ibid. 41.

Chapter 15
Beyond Talk Therapy: Family Therapy, the Maudsley Approach, and DBT

1. Berlinger, *Saving Your Child*, location 2234-41.

2. Wedge, *Suffer*, 215.

3. Ibid. 43.

4. Ibid. 155-6.

5. Lock and Le Grange, *Beat an Eating Disorder*, 121.

6. Daniel Le Grange and James Lock, "Family-based Treatment of Adolescent Anorexia Nervosa: The Maudsley Approach," Maudsley Parents, accessed March 8, 2014, http://www.maudsleyparents.org/whatismaudsley.html.; Lock and Le Grange, *Beat an Eating Disorder*, 53.

7. Blaise Aguirre, "Borderline Personality Disorder in Adolescents," *Psychology Today*, June 1, 2010, accessed March 8, 2014, http://www.psychologytoday.com/blog /stop-walking-eggshells/201006/borderline-personality-disorder-in-adolescents.

8. Ibid.

9. Linda Baird, "Childhood Trauma in the Etiology of Borderline Personality Disorder: Theoretical Considerations and Therapeutic Interventions," *Hakomi Forum* 19-20-21 (2008): 32, accessed October 11, 2014, http://www.hakomiinstitute. com/Forum/Issue19-21/4Linda%20Baird,%20Childhood%20Trauma2.pdf.

10. McKay, Wood, and Brantley, *Dialectical Behavior Therapy Skills Workbook*, 2.

11. Frances, *Saving Normal*, 178-179.

Part 5 • Optimizing Children's Mental Health

1. Lawrence Diller, *The Last Normal Child: Essays on the Intersection of Kids, Culture, and Psychiatric Drugs* (Westport, CT: Greenwood Publishing Group, 2006), 15.

2. Nina Björk, *Lyckliga i alla sina dagar: om pengars och människors värde* [Happily Ever After: On the Worth of People and Money] (Stockholm: Bonnier Pocket, 2013), 178.

Chapter 16 • A Society Designed to Optimize Mental Health

1. "Facts & Statistics," Anxiety and Depression Association of America, accessed August 8, 2014, http://www.adaa.org/about-adaa/press-room/facts-statistics.

2. "Chronic Diseases and Health Promotion," Centers for Disease Control and Prevention accessed February 14, 2015, http://www.cdc.gov/chronicdisease/overview/index.htm.

3. "Muhammad Yunus: Social Business," *Forbes*, June 15, 2010, accessed April 26, 2014, http://www.forbes.com/2010/06/15/forbes-india-muhammad-yunus-social-business-opinions-ideas-10-yunus.html.

4. Ibid.

5. Muhammad Yunus, *Building Social Business: The New Kind of Capitalism that Serves Humanity's Most Pressing Needs* (New York: PublicAffairs™, 2010), 9-10.

6. "About Us," Hometown Taxi, accessed April 26, 2014, http://www.hometowntaxidecorah.com/.

7. Alvarado Street Bakery, accessed April 26, 2014, http://www.alvaradostreetbakery.com/.

8. "About," Design Action Collective, accessed April 26, 2014, http://designaction.org/about/.

9. "What is a Worker Cooperative?" US Federation of Worker Cooperatives, accessed April 26, 2014, http://www.usworker.coop/about/what-is-a-worker-coop.

10. Alexander Eichler, "Pharmaceutical Companies Spent 19 Times More On Self-Promotion Than Basic Research: Report," *Huffington Post*, August 9, 2012, last modified May 8, 2013, http://www.huffingtonpost.com/2012/08/09/pharmaceutical-companies-marketing_n_1760380.html.

11. "Persuading the Prescribers: Pharmaceutical Industry Marketing and its Influence on Physicians and Patients," The Pew Charitable Trusts, accessed November 18, 2014, http://www.pewtrusts.org/en/research-and-analysis/fact-sheets/2013/11/11/persuading-the-prescribers-pharmaceutical-industry-marketing-and-its-influence-on-physicians-and-patients.

12. "Fact Sheet: Pharmaceutical Industry Marketing," The Pew Charitable Trusts, January 28, 2009, http://www.pewtrusts.org/~/media/legacy/uploadedfiles/phg/supporting_items/IBFSPPPPharmaceuticalIndustryMarketingpdf.pdf.

13. Bruce E. Levine, *Get Up, Stand Up: Uniting Populists, Energizing the Defeated, and Battling the Corporate Elite* (White River Jct., VT: Chelsea Green Publishing, 2011), location 1296.

14. Will Meek, "TV & ADHD," *PsychCentral*, accessed April 26, 2014, http://psychcentral.com/blog/archives/2007/09/08/tv-adhd/.

15. Marie Look, "Trash Planet: Germany," Earth911, July 13, 2009, accessed November 21, 2014, http://www.earth911.com/earth-watch/trash-planet-germany/.

16. *Happy*, Netflix streaming video, directed by Roko Belic (2011; Los Angeles:

Creative Visions Foundation, 2011).

17. "The 6 Defining Characteristics of Cohousing," The Cohousing Association, accessed November 21, 2014, http://www.cohousing.org/six_characteristics.

18. Jenny Isenman, "Should Parents Need a License to Procreate?" *The Huffington Post*, April 7, 2013, last updated April 7, 2013, http://www.huffingtonpost.com /jenny-isenman/parenting-humor_b_2615932.html.

19. Alfie Kohn, *Feel-Bad Education: And Other Contrarian Essays on Children and Schooling* (Boston: Beacon Press, 2011), 3.

20. "Universal Declaration of Human Rights," Office of the United Nations High Commissioner for Human Rights, accessed May 3, 2014, http://www.ohchr.org/EN/UDHR/Pages/Language.aspx?LangID=eng.

Chapter 17 · Creating a Culture of Enough

1. Leo Babauta, "How to Slow Down Now (Please Read Slowly)," *Zen Habits*, accessed May 3, 2014, http://zenhabits.net/how-to-slow-down-now-please-read-slowly/.

2. Leo Babauta, "18 Five-Minute Decluttering Tips to Start Conquering Your Mess," *Zen Habits*, accessed May 3, 2014, http://zenhabits.net/18-five-minute-decluttering-tips-to-start-conquering-your-mess/.

3. Leo Babauta, "The Ultimate Minimalist: 5 Powerful Lessons You Can Learn From Gandhi," Zen Habits, accessed May 3, 2014, http://zenhabits.net/gandhi-lessons/.

4. Tabita Green, "Reflections on the No New Clothes Experiment," *Simply Enough*, December 30, 2009, accessed May 3, 2014, http://tabitagreen.com /reflections-on-my-no-new-clothes-experiment/.

5. Björk, Lyckliga, 38.

6. Ibid. 53-55.

7. Ibid. 128.

8. Eric Holthaus, "Carbon Dioxide Levels in Atmosphere Reach Terrifying New Milestone," *Slate*, May 1, 2014, accessed May 4, 2014, http://www.slate. com/blogs/future_tense/2014/05/01/mauna_loa_atmosphere_measurements_carbon_dioxide_levels_above_400_ppm_throughout.html.

9. "How much do we waste daily?" Duke University, accessed May 4, 2014, http://center.sustainability.duke.edu/resources/green-facts-consumers /how-much-do-we-waste-daily.

10. "How many species are we losing?", WWF, accessed May 4, 2014, http://wwf.panda.org/about_our_earth/biodiversity/biodiversity/.

11. Jim Merkel, *Radical Simplicity: Small Footprints on a Finite Earth* (Gabriola Island, BC: New Society Publishers, 2003), 55.

12. Ibid. 93.

13. "What is an ecological footprint?" Global Living Project, accessed May 4, 2014, http://www.radicalsimplicity.org/footprint.html.

14. "Kantar Media Reports U.S. Advertising Expenditures Increased 0.9 Percent In 2013, Fueled By Larger Advertisers," *Kantar Media*, March 25, 2014, accessed August 24, 2014, http://kantarmedia.us/press/kantar-media-reports-us-advertising-expenditures-increased-09-percent-2013.

15. "Mission," The Center for a New American Dream, accessed May 4, 2014, http://www.newdream.org/about/mission.

16. Tori DeAngelis, "Consumerism and its discontents," *Monitor on Psychology* 35 (2004): 52, accessed August 10, 2014, http://www.apa.org/monitor/jun04/discontents.aspx.

17. "Circle of Simplicity: Return to the Good Life," Cecile Andrews, accessed May 9, 2014, http://www.cecileandrews.com/Topics.htm.

18. "Circle of Simplicity: Return to the Good Life," Cecile Andrews, accessed May 9, 2014, http://www.cecileandrews.com/index.htm.

19. Lucien Tessler, "Boy Scouts: Vote to end your anti-gay policy so my brother can earn his Eagle award," Change.org, accessed May 10, 2014, http://www.change.org/petitions/boy-scouts-vote-to-end-your-anti-gay-policy-so-my-brother-can-earn-his-eagle-award.

20. Dominique Kalata, "Stop using styrofoam coffee cups on flights," Change.org, accessed May 10, 2014, http://www.change.org/petitions/united-airlines-stop-using-styrofoam-coffee-cups-on-flights.

21. Sarah Kavanagh, "Powerade: If Gatorade can take crazy chemical BVO out of sports drinks, so can you," Change.org, accessed May 10, 2014, http://www.change.org/petitions/powerade-if-gatorade-can-take-crazy-chemical-bvo-out-of-sports-drinks-so-can-you.

22. "Other stuff relating to Reduce, Reuse, Recycle," Pinterest, accessed May 10, 2014, http://www.pinterest.com/sdrecycle/other-stuff-relating-to-reduce-reuse-recycle/.

23. Wen Lee, "PHOTOS: What Does "More Fun, Less Stuff" Mean to You?" The Center for a New American Dream, March 13, 2014, accessed May 10, 2014, http://www.newdream.org/blog/more-fun-less-stuff-photos.

Chapter 18 • Establishing a Just Republic

1. "Our Hidden History of Corporations in the United States," Reclaim Democracy!, accessed May 18, 2014, http://reclaimdemocracy.org/corporate-accountability-history-corporations-us/.

2. Jeff Clements, *Corporations Are Not People: Why They Have More Rights Than You Do and What You Can Do About It* (San Francisco: Berrett-Koehler Publishers, 2012), xiii.

3. "Top Industries," OpenSecrets.org, accessed May 18, 2014, http://www.opensecrets.org/lobby/top.php?showYear=2013&indexType=i.

4. "Revolving Door," OpenSecrets.org, accessed May 18, 2014, http://www.opensecrets.org/revolving/.

5. Robert Kyriakides, "The influence of big business on democracy," *Robert Kyriakides's Weblog*, March 31, 2011, accessed May 18, 2014, https://robertkyriakides.wordpress.com/2011/03/31/the-influence-of-big-business-on-democracy/.

6. Clements, *Corporations*, 3.

7. Ibid., 8.

8. Fernando Pargas, *Stopping Big Business and Politics From Bleeding America* (Silver Spring, MD: Beckham Publications Group, 2011), Kindle edition, location 2687.

9. "The Story of Citizens United v. FEC," YouTube video, 8:50, posted by "storyofstuffproject," February 25, 2011, http://youtu.be/k5kHACjrdEY.

10. Martin Gilens and Benjamin I. Page, "Testing Theories of American Politics: Elites, Interest Groups, and Average Citizens," *Perspectives on Politics* 12 (2014): 566, accessed November 21, 2014, doi: 10.1017/S1537592714001595.

11. Clements, *Corporations*, 145.

12. Deepa Fernandes, "Half of the nation's children have suffered trauma, report says,"

89.3 KPCC, accessed August 24, 2014, http://www.scpr.org/blogs/education
/2014/07/31/17084/report-half-of-the-nation-s-children-have-suffered/.

13. Björk, *Lyckliga*, 128.

14. Danielle Kurtzleben, "2010 Set Campaign Spending Records," *U.S. News & World Report*, accessed May 18, 2014, http://www.usnews.com/news/articles /2011/01/07/2010-set-campaign-spending-records.

15. "Voting and Registration in the Election of November 2010 - Detailed Tables," last modified October, 2011, http://www.census.gov/hhes/www/socdemo/voting /publications/p20/2010/tables.html.

16. Clements, *Corporations*, 146.

17. John Nichols, "The Senate Judiciary Committee Just Backed an Amendment to Overturn 'Citizens United'," *Moyers & Company*, July 14, 2014, accessed September 6, 2014, http://billmoyers.com/2014/07/12/the-senate-judiciary-committee-just-backed-an-amendment-to-overturn-%E2%80%98citizens-united%E2%80%99/.

18. Ibid. 146.

19. "Fair Elections Now Act," Public Campaign, accessed May 18, 2014, http://www.publicampaign.org/fair-elections-now-act.

20. Clements, *Corporations*, 155-157.

21. Ibid. 157-159.

22. Ibid. 156.

23. Ibid. 157.

24. "Business FAQ's," Benefit Corp Information Center, accessed May 18, 2014, http://benefitcorp.net/business.

25. Ibid.

26. Mike P. Zinn, "Government Spends More on Corporate Welfare Subsidies than Social Welfare Programs," *Think by Numbers*, accessed May 24, 2014, http://thinkbynumbers. org/government-spending/corporate-welfare/corporate-welfare-statistics-vs-social-welfare-statistics/.

27. Martin Lobel, "Should We Subsidize Multinationals or Repair Our Infrastructure?" *Huffington Post*, January 28, 2014, last modified March 30, 2014, http://www.huffingtonpost.com/martin-lobel/should-we-subsidize-rax-reform_b_4674126.html.

28. Emily Atkin, "Fossil Fuels Receive $500 Billion A Year In Government Subsidies Worldwide," *ThinkProgress*, November 7, 2013, last modified November 12, 2013, http://thinkprogress.org/climate/2013/11/07/2908361 /rich-countries-fossil-fuel-subsidies/.

29. Bonnie Kavoussi, "General Electric Avoids Taxes By Keeping $108 Billion Overseas," *Huffington Post*, March 11, 2013, last modified March 11, 2013, http://www. huffingtonpost.com/2013/03/11/general-electric-taxes_n_2852094.html.

30. Paul Buchheit, "Add It Up: The Average American Family Pays $6,000 a Year in Subsidies to Big Business," *Common Dreams*, September 23, 2013, accessed May 24, 2014, http://www.commondreams.org/view/2013/09/23.

31. "Deere Announces Record First-Quarter Earnings of $681 Million," John Deere, accessed May 24, 2014, http://www.deere.com/wps/dcom/en_US/corporate/ our_company/investor_relations/financial_data/earnings_releases/2014/ firstqtr14.page; Maggie McGrath, "DuPont Sees Profit Double, Authorizes $5 Billion Share Repurchase," Forbes, January 28, 2014, accessed May 24, 2014, http://www.forbes.

com/sites/maggiemcgrath/2014/01/28/dupont-sees-profit-double-authorizes-5-bil-lion-share-repurchase/; Carey Gillam, "Monsanto profit beats expectations on strong corn, soybean demand," Reuters, April 2, 2014, accessed May 24, 2014, http://www.reuters.com/article/2014/04/02/us-monsanto-results-idUSBREA310YU20140402.

32. Frank Morris, "Largely unpopular, direct payment subsidies persist," *Harvest Public Media*, September 24, 2013, accessed May 24, 2014, http://harvestpublicmedia.org/article/largely-unpopular-direct-payment-subsidies-persist.

33. *We're Not Broke*, Netflix streaming video, directed by Karin Hayes and Victoria Bruce (2013; Onshore Productions, 2013).

34. "2014 Poverty Guidelines," U.S. Department of Health & Human Services, accessed May 24, 2014, http://aspe.hhs.gov/poverty/14poverty.cfm.

35. *A Place at the Table*, Netflix streaming video, directed by Kristi Jacobson and Lori Silverbush (2013; New York: Magnolia Pictures, 2013).

36. Robert C. Whitaker, Shannon M. Phillips, and Sean M. Orzol, "Food Insecurity and the Risks of Depression and Anxiety in Mothers and Behavior Problems in their Preschool-Aged Children," *Pediatrics* 118 (2006): e859-e868, accessed November 21, 2014, doi: 10.1542/peds.2006-0239.

37. Clare O'Connor, "Report: Walmart Workers Cost Taxpayers $6.2 Billion In Public Assistance," *Forbes*, April 15, 2014, accessed May 24, 2014, http://www.forbes.com/sites/clareoconnor/2014/04/15/report-walmart-workers-cost-taxpayers-6-2-billion-in-public-assistance/.

38. Carla Murphy, "McDonald's Campus Closes Because of Fast Food Protests," *Colorlines*, May 21, 2014, accessed February 15, 2015, http://colorlines.com/archives/2014/05/mcdonalds_campus_closes_because_of_fast_food_protests.html.

39. Christina D. Romer, "The Business of the Minimum Wage," *New York Times*, March 2, 2013, accessed May 24, 2014, http://www.nytimes.com/2013/03/03/business/the-minimum-wage-employment-and-income-distribution.html.

40. "Michael T. Duke," Executive Paywatch, accessed May 24, 2014, http://www.aflcio.org/Corporate-Watch/Paywatch-2014#!/search/WMT.

41. "'Inequality is bad for everyone': Robert Reich fights against economic imbalance," *PBS*, October 11, 2013, accessed May 24, 2014, http://www.pbs.org/newshour/rundown/inequality-is-bad-for-everyone-robert-reich-fights-against-economic-imbalance/.

Chapter 19 · Compassionate Parenting

1. Elliot S. Valenstein, *Blaming the Brain: The Truth About Drugs and Mental Health* (New York: Free Press, 2002), 223.

2. Bob Murray and Alicia Fortinberry, *Raising and Optimistic Child: A Proven Plan for Depression-Proofing Young Children—for Life* (New York: McGraw-Hill, 2006), 5.

3. Ibid. 6.

4. Ibid. 25-26.

5. Ibid. 26.

6. Nara Schoenberg, "Some mothers can't breast-feed," *Chicago Tribune*, April 3, 2013, accessed May 30, 2014, http://articles.chicagotribune.com/2013-04-03/health/sc-health-0403-breast-feeding-20130403_1_milk-supply-lactation-breast.

7. Karleen D Gribble, "Mental health, attachment and breastfeeding: implications for adopted children and their mothers," *International Breastfeeding Journal* 1 (2006): 2, accessed May 30, 2014, doi: 10.1186/1746-4358-1-5.

8. Murray, *Raising*, 8.

9. Kabat-Zinn, *Full Catastrophe*, location 4987.

10. Pinka Chatterji, Sara Markowitz, and Jeanne Brooks-Gunn, "Early Maternal Employment and Family Wellbeing," NBER Working Paper No. 17212, *NBER Working Paper Series*, July, 2011, accessed November 22, 2014, http://www.nber.org/papers/w17212.pdf.

11. Jesper Juul, *Your Competent Child: Toward a new paradigm in parenting and education* (Bloomington, IN: Balboa Press, 2011), Kindle edition, location 579.

12. Ibid., location 595.

13. Ibid., location 603-611.

14. Scott M. Shannon, *Parenting the Whole Child: A Holistic Child Psychiatrist Offers Practical Wisdom on Behavior, Brain Health, Nutrition, Exercise, Family Life, Peer Relationships, School Life, Trauma, Medication, and more* (New York: W. W. Norton & Company, 2014), 27-28.

15. Juul, *Competent*, location 1141.

16. Ibid., location 1310.

17. Shefali Tsabary, *The Conscious Parent* (Vancouver: Namaste Publishing, 2010), Kindle edition, location 2572.

18. Ibid., location 264.

19. Shannon, *Parenting*, 200.

20. Juul, *Competent*, location 2374.

21. Ibid., location 1473.

22. Tsabary, *Conscious*, location 579.

23. Juul, Competent, location 1799.

24. Ibid., location 1826.

25. Ibid., location 2098.

26. Ibid., location 2811.

27. Ibid., location 2819.

28. Ibid., location 1716.

29. Murray, *Optimistic*, 21.

30. Michael Hollander, *Helping Teens Who Cut: Understanding and Ending Self-Injury* (New York: The Guilford Press, 2008), Kindle edition, location 689.

31. "Center for Nonviolent Communication: An International Organization," last modified September 30, 2013, http://www.cnvc.org/.

32. Tsabary, *Conscious*, location 427.

33. Ibid., location 542.

34. Ibid., location 4070.

35. Shannon, *Parenting*, 203.

36. Tsabary, *Conscious*, location 2995.

37. "Children's Wellbeing Manifesto," Our Emotional Health, accessed February 15, 2015, http://www.our-emotional-health.com/manifesto.

38. Murray, *Optimistic*, 24.

Chapter 20 • Student Centered Education

1. Kohn, Feel-Bad, 150.

2. "Fast Stats: Attention Deficit Hyperactivity Disorder (ADHD)," Centers for Disease Control and Prevention, last modified May 14, 2014, http://www.cdc.gov/nchsfastats /adhd.htm.

3. Alfie Kohn, *No Contest: The Case Against Competition* (Boston: Houghton Mifflin Company, 1986), 113.

4. Shannon, *Parenting*, 157.

5. Alfie Kohn, "Unconditional Teaching," *Educational Leadership*, September, 2005, accessed November 22, 2014, http://www.alfikohn.org/teaching/uncondtchg.htm.

6. Ibid., 21, 45-78.

7. Ibid., 21.

8. Ibid., 106-113, 120-125.

9. Joshua Davis, "How a Radical New Teaching Method Could Unleash a Generation of Geniuses," *Wired*, October 15, 2013, accessed June 2, 2014, http://www.wired.com/2013/10/free-thinkers.

10. School in the Cloud, accessed June 2, 2014, https://www.theschoolinthecloud.org/.

11. "Why Student-Centered Learning?" Students at the Center, accessed November 22, 2014, http://www.studentsatthecenter.org/.

12. "How a Radical New Teaching Method Could Unleash a Generation of Geniuses"

13. Kohn, *Feel-Bad*, 50.

14. "How a Radical New Teaching Method Could Unleash a Generation of Geniuses"

15. Levine, *Get Up*, location 2012.

16. Ken Robinson, "How Schools Kill Creativity," TED video, 19:24, TED2006, filmed February, 2006, http://www.ted.com/talks/ken_robinson_says_schools_kill_creativity.

17. "Students at the Center: Teaching and Learning in the Era of the Common Core," Students at the Center, accessed November 22, 2014, http://www.studentsatthecenter.org/about.

18. Shannon, *Parenting*, 145.

19. "Adverse Childhood Experiences in Iowa: A New Way of Understanding Lifelong Health," accessed November 22, 2014, http://www.iowaaces360.org/uploads/1/0/9/2 /10925571/iowa_aces_360_pdf_web_new.pdf.

20. "What Is Social and Emotional Learning?" CASEL, accessed November 22, 2014, http://www.casel.org/social-and-emotional-learning.

21. "State Scan Scorecard Project," CASEL, accessed November 22, 2014, https://casel.squarespace.com/state-scan-scorecard-project/.

22. Eluned Gold et al., "Mindfulness-Based Stress Reduction (MBSR) for Primary School Teachers," *Journal of Child and Family Studies* 19 (2010): 187.

23. Shannon, *Parenting*, 145.

24. Juul, *Competent*, location 2807.

25. *Race to Nowhere.*

26. Etta Kralovec, "Healthy Homework Guidelines: A New Vision for Homework," YouTube video, 5:03, posted by "Race to Nowhere," June 19, 2012, http://youtu.be/ZONH4B-qCAs.

27. Ibid.

28. "Homework Guidelines Supporting Student Health, Family Engagement and Active Learning Nationwide," accessed November 22, 2014, http://www.racetonowhere.com /sites/default/files/RTN-Homework-Guidelines.pdf.

29. Marjorie Hansen Shaevitz, "What College Admissions Offices Look for in Extracurricular Activities," *Huffington Post,* April 11, 2013, last modified June 11, 2013, http://www.huffingtonpost.com/marjorie-hansen-shaevitz /extra-curricular-activities-college-admission_b_3040217.html.

30. *Race to Nowhere.*

31. *Fame,* DVD, directed by Kevin Tancharoen (2009; Los Angeles: Fox Searchlight, 2010).

32. "Our History: School Lunch Initiative," The Edible Schoolyard Project, accessed November 22, 2014, https://edibleschoolyard.org/node/78.

33. Saint Therese de Lisieux, *The Story of a Soul (L'Histoire d'une Âme): The Autobiography of St. Therese of Lisieux,* Kindle edition, location 768.

34. "AAP Considers Recess a Necessary Break From the Demands of School," American Academy of Pediatrics, December 31, 2012, accessed November 22, 2014, http://www.aap.org/en-us/about-the-aap/aap-press-room/Pages/AAP-Considers-Recess-a-Necessary-Break.aspx#sthash.aRsrjJim.dpuf; "The Crucial Role of Recess in Schools," *The Journal of School Health* 80 (2010): 517-26, accessed November 22, 2014, http://www.ncbi.nlm.nih.gov/pubmed/21039550.

35. Murray, *Raising,* 146.

36. Sonja Lyubomirsky, Laura King, and Ed Diener, "The Benefits of Frequent PositiveAffect: Does Happiness Lead to Success?" *Psychological Bulletin* 131 (2005): 825, accessed November 22, 2014, doi: 0.1037/0033-2909.131.6.803.

Chapter 21 • Putting Vision Into Action

1. "Prozac Lawsuit," *Injury Lawyer News,* last modified August 19, 2014, http://injurylawyer-news.com/prozac/lawsuit/.

2. Alex Berenson, "Lilly Settles With 18,000 Over Zyprexa," *New York Times,* January 5, 2007, accessed June 17, 2014, http://query.nytimes.com/gst/fullpage.html?res= 9F00E5DB1430F936A35752C0A9619C8B63.

3. "Eli Lilly settles Zyprexa lawsuit for $1.42 billion," *NBCNEWS.com,* updated January 15, 2009, accessed June 17, 2014, http://www.nbcnews.com/id/28677805 /ns/health-health_care/t/eli-lilly-settles-zyprexa-lawsuit-billion/.

4. Marilyn Wedge, "Why French Kids Don't Have ADHD," *Psychology Today,* March 8, 2012, accessed June 17, 2014, http://www.psychologytoday.com /blog/suffer-the-children/201203/why-french-kids-dont-have-adhd.

5. "What is Integrated Care?" SAMHSA, accessed September 6, 2014, http://www.integration.samhsa.gov/about-us/what-is-integrated-care.

6. Levine, *Get Up,* location 2781.

7. Robison and Carrier, *The Spirit,* 9.

For Further Exploration

(Books, Films, Blogs)

Psychiatry and Psychotropic Drugs

Diller, Lawrence. *The Last Normal Child: Essays on the Intersection of Kids, Culture, and Psychiatric Drugs.* Westport, CT: Greenwood Publishing Group, 2006.

Frances, Allen. *Saving Normal: An Insider's Revolt Against Out-of-Control Psychiatric Diagnosis, DSM-5, Big Pharma, and the Medicalization of Ordinary Life.* New York: HarperCollins, 2013.

Mad in America. http://www.madinamerica.com/.

Sharpe, Katherine. *Coming of Age on Zoloft: How Antidepressants Cheered Us Up, Let Us Down, and Changed Who We Are.* New York: Harper Perennial, 2012.

Valenstein, Elliot S. *Blaming the Brain: The Truth About Drugs and Mental Health.* New York: Free Press, 2002.

Warner, Judith. *We've Got Issues: Children and Parents in the Age of Medication.* New York: Penguin Group, 2010.

Watters, Ethan. *Crazy Like Us: The Globalization of the American Psyche.*

New York: Free Press, 2011.

Whitaker, Robert. *Anatomy of an Epidemic: Magic Bullets, Psychiatric Drugs, and the Astonishing Rise of Mental Illness in America.* New York: Random House, 2010.

Helping Your Child

Berlinger, Norman T. *Rescuing Your Teenager from Depression.* New York: HarperCollins, 2009.

Dorfman, Kelly. *What's Eating Your Child?* New York: Workman Publishing, 2001.

Herrin, Marcia and Nancy Matsumoto. *The Parent's Guide to Eating Disorders: Supporting Self-Esteem, Healthy Eating, & Positive Body Image at Home.* Carlsbad, CA: Gurze Books, 2007.

Hollander, Michael. *Helping Teens Who Cut: Understanding and Ending Self-Injury.* New York: The Guilford Press, 2008.

Kaiser Greenland, Susan. *The Mindful Child: How to Help Your Kid Manage Stress and Become Happier, Kinder, and More Compassionate.* New York: Attria Books, 2010.

Lock, James. *Help Your Teenager Beat an Eating Disorder.* New York: Guilford Press, 2004.

Louv, Richard. *Last Child in the Woods: Saving Our Children From Nature-Deficit Disorder.* Chapel Hill, NC: Algonquin Books, 2008.

McKay, Matthew, Jeffery C. Wood, and Jeffrey Brantley. *The Dialectical Behavior Therapy Skills Workbook: Practical DBT Exercises for Learning Mindfulness, Interpersonal Effectiveness, Emotion Regulation & Distress Tolerance.* Oakland, CA: New Harbinger Publications, 2007.

Saltzman, Amy. *A Still Quiet Place: A Mindfulness Program for Teaching Children and Adolescents to Ease Stress and Difficult Emotions.* Oakland, CA: New Harbinger Publications, 2014.

Wedge, Marilyn. *Suffer the Children: The Case Against Labeling and Medicating and an Effective Alternative.* New York: W. W. Norton & Company, 2011.

Wolfson, Jeanie. It's Not Mental: Finding Innovative Support and Medical Treatment for a Child Diagnosed with a Severe Mental Illness. Cerebella Publishing, 2010.

Health and Wellness

Beuttner, Dan. The Blue Zones: *Lessons for Living Longer from the People Who've Lived the Longest.* Washington, D.C.: National Geographic Books, 2008.

Cohen, Rebecca. *Fifteen Minutes Outside: 365 Ways to Get Out of the House and Connect with Your Kids.* Naperville, IL: Sourcebooks, 2011.

Food Matters. DVD. Directed by Carlo Ledesma and James Colquhoun. McHenry, IL: Permacology Productions, 2008.

Happy. Streamed on Netflix. Directed by Roko Belic. Los Angeles: Creative Visions Foundation, 2011.

Kabat-Zinn, Jon. *Full Catastrophe Living: Using the Wisdom of Your Body and Mind to Face Stress, Pain, and Illness.* New York: Bantam Books, 2013.

Perlmutter, David. *Grain Bran: The Surprising Truth about Wheat, Carbs, and Sugar--Your Brain's Silent Killers.* New York: Little, Brown and Company, 2013.

Ratey, John J. *Spark: The Revolutionary New Science of Exercise and the Brain.* New York: Little, Brown and Company, 2008.

Ratey, John J. and Richard Manning. *Go Wild: Free Your Body and Mind from the Afflictions of Civilization.* New York: Little, Brown and Company, 2014.

Reed Stitt, Barbara. *Food and Behavior: A Natural Connection.* Manitowoc, WI: Natural Press, 2004.

Robison, Jon and Karen Carrier. *The Spirit and Science of Holistic Health.* Bloomington, IN: AuthorHouse, 2004.

Rosenthal, Joshua. *Integrative Nutrition: Feed Your Hunger for Health and Happiness.* New York: Integrative Nutrition Publishing, 2012.

Satter, Ellyn. *Secrets of Feeding a Healthy Family: How to Eat, How to Raise Good Eaters, How to Cook.* Madison, WI: Kelcy Press, 2008.

Shedinger, Robert. *Radically Open: Transcending Religious Identity in an Age of Anxiety.* Eugene, OR: Cascade Books, 2012.

Smith, Melinda, et. al. "Improving Emotional Health." *Helpguide.org*. http://www.helpguide.org/articles/emotional-health/improving-emotional-health.htm.

Simple Living

Andrews, Cecile. *The Circle of Simplicity: Return to the Good Life.* New York: HarperCollins, 1997.

Luhrs, Janet. *The Simple Living Guide: A Sourcebook for Less Stressful, More Joyful Living.* New York: Broadway Books, 1997.

Merkel, Jim. *Radical Simplicity: Small Footprints on a Finite Earth.* Gabriola Island, BC: New Society Publishers, 2003.

The Minimalists. http://www.theminimalists.com/.

Robin, Vicky and Joe Dominquez. *Your Money or Your Life: 9 Steps to Transforming Your Relationship with Money and Achieving Financial Independence.* New York: Penguin Books, 2008.

Rowdy Kittens. http://www.rowdykittens.com/.

Schulte, Brigid. *Overwhelmed: Work, Love, and Play When No One Has the Time.* New York: Picador, 2015.

Wann, David. *Simple Prosperity: Finding Real Wealth in a Sustainable Lifestyle.* New York: St. Martin's Griffin, 2007.

Zen Habits. http://www.zenhabits.net.

Economics and Politics

Bornstein, David. *How to Change the World: Social Entrepreneurs and the Power of New Ideas.* New York: Oxford University Press, 2007.

Capitalism: A Love Story. DVD. Directed by Michael Moore. New York: Dog Eat Dog Films, 2009.

Clements, Jeff. *Corporations Are Not People: Reclaiming Democracy from Big Money and Global Corporations.* San Francisco: Berrett-Koehler Publishers, 2012.

Inequality for All. DVD. Directed by Jacob Kornbluth. San Francisco: 72 Productions, 2013.

Levine, Bruce E. *Get Up, Stand Up: Uniting Populists, Energizing the Defeated, and Battling the Corporate Elite.* White River Jct, VT: Chelsea Green Publishing, 2011.

Martinez, Dawn B. "Mental Health Care After Capitalism." *Radical Psychology* Winter (2005). http://www.radicalpsychology.org/vol4-2/Martinez4.html.

Mycoskie, Blake. *Start Something That Matters.* New York: Spiegel & Grau, 2011.

Of-Hearts, Saul. *The Lateral Freelancer: How to Make A Living in the Share Economy.* Seattle: CreateSpace, 2013.

Pargas, Fernando. *Stopping Big Business and Politics From Bleeding America.* Silver Spring, MD: Beckham Publications Group, 2011.

A Place at the Table. Streamed on Netflix. Directed by Kristi Jacobson and Lori Silverbush. New York: Magnolia Pictures, 2013.

We're Not Broke. Streamed on Netflix. Directed by Karin Hayes and Victoria Bruce. Onshore Productions, 2013.

Yunus, Muhammad. *Building Social Business: The New Kind of Capitalism that Serves Humanity's Most Pressing Needs.* New York: PublicAffairs™, 2010.

Education and Parenting

Hanh, Thich Nhat and Chan Chan Nghiem. *Planting Seeds: Practicing Mindfulness with Children.* Berkley: Parallax Press, 2011.

Healthy Habits of Mind. Streamed Online. Directed by Mette Bahnsen. Århus: Persona Film, 2013.

Juul, Jesper. *Your Competent Child: Toward a new paradigm in parenting and education.* Bloomington, IN: Balboa Press, 2011).

Kabat-Zinn, Myla and Jon Kabat-Zinn. *Everyday Blessings: The Inner Work of Mindful Parenting.* New York: Hyperion, 1998.

Kohn, Alfie. *Feel-Bad Education: And Other Contrarian Essays on Children and Schooling.* Boston: Beacon Press, 2011.

Kohn, Alfie. *No Contest: The Case Against Competition.* Boston: Houghton Mifflin Company, 1986.

Murray, Bob and Alicia Fortinberry. *Raising and Optimistic Child: A Plan for Depression-Proofing Young Children—for Life.* New York: McGraw-Hill, 2006.

Nabhan, Gary Paul and Stephen Trimble. *The Geography of Childhood: Why Children Need Wild Places.* Boston: Beacon Press, 1994.

Pozatek, Krissy. *Brave Parenting: A Buddhist-Inspired Guide to Raising Emotionally Resilient Children.* Somerville, MA: Wisdom Publications, 2014.

Race to Nowhere. DVD. Directed by Vicki Abeles and Jessica Congdon. LaFayette: Reel Link Films, 2009.

Room to Breathe. DVD. Directed by Russell Long. Sacred Planet Films, 2012.

School's Out: Lessons from a Forest Kindergarten. DVD. Directed by Lisa Molomot. Bullfrog Films, 2014.

Shannon, Scott M. *Parenting the Whole Child: A Holistic Child Psychiatrist Offers Practical Wisdom on Behavior, Brain Health, Nutrition, Exercise, Family Life, Peer Relationships, School Life, Trauma, Medication, and more.* New York: W. W. Norton & Company, 2014.

Snel, Eline. *Sitting Still Like a Frog: Mindfulness Exercises for Kids (and Their Parents).* Boston: Shambhala Publications, 2013.

Srinivasan, Meena. *Teach, Breathe, Learn: Mindfulness in and out of the Classroom.* Berkley: Parallax Press, 2014.

Tsabary, Shefali. *The Conscious Parent.* Vancouver: Namaste Publishing, 2010.

Take Action

Progressive Change

Change.org
Change.org is a website that allows anybody to create a petition for change.

    http://www.change.org/

Collective Impact Forum
Collective impact brings people together, in a structured way, to achieve social change.

    http://collectiveimpactforum.org/

CREDO Action
CREDO is a social change organization that supports activism and funds progressive nonprofits. Funding is made possible by the revenues from CREDO mobile.

    http://www.credoaction.com

Empowerment Institute
Empowerment Institute is the world's preeminent consulting and training organization specializing in the practice of empowerment.

    http://www.empowermentinstitute.net

Hidden Driver
Hidden Driver is the creative home of Laura Hanna and Astra Taylor, who use every medium at their disposal to better understand the world, connect with

others, and challenge the status quo.
http://www.hiddendriver.com/

MoveOn

MoveOn is a community of more than 8 million Americans who use innovative technology to lead, participate in, and win campaigns for progressive change.
http://front.moveon.org/

Random Acts of Kindness

The Random Acts of Kindness Foundation encourages members to engage in kind actions. Includes a resource area for teachers.
http://www.randomactsofkindness.org/

Resilience.org

Resilience.org is both an information clearinghouse and a network of action-oriented groups.
http://www.resilience.org/

Wellstone Action

Wellstone Action trains grassroots leaders to create lasting progressive change.
http://www.wellstone.org

Holistic Health/Mental Health

The Center for Investigating Healthy Minds (CIHM)

CIHM is a global leader in conducting novel research that has revolutionized how we understand the mind, our emotions, and how to nurture well-being for ourselves and others.
http://www.investigatinghealthyminds.org/

Integrative Healthcare Policy Consortium (IHPC)

IHPC envisions a national healthcare system devoted to optimal health and well-being.
http://www.ihpc.org/

Mad in America Continuing Education

Provides on-line courses based on research that is free of commercial interest on topics such as psychiatric medications, including their long-term effects, and alternatives that promote long-term recovery.
http://madinamericacontinuinged.org/

MindFreedom International

MindFreedom International works to win human rights and alternatives for people labeled with psychiatric disabilities.

http://www.mindfreedom.org/

Mindful

The Mindful network provides information on the importance of diet, nutrition and lifestyle in optimizing children's mental health.

http://mindfulcharity.ca/

National Technical Assistance Center for Children's Mental Health (TA Center)

The TA Center is dedicated to working in partnership with families and many other leaders across the country to transform systems and services for children, adolescents, and young adults who have, or are at risk for, mental health problems and their families.

http://gucchdtacenter.georgetown.edu/

National Wellness Institute (NWI)

NWI aims serve the professionals and organizations that promote optimal health and wellness in individuals and communities.

http://www.nationalwellness.org/

Partnership for Prevention

Partnership for Prevention is a nonpartisan organization of business, nonprofit and government leaders working to make evidence-based disease prevention and health promotion a national priority.

http://www.prevent.org/

Physicians Committee for Responsible Medicine (PCRM)

The Physicians Committee is leading a revolution in medicine—putting a new focus on health and compassion.

http://www.pcrm.org/

RxISK

Research a prescription drug to see what side effects have been reported in the 5.5 million reports submitted to the FDA, Health Canada, and RxISK.

RxISK.org

Youth M.O.V.E. National

Youth M.O.V.E National is a youth-led national organization devoted to improving services and systems that support positive growth and development by uniting the voices of individuals who have lived experience in various systems including mental health, juvenile justice, education, and child welfare.

http://www.youthmovenational.org/

Environment/Nature

350.org
A global climate movement with campaigns, projects, and actions led from the bottom-up by people in 188 countries.

http://350.org/

Carbonfund.org
Tools to reduce and offset your carbon footprint.

https://www.carbonfund.org/

Children & Nature Network
Together we can create a world where every child can play, learn and grow in nature.

http://www.childrenandnature.org/

Collective Evolution (CE)
CE is a community of people who encourage and inspire each other to take action with the goal of bringing to life a bright future for us all.

http://www.collective-evolution.com/

Earth Day Network
The Earth Day Network aims to broaden, diversify and activate the environmental movement worldwide, through a combination of education, public policy, and consumer campaigns.

http://www.earthday.org/

Great American Campout
Every June, thousands of people across the nation gather in their backyards, neighborhoods, communities and parks to get outside and connect with nature.

http://www.nwf.org/Great-American-Backyard-Campout.aspx

National Get Outdoors Day
National Get Outdoors Day is an annual event to encourage healthy, active outdoor fun.

http://www.nationalgetoutdoorsday.org/

NATURE ROCKS

Inspiring families to explore nature.

http://www.naturerocks.org/

Natural Resources Defense Council (NRDC)

Check out the link below for NRDC resources for kids.

http://www.nrdc.org/reference/kids.asp

Slow Food USA

Part of the global Slow Food Network, Slow Food USA works for good, clean, and fair food for all.

http://www.slowfoodusa.org/

Take a Child Outside Week

An annual event that occurs in September, this is a program designed to encourage children and adults to spend time together outdoors.

http://www.takeachildoutside.org/

Economy/Simple Living

AFL-CIO: Americas Unions

AFL-CIO exists to represent people who work and envisions a future in which work and all people who work are valued, respected and rewarded.

http://www.aflcio.org/

American Sustainable Business Council

The American Sustainable Business Council offers programs that educate and inform the public and policy makers about the benefits of a more sustainable economy, and about policies and practices that can help the economy become more sustainable.

http://asbcouncil.org/

B Corporation

Certified B Corporations are leading a global movement to redefine success in business.

https://www.bcorporation.net/

Center for a New American Dream

The Center for a New American Dream helps Americans to reduce and shift their consumption to improve quality of life, protect the environment, and promote social justice. • http://www.newdream.org/

Changers of Commerce

Changers of Commerce is a movement of leaders who believe there is a better way of practicing Capitalism that results in a higher likelihood that the benefits of capitalism can continue.

http://changersofcommerce.com/

Fair Trade USA

Quality products. Improving lives. Protecting the environment.

http://fairtradeusa.org/

The Forum for Sustainable and Responsible Investment

The Center provides investors, investment advisors, consultants, analysts, and other financial professionals with access to high quality education, research and thought leadership on sustainable investment.

http://www.ussif.org/

Inequality for All

Learn the facts about income inequality and take action for change. http://inequalityforall.com/

Occupy Wall Street

Occupy Wall Street is a leaderless resistance movement with people who have in common that they are the 99% and will no longer tolerate the greed and corruption of the 1%.

http://occupywallst.org/

Postconsumers

Postconsumers is an educational company helping to move society beyond addictive consumerism.

http://www.postconsumers.com/

The Simple Way

The Simple Way is a web of subversive friends conspiring to spread the vision of 'Loving God, Loving People, and Following Jesus' in our neighborhoods and in our world.

http://www.thesimpleway.org/

Slow Money

Slow Money is bringing people together around a shared vision about what it means to be an investor in the 21st Century. • https://slowmoney.org/

The Story of Stuff Project

This is a community of 750,000 changemakers worldwide, working to build a more healthy and just planet. Check out their awesome videos!

http://storyofstuff.org/

Politics

Americans for Tax Fairness

Americans for Tax Fairness (ATF) is a diverse campaign of national, state and local organizations united in support of a tax system that works for all Americans.

http://www.americansfortaxfairness.org/

Common Cause

Common Cause is the original citizens' lobby and battles for open, honest and accountable government in Washington, D.C. and in all 50 states. http://www.commoncause.org/

Free Speech for People

Free Speech For People works to challenge the misuse of corporate power and restore republican democracy to the people.

http://freespeechforpeople.org

Move to Amend

Move to Amend is a coalition of organizations and individuals committed to social and economic justice, ending corporate rule, and building a vibrant democracy that is genuinely accountable to the people, not corporate interests.

https://movetoamend.org/

Open Secrets

OpenSecrets.org is your nonpartisan guide to money's influence on U.S. elections and public policy.

http://www.opensecrets.org/

OurTime.org

OurTime.org empowers and speaks for the interests of young Americans.

http://www.ourtime.org/

Project Vote

Project Vote is a national nonpartisan organization that works to empower, educate, and mobilize low-income, minority, youth, and other marginalized

and under-represented voters.
http://projectvote.org

Public Campaign

Public Campaign is dedicated to sweeping campaign reform that aims to dramatically reduce the role of big special interest money in American politics.
http://www.publiccampaign.org/

Reclaim Democracy!

Reclaim Democracy! is dedicated to restoring democratic authority over corporations, reviving grassroots democracy, and establishing appropriate limits on corporate influence.
http://reclaimdemocracy.org/

U.S. PIRG

U.S. PIRG is a consumer group that stands up to powerful interests whenever they threaten our health and safety, our financial security, or our right to fully participate in our democratic society.
http://www.uspirg.org

We the People: Your Voice in Our Government

Giving all Americans a way to engage their government on the issues that matter to them. Start or sign a petition!
https://petitions.whitehouse.gov/

Family/Parenting

The Association for Prenatal and Perinatal Psychology and Health (APPPAH)

APPPAH educates professionals and the public, worldwide, that a baby's experience of conception, pregnancy, and birth creates lifelong consequences for individuals, families, and society.
https://birthpsychology.com/

Attachment Parenting International (API)

API promotes parenting practices that create strong, healthy emotional bonds between children and their parents.
http://www.attachmentparenting.org/

Families for Conscious Living

This organization is determined to bring forward the practical wisdom of holistic and whole systems living in creative and collaborative outreach projects with like-hearted organizations.

http://www.familiesforconsciousliving.com/

Family Lab International (FLI)

Professional and parents work together to figure out how to transform emotional love and commitment into loving behavior.

http://www.family-lab.com/

Holistic Moms Network

Connects parents interested in holistic health and green living.

http://www.holisticmoms.org/

MomsRising.org

Where moms and people who love them go to change the world. This organization tackles issues such as parental leave, flexible work, and paid sick days.

http://www.momsrising.org/

Too Small to Fail

Too Small to Fail aims to help parents and businesses take meaningful actions to improve the health and well-being of children ages zero to five, so that more of America's children are prepared to succeed in the 21st century.

http://toosmall.org/

Progressive Education/School Food

Alliance for a Healthier Generation

This organization works with schools, companies, community organizations, healthcare professionals and families to transform the conditions and systems that lead to healthier kids.

https://www.healthiergeneration.org/

Blue School

This is a downtown NYC independent school. Featured in Race to Nowhere.

http://www.blueschool.org/

Center for Education Reform

The destination and leading voice and advocate for lasting, substantive and structural education reform in the U.S. • edreform.com

Challenge Success

This organization believes that our society has become too focused on grades, test scores and performance, leaving little time and energy for our kids to become resilient, successful, meaningful contributors for the 21st century.

http://www.challengesuccess.org/

Edutopia

This website shares evidence- and practitioner-based learning strategies that empower teachers to improve K-12 education.

http://www.edutopia.org/

FoodCorps

FoodCorps is a nationwide team of AmeriCorps leaders who connect kids to real food and help them grow up healthy.

https://foodcorps.org/

Goddard College: Master of Arts in Education

A holistic, interdisciplinary and student-centered approach to learning that is personally and socially relevant and transformative.

http://www.goddard.edu/

The Lunch Box

Chef Ann Cooper's website about school lunch.

http://www.thelunchbox.org/

National Farm to School Network

Farm to school enriches the connection communities have with fresh, healthy food and local food producers by changing food purchasing and education practices at schools and preschools.

http://www.farmtoschool.org/

National Institute for Student-Centered Education (NISCE)

NISCE has a vision of education where students—not politics, not tests, not expediency—are at the center of learning, and where all students have the opportunities and resources they need to succeed.

http://nisce.org/

NewSchools

NewSchools is a nonprofit venture philanthropy firm working to transform public education for low-income children.

http://www.newschools.org/

PE4Life

PE4life advocates for and assists in the development and enhancement of physical education programs and physical activity opportunities in schools and communities.

http://www.pe4life.org

Race to Nowhere

This organization, connected with the film with the same name, is transforming education from the ground up.

http://www.racetonowhere.com/

Zinn Education Project

The Zinn Education Project promotes and supports the use of Howard Zinn's best-selling book A People's History of the United States and other materials for teaching a people's history in middle and high school classrooms across the country.

https://zinnedproject.org/

Mindfulness in Education/Social and Emotional Learning (SEL)

Association for Mindfulness in Education (AME)

AME is a collaborative association of organizations and individuals working together to provide support for mindfulness training as a component of K-12 education.

http://www.mindfuleducation.org

Collaborative for Academic, Social, and Emotional Learning (CASEL)

CASEL's mission is to help make social and emotional learning an integral part of education from preschool through high school.

http://www.casel.org

The Garrison Institute: CARE for Teachers

CARE for Teachers is a unique program designed to help teachers reduce stress and enliven their teaching by promoting awareness, presence, compassion, reflection, and inspiration—the inner resources they need to help students flourish, socially, emotionally and academically.

http://www.garrisoninstitute.org/contemplation-and-education/care-for-teachers

Inward Bound Mindfulness Education (iBme)

iBme offers transformative retreats for teens, parents, and professionals.

http://ibme.info/

KidsMatter

KidsMatter is an Australian mental health and wellbeing initiative set in primary schools and early childhood education and care services.

http://www.kidsmatter.edu.au/

Mindfulness in Education Network (MiEN)

This organizations mission is to support and cultivate the practice of mindfulness in educational settings.

http://www.mindfuled.org/

Mindful Schools

Mindful Schools provides mindfulness training for educators.

http://www.mindfulschools.org/

MindUP

MindUP™ teaches social and emotional learning skills that link cognitive neuroscience, positive psychology and mindful awareness training utilizing a brain centric approach.

http://thehawnfoundation.org/mindup/

Project Happiness

Project Happiness spreads happiness through classrooms and communities globally.

http://projecthappiness.org/

The Smart Living Program

Based in Europe, this is a Chinese medicine-based preventive medicine program for teachers, who in turn teach their students.

http://www.luohan.com/luohan-gong-for-children/

Yoga 4 Classrooms

Yoga 4 Classrooms™ provides school yoga and mindfulness based programs, teacher inservice workshops, and staff development workshops.

http://www.yoga4classrooms.com/

Yoga Calm

Yoga Calm® is an integrated approach to wellness curriculum used in schools, hospitals and community-based settings.

http://www.1000-petals.com/what-is-yoga-calm/

Join the Conversation

Website: http://tabitagreen.com/

Twitter: https://twitter.com/tabitag/

Google+: https://plus.google.com/+TabitaGreen/

Facebook: https://facebook.com/annatabitagreen/

CPSIA information can be obtained
at www.ICGtesting.com
Printed in the USA
FFOW02n1128220318
45796337-46689FF